PRAISE FOR

ENOUGH ABOUT ME

Enough About Me is a must-read for business leaders that is surprisingly entertaining. This book will forever change the way you think about selflessness.

> RON INSANA, CNBC senior
> analyst and commentator

Selflessness is an asset for every community. In South Africa, we call it the spirit of "Ubuntu." Selflessness has been fundamental to building a sense of human solidarity, caring for and believing in each other, and embracing the belief that we are all better off when one of us is affirmed, treated well, and cherished.

> PHUMZILE MLAMBO-NGCUKA,
> Under-Secretary-General of the United
> Nations, executive director of UN Women

The ups and downs of Richard Lui's life are somehow simultaneously a truly remarkable and yet all too familiar human story. Part humorous personal memoir, part journalism career guidebook, part introspective man's hard-earned life lessons, *Enough About Me* provides a great opportunity to get a concentrated shot of almost fifty years of life experience in one book.

> RONNY CHIENG, comedian and correspondent
> on *The Daily Show with Trevor Noah*

To successfully navigate these racially divisive times, we must think outside ourselves and not isolate on the basis of race. Racism is selfish. *Enough About Me* helps us steer clear of the shoals of selfishness by instead making others a priority.

> PAULA MADISON, executive vice president,
> NBCUniversal (retired), named one of the
> "75 Most Powerful African Americans
> in Corporate America" in 2005

Timely, emotional, and authentic, *Enough About Me* provides enjoyable content from a leading influencer. #EnoughAboutMe is worth sharing!

WES FINLEY, head of global social marketing, Facebook

Ambitious and extremely well researched, *Enough About Me* is an essential read for those who want to explore new thinking on one of today's most pressing societal issues.

COLONEL JACK JACOBS,
US Army (Ret.), Medal of Honor

Richard Lui underscores the importance of sharing stories to bring people together through selfless acts for the greater good.

BETH KALLMYER, vice president of Care
and Support, Alzheimer's Association

Richard Lui is living a life of service. What an extraordinary testament to the best in human character. So many life lessons learned! This is a jewel of a book, a celebration of the best of the human spirit and of the good that emerges from sacrifice. Richard Lui is a beacon of light in these dark times.

JOSÉ DÍAZ-BALART, anchor, *Noticias
Telemundo* and *NBC Nightly News Saturday*

When I first met Richard Lui many years ago, it was immediately evident that he possessed the rare combination of shining intelligence and self-confidence, mixed with humility and a genuine vulnerability. *Enough About Me* is a reflection of these qualities exhibited over decades. In these narcissistic and individualistic times, Richard's storytelling provides insight and perspective into how to find the best part of ourselves.

TOM GARFINKEL, vice chairman, CEO of
the Miami Dolphins and Hard Rock Stadium

Enough About Me is an everyman's and everywoman's book—down-to-earth and practical from beginning to end. Richard Lui shares his humble upbringing in a fun but vulnerable way that reminds me of my own family's experiences.

JAY ALLEN, country music singer

I wish *Enough About Me* had been around when I began my journey as a caregiver. As I learned, a good laugh can make a big idea fresh—and this book does just that.

> JESUS TREJO, comedian

Richard Lui makes selflessness a necessity. Personal stories and science bring the idea of selflessness to life. Lui helps us see that selflessness is not simple. It is an essential way of being that needs to be built and practiced over our lifetimes. All of us—leaders, employees, citizens, parents, children—can use a guide for becoming more selfless. This book is an answer to what we most need right now.

> JANE DUTTON, PhD, cofounder, Center for
> Positive Organizations, Ross School of Business

I'm a five-book-a-month kind of reader, and *Enough About Me*, part business and part personal, is constructive, workable, and mirthful in a mix I haven't seen before.

> VENKAT NAGASWAMY, global vice
> president of marketing, 8x8 Inc.

ENOUGH ABOUT ME

THE UNEXPECTED POWER OF SELFLESSNESS

RICHARD LUI

WITH NANCY FRENCH

ZONDERVAN BOOKS

ZONDERVAN BOOKS

Enough About Me
Copyright © 2021 by Richard Lui

Requests for information should be addressed to:
Zondervan, *3900 Sparks Dr. SE, Grand Rapids, Michigan 49546*

Zondervan titles may be purchased in bulk for educational, business, fundraising, or sales promotional use. For information, please email SpecialMarkets@Zondervan.com.

ISBN 978-0-310-36239-5 (hardcover)
ISBN 978-0-310-36247-0 (audio)
ISBN 978-0-310-36246-3 (ebook)

Published in association with Pilar Queen / United Talent Agency.

Cover direction: Curt Diepenhorst
Cover and section title pages art: Lorraine Nam
Author photo: Courtesy of New Abolitionists
Unless noted otherwise, all graphics and charts are based on reference matter and illustrated by Paul Cheung / Io Kurihara
Interior design: Kait Lamphere

Printed in the United States of America

21 22 23 24 25 26 27 28 29 30 31 /LSC/ 15 14 13 12 11 10 9 8 7 6 5 4 3 2 1

To Rose and Stephen

The author plans to donate portions of his proceeds from this book to charitable organizations supporting Alzheimer's care and research, advocacy for senior citizens, and AAPI (Asian American and Pacific Islander) representation in journalism.

CONTENTS

Section Four:
FINDING THE POWER

Section Five:
GREEN PATCHES

Section One

UNEXPECTED

Chapter One

HALFTIME

I looked out the window. The neon CNN logo—right there. Every sixty seconds, "CNN" went dark and then pulsed on again, one red letter at a time: C-N-N. It was August 2004. I was exhausted from traveling from Singapore to Atlanta. The logo woke me up.

I had been working in Singapore as an anchor at Channel News Asia, a regional English-language network, during a turbulent period—covering the South Asian tsunami that killed more than 200,000 people, the SARS epidemic, and the shooting of Taiwan's president. Now I was in a Georgia hotel room, about to audition for an anchor job at CNN International.

I called my dad. Although my two brothers and sister and I referred to my mother with the typical "Mom," we called my father "Baba"—an informal Chinese term of affection, sort of like the way a kid says "Daddy." It had been a long time since they tried to get us to learn Chinese, but that one word stuck.

"Baba, you're not going to believe what I'm looking at," I said, staring at the blinking logo. My stomach was uneasy when I thought about sitting on CNN International's anchor set. Their broadcasts reached more than 380 million households. "My room is facing CNN's *world* headquarters right now."

I set my alarm but struggled to sleep because of jet lag and flashing, logo-induced adrenaline. The next day, I walked to the sprawling building and was taken directly to makeup. I watched in amusement as the two makeup artists experimented with how to match my skin tone. I'm pretty sure I saw one of them Googling "best makeup hacks for Asian males," which surprisingly doesn't bring up a lot of results. It was pre–*Crazy Rich Asians*.

Then—*the* desk. The one seen by those 380 million households. This was where I was supposed to work my way through a twenty-minute, uninterrupted "live" (but not broadcasted) show that executives would evaluate.

"We're going to put some stories in the teleprompter," the producer explained. "Just start reading. I'm going to go into the control room, where I'll be following along. Any questions?"

Yes, how do I stop this out-of-nowhere sweating?

"Do I read straight through until told to stop?"

The floor director nodded and pointed to a camera. The opening animation rolled. The familiar theme song played. The teleprompter operator jiggled the text a little to check on whether it was working.

"Cue," the director in the control room said in my ear. The text rolled across the screen like a reverse waterfall. My brow was catching all the mist. The audition had begun.

Because words on a teleprompter appear right above the camera lens, anchors look directly at them, but it appears they are looking at the viewers. I had done this for a year by then, but it still felt new. The way I remember it, I didn't stumble over any unfamiliar words or names. Then a sound bite came up. A moment to rest off camera.

The producer's voice popped into my earpiece: "Richard, we're getting news in. A plane crashed in Siberia." She told me scant details but included the fact the plane had been carrying 130 people. "We don't have a lot of information."

More nervous sweat. *How was I supposed to deal with this? I hadn't done the best job jotting down details.* "How many people on board again? What was the airline? Do we know why?"

She replied into my earpiece. "Don't know airline, only that it's European, and . . . no, we don't know cause yet. After this sound bite is done, we'd like you to summarize. You have forty-five seconds." That's like forty-five minutes when ad-libbing without a teleprompter.

I jotted down more details as the tape played. "Twenty seconds,"

I heard her voice say in my ear again. I grabbed one of the script pages and pressed it into my face to sop up the moisture on my face. Not conventional and barely ecological, but scripts are always around; the makeup team isn't.

Why were they giving me breaking news in the middle of an audition? It seemed unfair. Like showing up to interview for an accountant position and suddenly being asked to pirouette. "Ten seconds." I shook my head, taking advantage of the off-camera time to do a couple of "bumble bees" out loud to loosen my lips, and I let out a couple of performative coughs and some meditative "aahs."

"Five seconds." Last move—a throat clearing, replanting myself in the chair.

Then the sound bite was finished. I felt ready. "And cue." At that word, the rattled Mr. Hyde became the calmer Dr. Jekyll.

"We'll get back to that story in a moment, but I need to get to some breaking news just in on CNN. We're getting word that a plane has crashed in Siberia approximately one hour ago." So far so good. "One hundred thirty people were on board, though we have no additional information at this time. We'll keep you updated as we learn more." The breaking story was done. I continued reading from the teleprompter.

Then the producer's voice in my earpiece. *Again?*

"There's been a flare-up in the Middle East on the West Bank. SCUD missiles landed, unknown actor, but believed to be part of recent skirmishes between IDF and insurgents from an offshoot of Hezbollah."

All of this is happening during my screen test? What's next? Is the control room going to hit a button to set off the sprinklers so I can practice reporting in the middle of a hurricane, like the quintessential Al Roker?

I scribbled down the details. I couldn't get this wrong. I was sweating badly. I wasn't on air. I had twenty seconds to dry my face without ruining my makeup.

Get yourself together, Richard. Enunciation. "Bumble bee, bumble bee." I looked like a crazed man on the subway, rambling about his favorite brand of tuna. I jabbed the air like a boxer. I spit nervously. I blew my nose, honking with gusto to get out all the good bits. "Ten seconds, five . . . cue." The cameras rolled. I went from frenetic to calm. Like Jim Carrey in the 1994 anti-superhero classic *The Mask*—or Jim Carrey as I imagine him on an ordinary Tuesday.

I delivered the breaking news and then read four more stories. The producer came out, smiled, and shook my hand. "Thanks for coming in. We appreciate your time." It appeared I had done okay.

A week later, my agent called. I didn't get the job.

"What did I do wrong?" I asked.

"Well, they don't tell you what they don't like, only that now is not the right time and to let them know when you have more tape in the next year."

The next year? My agent could tell I was disappointed.

"How did *you* think the audition went?" he asked. I told him I'd been asked to deal with two unexpected breaking news stories. I admitted I was nervous but felt like I was able to work through it by doing my off-camera face yoga and unorthodox printer paper blotting.

"Wait a minute," my agent said and then went silent for a few beats. "You know, when the sound pieces play, even though you're not technically on camera, you're actually on camera for the audition, right? That's when executives watch you quite closely."

"I wasn't on camera."

"You're *always* on," he corrected. "Even if the viewer can't see what's going on, the execs want to know how you handle the pressure of breaking news. They watch what you do as much off camera as they do when you're on. In fact, what happens off camera could be even more important than what happens on camera."

It took a moment to digest that. I figured they'd judge my performance based on how well I read and the intonation and quality of my voice, so I wasn't worried when the camera wasn't on. Images of the nose blowing, the gibberish, the face stretches, the bumble bees, the arm jabs, and the script face blotting flashed before my eyes like a slow-motion *Three Stooges* highlight reel.

A year later, I came back to the CNN headquarters for another audition. I did better. I got the job. And thus began the 10,000-mile journey home to America and my first US anchor job.

Five years later, I moved to MSNBC in New York. I wanted to cover political news. I live close enough to 30 Rockefeller Plaza that I can walk to work. Four years passed in New York, and my career had been moving along. Then life off camera came at me with an uppercut.

My father was diagnosed with Alzheimer's disease, and his condition was worsening. I had begun to travel more frequently from New York to my parents' home in California, but I was struggling to keep up with my job while also giving him—and my mother—the support they needed. *How would I keep my job and also fulfill my responsibilities as a son?* My dad's condition was horrible for him. It was challenging and taxing for my mother. It was awful for my siblings. For me, it felt like a compounded loss—I was losing my dad *and* potentially giving up a career he had supported me in for years.

As I weighed the pros and cons of leaving my career to care for my dad, I remembered the hard-learned lesson from long ago: what happens off camera is more important than what happens on camera. It's one of those principles that sounds good, but at the time, it felt about as meaningful as the sentiment on a dollar bin greeting card.

Growing up in a household of a minister, like some of us do, I did the opposite of what might have been expected—I went through phases of rejecting what my dad told me I should believe. At that point, I actively believed. Then I didn't. And then I did, but differently. One thing's for sure, it stuck at least enough to remember something he often said from the pulpit: "It is more blessed to give than to receive."[1] Of course, he wasn't making an original statement. He was reading from the Bible, but the idea behind these words are shared in many places.

- "When you get, give."—American author and activist Maya Angelou
- "The sole meaning of life is to serve humanity."—Russian author Leo Tolstoy
- "If you pick up one end of the stick you also pick up the other."—Ethiopian proverb
- "From what we get, we can make a living; what we give, however, makes a life."—American professional tennis player Arthur Ashe
- "Helping those in need is not only part of our duty but of happiness."—Cuban philosopher José Martí

The collective wisdom of nearly every society over time seems to agree: selflessness ties us together and benefits both self and community.

When faced with a decision to aid my dad in his slow-moving, life-and-death battle, did I believe all this? Would I deny myself, put aside ambition, and sacrifice my plans for someone who may or may not even know I was doing so? I had two options: stay on my path of living for myself or become a caregiver, like 53 million other Americans. My mind and heart did not agree.

. . . .

Turns out most of us believe being selfless has too high of a price.

When I surveyed 1,012 Americans, 73 percent said being selfless requires making sacrifices in their lives. A similar number thought it would mean changing their lifestyle altogether.

This despite the fact that 91 percent of us believe living selflessly can be done in small ways.

There is a perception gap—selfless acts are for people like Mother Teresa.

Turns out moving the dial isn't always that mythical, gargantuan Mother Teresa–sized act. (Though she barely reached five feet.)

Try as accessible as every fifteen minutes. That's how often we make a conscious choice.[2] If we choose more selflessly for just one of these decisions each day, we've done something. It doesn't have to involve huge sacrifices or a lifestyle redefinition. Small and steady can change the world.

And now I had one of those decisions right in front of me.

. . . .

The choice reminded me of another turning point that happened when I was nine years old. I approached my dad and reluctantly admitted that kids in my class were bullying me. They made fun of me for not looking like they did. My father told me I had two options. "What are you going to do—get beaten up or learn to defend yourself?"

I chose to fight. My father enrolled my scrawny, four-foot-ten-inch self in martial arts classes, which felt a little on the nose. *Baba, you're suggesting I take kung fu lessons because other kids call me Kung Fu Kid? What's next, fortune cookies in my lunch box?*

There I was—training with a former monk from the famed Shaolin

Temple in China, where masters have trained since the sixth century AD. I was nine years old, and like people in generations before me, I was doing splits and roundhouse kicks in the early mornings. After five years—ta-da—I became a chiseled, quarter-scale Bruce Lee. A tiny crouching tiger, an easily hidden dragon. I was ready to fight.

And now, many years later, my father needed someone to fight for him. He could no longer do it for himself. It was time for me to step up and do what he taught me. I was as scared as that kid on the playground.

After several weeks, I took a deep breath and walked into my boss's office to have the conversation that could end my career. There were no part-time field journalists. Nobody dabbles in hurricane reporting. It's a twenty-five-hours-a-day, eight-days-a-week job. I could be leaving it all behind.

"My father is not well." It pained me to say it. "I think I may need to spend more time flying from New York to California to help care for him." My boss, Yvette Miley, sat up in her chair and looked me in the eye the way a news editor does, listening for facts. Not many broadcast journalists ask for less screen time, less money.

"I feel you. I also take care of my mom in Florida," Yvette shared. "Let's come up with some ideas." She pulled out her reporter's notebook and jotted down ideas based on what she was living through. Wow!

She worked with me on this plan for months. She didn't have to. This would not make her job easier—in fact, probably the opposite. Plenty of talented broadcast journalists could fill my spot. And what I had expected to be difficult turned out to be about creative kindness.

When I first started at 30 Rock, I had worked thirty days straight with no days off. I loved it. After this talk with my boss, I was no longer working on a daily show or going on location to places where breaking news was taking place around the country and the world. My speaking schedule was cut dramatically. My annual earnings were slashed. I thought I was trading a life that I had invested years to develop, giving it up for my dad—for whatever time he had left. I was torn by this new, ironic work-life balance. The longer I was successful in fighting for my father to live, the longer my career would be slowed. What I didn't realize is that my life would also change in ways I couldn't have previously imagined.

This book is an exploration of that change and what it taught me, of being challenged to think outside myself in big ways, of doing the small things, and of the personal foibles I encountered along the way. It's a halftime review. From the past—what had I done and what had I learned? For the future—what will I have to do and what might I learn?

In any bookstore, the bestsellers sit on the self-help shelves and promise to give us advice for such reflections. However, the focus of many is less on personal growth and more on how to "truly" love ourselves. Recent titles include:

- *Radical Self-Love: A Guide to Loving Yourself and Living Your Dreams*
- *I Heart Me: The Science of Self-Love*
- *How to Love Yourself (and Sometimes Other People): Spiritual Advice for Modern Relationships*

Oh, and a couple of other (tongue-in-cheek) titles:

- *I'm Super Great: What the Hell's Wrong with You?*
- *Me, Me, Me: A Love Story*, with a foreword by "My Mirror"

Admittedly, I have loved self-help books for years. Why wouldn't I want to make myself better? Everyone could use a little improvement. (Two exceptions—the legends Judy Woodruff and Andrea Mitchell.)

So here I am—writing an anti-self-help self-help book. A book on selflessness, just when self-love is all the rage. Maybe for my next trick I can open a video rental store. Or sell waterbeds or pet rocks. Get into disco. Transfer my cloud data to floppy disks.

Here in this halftime breather, we find a place to jot down notes that will put things in context. What's working? What isn't? Like the 360 reviews some of us do at work every six months. Except this 360 reveals it's about the 360. It's about *we*.

As I set out to learn about selflessness, I realized I'm a "swing doer," a person who wants to hear and learn more before deciding, not just be quick to the draw. I need logical, reasoned thinking, not hyperbole, polarizing words or ideas. I don't like ivory towers. I like to hear from practitioners. I read books on how to build things around the house. I like YouTubing how to change the kitchen tile or fix broken eyeglasses. I like solutions to problems. I'm kind of a life do-it-yourselfer, learning from the contractors of human spirit. You might call it a blue-collar approach to a white-collar topic.

I'm the type of guy who doesn't buy the car without looking under the hood. But even though I looked under the hood of selflessness and decided to buy into the concept, I didn't, and still don't, know what the road ahead may bring.

I am no saint. That's Mother Teresa, who tended to the dying on the streets of Calcutta. Or Desmond Tutu, who strove for equality for all. I'm just a drop in a pail, a guy who was presented with a challenge and decided to figure out how to help his dad by slowly understanding what he had been saying all along: Being ordinary can be extraordinary. Live off camera. Is this old-fashioned principle still relevant today? I wasn't sure. As I walked out of my boss's office, so began the fight for the man who had taught me how to fight.

Chapter Two

IS SELFLESSNESS POSSIBLE?

I think we have shots fired, possible shots fired, 1200 building," the former county sheriff deputy could be heard saying on dispatch.

The deputy reached the high school building and then retreated to another position for safety. The gunman fired approximately seventy-five more times. The deputy did not enter the building. The gunman killed seventeen people, mostly teens. The deputy, a veteran officer, had received "many hours" of active shooter training to learn how to respond to these difficult situations. Later, critics called him the "Coward of Broward County," citing his failure to act at Marjory Stoneman Douglas High School, which is now the site of the deadliest school shooting in American history.

While the bullets flew, fifteen-year-old student Peter Wang, an Army Junior Reserve Officers Training Corps cadet, didn't run. In fact, he stood still, holding the door open for his classmates so they could escape.

Then one of the bullets accomplished its goal, piercing Peter's gray JROTC uniform and killing him. When America heard of his death, we all wished his uniform had been made of steel or Kevlar or something that would have stopped that bullet. His story, along with those of the other teens who died that day, conjured up a new brew of collective national grief.

No one who knew Peter was surprised that he died saving others. "He is so brave," his cousin said. "He is the person who is genuinely kind to everyone. He doesn't care about popularity. He always liked to cheer people up. He is like the big brother everyone wished they had."[1]

Peter had wanted to go to West Point, his dream school. So a week later at his funeral, the hallowed military academy notified Peter's parents that they were admitting him posthumously to the revered military academy for his heroism. In addition, the United States army posthumously awarded him the Medal of Heroism, the highest award given to ROTC cadets.

His parents decided to bury their son in his gray JROTC uniform, his heroism medal pinned neatly beside his other ribbons. The Patriot Guard Riders who normally pay tribute to fallen enlisted military attended his funeral, as is their tradition, roaring by with full-sized American flags on the back of their motorcycles.[2]

Why would a teen risk—and ultimately give—his own life to help others? At that age, I would barely hold the front door open for my grandparents. His parents immigrated to America because of its freedom, so this was something Peter was built to defend, but it was also something that couldn't safeguard him that Wednesday.

PHYSIOLOGY AND NATURE

Some scholars have argued for years that humans are not naturally selfless. And some social scientists went beyond this claim. They said pure altruism does not exist. They claimed that selflessness, like Bigfoot, the Loch Ness Monster, and a stylish fanny pack, is a myth. Survival, not virtue, is what motivates us.

The British naturalist Charles Darwin, who wrote *On the Origin of Species*, explained our behavior simply as the struggle to survive. We do what it takes to get the evolutionary edge. Our genetic makeup changes (Is this the tenth time I've mentioned makeup? I'm on camera a lot, okay?) to help organisms survive over generations. Even the slightest evolutionary advantage becomes permanent over time. To evolve, species put survival first. Consider these examples:

- After arriving in the Nebraska Sandhills, deer mice changed from dark brown to light brown to better blend in and increase their chances of survival.

- After being killed by pesticides, insects become resistant to the chemicals and pass the resistance on to offspring. Since insects have such short lifespans, this evolutionary change can be observed over the course of months. (I can see the roach ancestors laughing at Raid!)
- Female peahens (NBC has a male peacock icon) prefer mates with the largest and brightest tails, so much so that it's hard to find males that don't have bright feathers. A larger tail suggests a healthier male peacock with better genes.[3] (As far as I know, the NBC mascot is still single, so let me know if you know any good female peahens. Our peacock's feathers are pretty bright!)

Evolution favors survival because organisms want to live and thrive. So choices are based on long-term survival, as well as the survival of offspring, and *not* based on what might benefit or harm other species. That's why bird nests rarely welcome outside visitors. This means sex may have to do less with Axe body spray and organic shampoos and more to do with improving evolutionary success. Humans are not different from field mice, insects, and peacocks in that respect.

In 1976, Richard Dawkins claimed in his bestselling book *The Selfish Gene* that we can't expect humans to be anything but selfish: "We are survival machines—robot vehicles blindly programmed to preserve the selfish molecules known as genes."[4] Even though we'd love to believe in "universal love" and the "welfare of the species as a whole," these concepts simply do not make sense, according to Dawkins. Altruism only makes sense when it's shown to close relatives who share copies of our own genes, or others who might owe us. In *The God Delusion*, Dawkins describes all of our Good Samaritan acts as "misfirings."[5]

In *The Selfish Gene*, he compared the brutal selfishness of our genes to Chicago gangsters. "You can make some inferences about a man's character if you know something about the conditions in which he has survived and prospered," Dawkins wrote. "We, and all other animals, are machines created by our genes. Like successful Chicago gangsters, our genes have survived . . . in a highly competitive world."[6] Unlike the gangster Al Capone, who ended up in Alcatraz and died in 1947, genes can survive in some cases for millions of years.

One of Dawkins's fans was Enron CEO Jeffrey Skilling, who pulled off the largest accounting and corporate fraud ever, resulting in shareholders losing $74 billion. Skilling said his favorite book was Dawkins's *The Selfish Gene*, which was in the evolutionary spirit of Darwin's theory of natural selection.[7] Even though Darwin was by all accounts a kindhearted man, his theory ultimately inspired some controversial philosophical and political positions, such as social Darwinism and eugenics.

Social Darwinism. The late-nineteenth-century English professor Herbert Spencer coined the phrase "survival of the fittest,"[8] because he saw natural selection as "red in tooth and claw,"[9] a brutal description of the competition for scant resources. He didn't value protecting the weak. If more weak people died, more beautiful, healthy, strong, and smart people could thrive. Spencer believed this would improve the condition of humanity over time.

Eugenics. In the 1920s and 1930s, books, films, fairs, and exhibitions promoted eugenics, a movement to rid the population of undesirable traits by preventing "unfit" people from having children. Thirty-two states passed laws that resulted in 64,000 Americans (including African Americans, immigrants, unmarried mothers, and people with mental illness) to be forcibly sterilized. (Charles Darwin himself did not promote laws to regulate marriage, reproduction, or segregation and didn't think they would be effective.)

You can see how the argument that selflessness may not even be real but instead the extreme opposite—survival of the fittest—has supporting theories and examples. One theory has been working itself out recently. As the deadly COVID-19 spread throughout the globe, people everywhere were isolated, sacrificing convenience, financial success, and comfort in order to preserve (in Darwinian terms) the weakest members of our society—the elderly and other immunocompromised people.

For instance, I was about to take my first trip in four months back to California to care for my parents. My father was hospitalized for the tenth time. My mother fell for the third time. I faced certain exposure as I made that ten-hour, door-to-door trip. They needed my support, and I wanted to give it. So I went.

Southern Baptist leader Russell Moore wrote in the *New York Times* that we needed to put the emphasis less on the economy and more on the lives of the vulnerable portions of society. Instead of survival of the fittest, he argued we must fight for survival of all of us. "Vulnerability is not a diminishment of the human experience, but is part of that experience," he wrote. "A life in a nursing home is a life worth living. A life in a hospital quarantine ward is a life worth living. The lives of our grandparents, the lives of the disabled, the lives of the terminally ill, these are all lives worth living."[10]

And there we were, economy versus health. Grand perennial battles that also reflected a collision between the utilitarian "survival of the fittest" mindset and the "let's take care of others" philosophy. It brought to the surface the question of whether we should put value on saving lives versus returning to our livelihoods. The "open the states" supporters' remarks were seemingly informed by real economic concerns, while Moore's were motivated by the spiritual values and obligations he possesses.

Biologist J. B. S. Haldane offers something in between. According to legend, one night in the 1950s while drinking at a pub in the West End of London, he was presented with a philosophical question: *How far would you go to save the life of another person?* "I would jump into a river to save two brothers, but not one," Haldane said after feverishly calculating on the back of a napkin. "Or to save eight cousins but not seven."[11]

However, Haldane's drunken calculation may have pointed to a way out of the "altruism conundrum" for evolutionary psychologists. If a person performs a selfless act for someone in their own family, they are still promoting the survival of their own DNA, right? Sociobiologists in Western Europe decided it can only be explained among people and organisms who were related by blood.

Marjory Stoneman Douglas High's Peter Wang would disagree with this. Instead, he might have agreed with examples in the animal kingdom: bats feed other bats that haven't gotten enough food to live; honeybees deliver a sting to defend the hive, even though it results in their own death; birds raise the offspring of other birds; ants cooperate to dig huge nests, form rafts, sew leaves together, create bridges, and farm for food; and young male Australian gray-crowned babblers stay in the nest to gather food, incubate eggs, and take care of the young. (These ain't your grandparents' male Australian gray-crowned babblers.) All of these different types of creatures that live together in selflessness indicates selfless communities survive adeptly. There *must* be some advantages to it.

And yet if selflessness is so amazing, why aren't all living beings organized like the ants? Why does humanity remain a relatively unorganized mess? It's pretty obvious that people aren't honeybees or ants. People are complicated, complex beings. And if you've read much about communes (or lived in one), you know they aren't well-oiled cultural machines like ant colonies.

Shorthand. Selflessness is not a binary, "real or not" proposition. There are more than two dishes at this cook-off.

LOGIC AND CHOICE

And so we come back to the selflessness of people like teenager Peter Wang. Logic probably told him he faced sure danger, but he still chose to hold open a door. An action that said, *You first, please; my life is after yours.* That was the snapshot of his life we all came to know. There are more in the photo album of ordinary people being extraordinary, doing what doesn't seem logical.

This was true in the case of the former New York City firefighter James Boyle. He was working in Brooklyn when terrorists flew planes into the World Trade Center.[12] His son Michael had decided to emulate his father's career and become a firefighter too. When Boyle got word that his son was working in the North Tower, he raced on foot to be close to his son, not get farther away. Though Boyle was retired, he was a "run toward the fire" kind of guy, a decision he had made thousands of times over his twenty-five-year career.

When I interviewed him on the fifth anniversary of 9/11, he shared his son's decision to become a firefighter, a career ranked in the top twenty-five most dangerous jobs in the United States.[13] Boyle knew this counter-instinctual choice himself. He talked about searching for his thirty-seven-year-old son that fateful day and not being able to find him. Four months later, after days of going through the rubble himself, Boyle found his son's fireman's turnout coat.

His recounts were always filled with sorrow, and I saw it in his eyes each time we spoke. The first time was about remembering his son on the five-year anniversary. The next interview was about being the fireman's union chief and advocate for all first responders' needs, not just his son's.

Boyle had at least three careers, each pushed by what he knew was right. His family says his repeated trips to Ground Zero to find his son and help others ultimately led to the cancer that took his life eighteen years later. Even as I tell his story, I hear Boyle telling me, "Don't talk about me. Write about the first responders; they're the ones who made the tough choices."

Boyle's approach to life reminded me of that of a member of George W. Bush's Secret Service detail, who later became a United States Immigration and Customs Enforcement officer. One of her everyday duties was to find undocumented immigrants and begin the process of deportation. She also kept her eye out for women who had been tricked into coming to the United States illegally and forced into sex slavery. I traveled to Georgia to interview this ICE agent. She told me how one of the women she had arrested appeared to have been trafficked. She put that into her report—and at that point, the agent's involvement is typically concluded.

This ICE officer decided to help the survivor apply for a T visa (as in "trafficking") that allows a survivor to stay and help prosecute her pimps and traffickers. Without this visa, people who are trafficked for sex are sent back to their home country, where their pimps' networks will either beat them and their families or return them into the slave pipeline. Most trafficking victims are unaware of the T visa, especially those who don't speak English and are not educated. So the agent's help is crucial.

But this agent didn't stop there. After the T visa was granted, she helped the survivor get a part-time job. The agent's decisions to operate in a way inconsistent with the stereotype of what ICE agents do no doubt raised some eyebrows in the proverbial locker room.

Both the FDNY veteran and the ICE officer were people dealing with their day-to-day imperatives. How and why did they move past selfish instincts?

HEART AND MIND

In the ongoing, complex discussion of whether selflessness is even real, we've talked about instinct and discussed how the brain may reject it to choose a middle ground. We've discussed "physiology and nature" and "logic and choice"; "heart and soul" is a third topic to consider when it comes to the question of why some seem to ignore instinct's warnings. One theory is this: people may look selfless, but they're hiding self-interest under a veneer of virtue.

If I bring in donuts for my coworkers, am I hoping they will like me more and do favors for "the donut guy"? When Facebook CEO Mark Zuckerberg and his wife, Priscilla Chan, promised to donate 99 percent of their Facebook shares to charity for the rest of their lives, was that because of altruism, a desire to save millions in taxes, or both? When we compliment someone on their appearance, do we want them to feel good, or do we want them to like us?

Researchers have used this complex ambiguity of motive to explain away any philosophical contradictions—essentially concluding that true selflessness doesn't exist. The American biologist and philosopher Michael Ghiselin bluntly and concisely expressed this duality: "Scratch an 'altruist' and watch a 'hypocrite' bleed."[14] There are lots of ways to read this, but for this conversation, let's say Ghiselin bluntly expresses the binary approach to the question of whether true selflessness exists. In other words, there are only two options—zero or one. But might there be a third option, something like the midpoint between the two—say, a 0.5?

Darwin saw selflessness as a potentially devastating blow to his theory. In *The Descent of Man*, he wrote:

> He who was ready to sacrifice his life, as many a savage has been, rather than betray his comrades, would often leave no offspring to inherit his noble nature. The bravest men, who were always willing to come to the front in war, and who freely risked their lives for others, would on an average perish in larger numbers than other men.[15]

Yet selfless, brave men are still around, not dying at high rates. Their instinct did not cause them to become extinct.

What evolutionary psychology may be missing is something my dad used to emphasize in his pastoral robe-wearing days. He and my mom stuck to their commitment to help others, which meant we didn't have a ton of money. But our family was doing better in other ways. I guess my folks practiced what they shared openly on Sundays about an "upside-down kingdom": "Whoever wants to become great among you must be your servant," and "The last will be first, and the first will be last."[16]

Like a Facebook relationship status, it's complicated. Life defies much of the way we expect the world should be—that it must be one or the other, a zero or a one. Instead, the challenge is how to thrive in the midpoint between the two—in greatness and servitude, when first and last and when rich and poor.

If we can never accomplish true selflessness or pure selfishness, we should find the ways to understand best practices between the two. Maybe that's why this topic seems so dangerous—it rarely looks like a win. Instead, it's about making progress, like making it to the opponent's forty-nine yard line. (Stick around, chapter 13 has some ideas about how to measure wins.) We don't make it our goal to land in that gray, in-between space, but we recognize that we may spend 80 percent of the game there.

. . . .

In 2019, I was filming in Michigan and was in line at a gas station paying for my tank of gas. A gentleman in front of me—in his mid-fifties, about six-foot-four-inches tall—noticed I was in a rush and waved me in front of him.

"Appreciate that." I was grateful for the gesture.

He was on the phone but made a point of speaking to me anyway. "No problem, buddy. I'm in no rush." While I waited for the person in front of me to finish, the guy behind me returned to his call.

"Yeah, sorry to hear about that—that's a bad day. Sounds tough," he said to the person on the phone. "Go on home, throw her around a little bit, punch her around a little bit, and you'll feel better." I froze. Was he encouraging someone to commit domestic violence? When I speak on gender inequality, I challenge audiences by asking, "When do you intervene?" Now I was being put to my own test.

"Take it out on her," he said, as if to remove all doubt. "It'll do you right." I took a deep breath as I watched the guy in front of me leave. As I stepped up to pay for my tank of gas, my mind was racing with the possibility of confronting the guy behind me. *Is that the right way to approach this?* I figured it wouldn't work out well. He was a big guy, and it had been a long time since those kung fu classes. As the cashier handed back my change, I could envision interrupting his phone call. *Excuse me, sir, but violence against women is never the right thing to do.*

I put my change in my pocket and walked out the door. I was disappointed in myself. I rationalized, *Would a random guy like me at a gas station change this guy's heart toward women?* Probably not. But maybe I was asking the wrong question. Maybe I should have been willing to do something smaller rather than nothing at all.

I consider myself a seven-year-old feminist. And no, that doesn't mean I sit at the kids' table at women's group dinners. After years of reporting on sex slavery, seven years ago I realized that women are systemically treated unfairly everywhere. So as a seven-year-old, I've still got a lot to learn.

I mention all this because I needed to realize two things when I was standing in line in that Michigan gas station: (1) I was still learning, and (2) at that age, I hadn't learned to see the gray, in-between area. It was too simplistic to pick from two choices: either tell him he was wrong *or* do nothing. I missed at least thirty-five other choices in that moment, I'm sure. Among these are the "Five Ds of Bystander Intervention," developed by the Southern Poverty Law Center: Direct, Distract, Delegate, Delay, Document.[17] These are all actions, but not the traditional all-or-nothing choices I had grown up operating from.

I could have done any number of things to engage the gentleman (who was kind enough to let me in front of him in line) and object to his advice to abuse someone. What if I had slowed him down by saying, "You got a cigarette I could bum off you? Thanks, it's for later. Go ahead in front of me. I realized I forgot to get a bag of chips. It's always something, isn't it. You don't mind, do you? Thanks again."

While I don't smoke but do make up for it with my love for chips, this approach *directs* (per the Five Ds) him away from talking to his friend, if only for a moment, so he might change the subject, and *distracts* him, since he'd get to the cashier faster and might have to get off the phone. Both actions might have reduced his abuse encouragement time.

In those few moments, none of my options were that great. The situation taught me the selflessness option isn't always an obvious one.

In that self-preservation, survival-of-the-fittest moment, I was like a deer in the headlights. Plagued by my lack of action, I vowed to do more to stop violence against women through my volunteer work. It also pushed me to think beyond the either-or thinking that conflicted me and to search for the better answer I was sure was out there.

When I share this story, I've found I'm not the only one who sees and experiences these unfortunate situations and then suffers selflessness paralysis as a result. At times, when we think of doing a selfless act for someone, we instantly doubt ourselves. We convince ourselves we'll do it next time because we're in a rush and don't have the time and money right now. "Although we may frequently feel an impulse to do something for others, we often suppress it," wrote Stefan Klein in *Survival of the Nicest*. "Altruism almost always seems riskier than acting exclusively for our own advantage."[18]

Though there are strong arguments from different camps around selflessness, some things seem clear. The world would be a cooler place if people—of all faiths or of no faith at all—thought strategically about serving others. Even if it feels awkward. Even if we do it imperfectly. And even if we end up with too many chips to eat and cigarettes to smoke. At some point, it will come naturally.

We are more than our biological instincts; we have a mind and a heart. Because these internal forces are at odds, pushing aside selflessness paralysis requires good old-fashioned work. The results are strong muscle reflexes. And then better choices—many of which may not be perfect, but will be in the gray.

Like Peter Wang's uniform.

Chapter Three

BEHIND THE
CAMERA

I n my twenty-five years of practicing journalism, many of the stories I've covered are about something bad—natural disasters, crimes, tragedies. And yet the people I've met in the aftermath have shown an inspirational goodness that often transcends the initially daunting bad stuff. They are instinctively helpful, self-sacrificing, and generous. It's an extraordinary thing to witness. In fact, there may be no such thing as an ordinary person. If you take the time to listen, the stories people tell reveal how extraordinary they truly are. And yet in the world around us, there's no denying that a lot of us still fall short on the spectrum of selflessness.

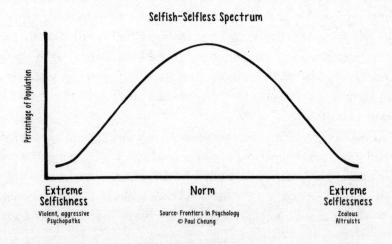

Selfish–Selfless Spectrum

Percentage of Population

Extreme
Selfishness
Violent, aggressive
Psychopaths

Norm
Source: Frontiers In Psychology
© Paul Cheung

Extreme
Selflessness
Zealous
Altruists

Researchers at the University of Kentucky and University of Central Florida who explored the neurobiology of the selfish-selfless spectrum found that most of us are neither extremely selfish (which results in becoming aggressive psychopaths) nor extremely selfless (which results in becoming zealous altruists). Most of us are between these extremes, moving closer to one side or the other on the spectrum depending on the circumstances. When it comes to selfishness and selflessness, it turns out we're not static, nor are we, incapable of moving toward one end or the other.[1]

Breaking stories often prove out this fluidity, as they often include someone on the psychopath end of the spectrum who has done something extremely selfish; the answer to that are the altruists who step up and remind us there are amazing people ready to act, to call a halt to the actions of those who epitomize selfishness.

So here are three stories of four extraordinary people—Tiffany, Bradley and Mohamad, and Anita. They don't know it, but they've been my unexpected mentors in selflessness. They've inspired me to work harder and better, to move toward what initially frightens me, to find ways to help even when there seems to be little to give, to stay strong even in the worst of storms.

TIFFANY

West Texas, August 31, 2019

It was a Saturday afternoon at 30 Rockefeller when things got busy. "Breaking news" is news about an unfolding event—something happening *right now*. As a breaking news anchor, I had handled many such stories, sometimes reporting for four, five, even six hours straight—to the point where going to the bathroom was a luxury. (In an awkward sort of way, an uncomfortable bladder is sometimes the measure of the severity of a breaking story.)

That day's breaking news story started like this: A state trooper tried to pull over a gold Honda for failing to signal a left turn on a highway near Midland and Odessa, Texas. Suddenly, the driver pointed a rifle out of his window, fired indiscriminately, and then took off—an active shooter in a moving car. This wasn't a typical scenario—most mass shooters I had covered tended to be on foot. This shooter was instead going from location to location across city lines, emptying out his rifle along the way at cars on the freeway. Most police officers aren't accustomed to dealing with a spree shooter in one jurisdiction, and now police in multiple jurisdictions had to coordinate to stop this bizarre active shooter scenario.

We didn't have much information, because most early reportable data comes from law enforcement and city administration. Eyewitness information was essential in characterizing what was happening but not confirmable most of the time.

I talked to a national law enforcement expert on air about the situation. Then our booker got Tiffany Parada on the phone—the gunman had shot at her and her family just moments earlier. She and her husband had been driving away from Midland when they saw the gold Honda on the freeway median.

"My husband saw him start shooting at us, and we got onto the median," Tiffany said calmly. "My husband was trying to control our Suburban because we had our kids in there; we were just freaking out, making sure our kids weren't hit or nothing."

Nevertheless, when they saw the shooter get back on the interstate, they did too. Not to flee, but to warn others. And to drive *toward* the shooter, who was now in front of them. They hoped to pass him and then warn the other cars that were in front of him.

Eventually, their Suburban's V8 engine allowed them to catch up to the suspect's Honda. The shooter apparently didn't appreciate their selflessness. He reloaded his gun and shot at them as they overtook him, miraculously escaping injury and excessive damage to their vehicle.

As heroic as this sounds, the reception from those the Paradas had hoped to help was, well, not what they expected. All that people saw was an old SUV with its windows down and people yelling at them frantically. It was hard to hear the couple's important message: "There's a shooter back there!" People thought the Paradas were crazy.

The big question is this: Why did Tiffany decide to warn others, with her four kids in the back seat and the car speeding forward at 110 miles an hour? She appeared to have zeroed in on my mention of the kids and began her answer by giving me their ages.

"My oldest is nine," she said, her voice catching as if the full extent of the danger they had faced was only now beginning to sink in. "My second is eight." She paused. "And five and two."

Throughout the interview, my producer was speaking to me through my earpiece—she wanted me to interrupt Tiffany. "Ask her about the gun. Your other guest, the law enforcement expert, wants you to ask her about the gun."

I wasn't going to interrupt her. It would take time for Tiffany to feel comfortable enough to tell her story of charging toward danger to help others. Asking her for details about the gun would derail her progress. Plus, it was information that law enforcement could get later.

"Ask her about the gun," I heard the producer say again a few seconds later. *Not yet.* I listened to Tiffany explain how she and her husband had attempted to warn others and even stopped to help a man who'd been injured. What none of us knew at the time was that the shooter would go on to kill seven people and injure twenty-five, including three police officers—all in the span of an hour.

The story needed to be handled like this. Allowing people to show their humanity in their own way as it's being tested is a lesson I learned from my first spree-killing press conference years earlier. At the time, the local and national reporters were asking the police chief for details of the crime, such as the caliber of the bullet. I was the only one there who hadn't previously worked for an affiliate or a local broadcast news station (my job was working as a cable news anchor), so I hadn't experienced the culture of covering shootings in local settings. Local reporters know all the ins and outs of the story, so usually if you're flown in, like I was, you let them lead because they know the community and the angles. So I stuck to what I knew.

"Captain, how is the department doing?" I asked. "How are the officers feeling?" It was day two of their investigation. The other reporters were probably thinking, *Why aren't you asking about the gun?* The chief paused before answering. "This is painful for us," he said. "This is a tight-knit community. We know every one of the people who died. We're working day and night to find out who this person is and why he did it." That was the sound bite. Even if my question didn't elicit the details of the crime scene, it did get to the essence of the story.

It was the same situation with Tiffany Parada and her four kids in the back seat. Spree killers want the story to be about them. We should not give them that. It's no accident that the killer's name isn't mentioned here but Tiffany Parada's is. The gunman's plan for achieving fame was foiled, like a second-rate Scooby-Doo villain. Instead, ironically, his killing spree revealed the stories of goodness, heroism, and selflessness of those around him. Tiffany's was one of those—though not on screen; we could only hear Tiffany's voice on her mobile phone.

Still, I saw her.

"I just feel like God was with us," Tiffany shared.

Now it was time to ask her about the gun and all the details she could recall about the shooter. But I and all the viewers who heard Tiffany Parada took away more than the details of evil that played out in West Texas that day; we learned about a selfless family that risked their lives to save strangers.

BRADLEY AND MOHAMAD

Ferguson, Missouri, August 9, 2014

Ferguson numbers barely twenty thousand residents. One of them, a Black teen, was shot and killed by a White police officer. The controversy around the moments before the killing led to local conflicts about the disparities between Black and White Americans in this Midwestern community. Fury grew and spread as I covered the story from my anchor seat. Protests erupted daily in the area, especially on West Florissant Avenue, near where the teen, Michael Brown, was shot.

In order to have a nearby base of operations for ongoing coverage of the unrest, NBC News and MSNBC rented a two-acre warehouse a few blocks from Brown's home and the street where he died. We didn't need more than a tenth of the large warehouse, but the location was ideal because it was right on the demonstration routes. Plus, it was surrounded by a new fence you could see through but not get through. MSNBC security suspected things could get dicey. In a rare construct, most live reporting would occur twenty feet behind the fence so rocks and other projectiles would have difficulty reaching us. It could house our broadcast trucks and security personnel who were armed with long rifles and bulletproof vests. It was the first conflict zone approach I had experienced on US soil. Soon after, I'd get my gas mask.

During the days, the marches were mostly peaceful. The elders tried to show the newer protesters what they had learned in the 1960s and 1970s during the civil rights movement. Pastors marched at the front of groups of young adults who were chanting as they passed our fence, "No justice, no peace!" Even though we set cameras farther back from the chain-link fences and the majority of protesters were peaceful, an occasional outlier would lob rocks and hit us. Those belligerents sometimes hid behind protestors at the front of the march who were nonviolent. Consequently, when police officers charged in to stop the projectiles, it was the innocent ones in front who took the brunt.

As a cub reporter twenty years before, I had covered the story of Rodney King, a Black man whose savage beating by Los Angeles police officers had been captured on videotape. The state of California erupted. Two decades later, it felt like the valleys of racism in our America were the same, if not deeper. Since the LA riots, no American city had felt more like a war zone than Ferguson. At night, anger flared, and even our security detail was shot at as they guarded our news "green zone."

Maybe the people throwing rocks didn't realize they were causing all of the protesters to be labeled as troublemakers—which only intensified the police response and worsened public perception. Or maybe the rock throwers didn't care.

The days of anchoring and reporting live from Ferguson melded together.

Then one sweltering afternoon, I interviewed a college student named Bradley, who was following in the footsteps of his broadcast photojournalist dad. Bradley was from the neighborhood. He lived in the middle of the unrest. On the first night, he saw the color of the sky change. One of the first major fires and lootings took place at Sam's Meat Market, located on the same street where Brown had been shot. Bradley captured footage of his neighborhood's burning skyline as he ran toward Sam's—its windows broken and its front door bashed in by looters. It was a dangerous location, with people running in and out of the small grocery store, almost trampling each other, lots of smoke, flames, and screaming. The scene on the street looked like one from a war zone. And Bradley ran into the store.

"Weren't you worried?" I asked.

He admitted he had been, but he told me this was the community where he had grown up and he was trying to step in to prevent further damage—and he felt he should tell the story. "Some were misguided; they didn't know what they were doing," he told me on air.

After we finished his interview, I went back inside our portable offices to escape the 99-degree heat and prep for the next broadcast. Not too much later, I noticed Bradley was still sitting outside.

"It's hot; you still here?" I poked my head outside.

"Can I just hang out and watch what you all are doing?" he asked. Turns out it was a great idea. When my boss arrived an hour later, I introduced her to Bradley. This connection wouldn't have been possible had the shooting and protests not brought my boss down to Missouri. "Show me your portfolio," she said. Right there in Ferguson, sitting inside a perimeter of chain-link fences, she began to mentor him.

And as Bradley found a mentor, I found Bradley inspiring for remaining so resilient. I decided to go to the meat market I'd seen burning in his video. The owner was a Middle Eastern American immigrant, Mohamad Yaacoub, who had built his grocery business with a partner over a period of nine years. His store was vandalized, not only the first night, but also the second night and the third. Every morning, he boarded up whatever had gotten damaged and reopened the store.

"Why do you keep opening?" I asked. People were looting, emptying the shelves and trying to set his store on fire.

"I have customers who need me," he explained. "They don't make a lot of money. This is the place they come. I want to be here for them."

"What does your wife think about you coming to work like this?"

"She doesn't like it, but I'm doing it," he smiled. "I am Muslim. This is the right thing to do."

He took a few minutes to show me the damage throughout the store, which he estimated to be a loss of $600,000. The meat counter had little meat, but he was ready to sell whatever was there.

"Mohamad, why do you come in?" I repeated my question. The majority of the restaurants on the strip had already closed and were boarded up. He had the same answer as before. "This is my job, my community."

Bradley and Mohamad were in the middle of widespread protest and violence. Their neighborhoods were getting crushed. But they still made commitments to do more. To go and take pictures, to keep the store open.

They had so little. And from one angle, they did ordinary things, yet from another angle, these were extraordinary things. They really had so much.

ANITA

Paris, France, November 13, 2015

The phone rang—a call from New York. I glanced at the time. It was 10:00 p.m. London time, which meant it was 5:00 p.m. back in Manhattan. Calls from this number usually meant there was an emergency. I was in England to give a speech and was meeting friends for dinner the night before the speech. I excused myself and answered the phone.

"Richard, can you get to 30 Rock now?" It was Jessica, the director who manages scheduling at MSNBC.

"Not quickly," I said, reminding her that I was out of the country. "I'm in London."

"A mass spree killing just happened in Paris," she said. There had been explosions, one after the other—at a concert, at a sports stadium— and shootings in other locations. If I had been in Manhattan, I'd have hauled butt to 30 Rock and been on camera in minutes.

"Hang tight," Jessica said, excusing herself to rejigger plans. She called back moments later. "We need to send you to Paris directly from London. You can get there pretty fast, right?"

I left dinner immediately—it was British cuisine, after all—and headed back to the hotel to pack and figure out how to get to Paris. The French government had shut down the Chunnel, which normally had trains leaving late and early to Paris. They had no idea where the terrorists were coming from, who they were, or how they had organized in order to strike so many locations at once. People speculated that flights could be prohibited from landing in France, so the wee hours of that Friday night were spent trying to figure out ways to get from London to Paris. The first available Chunnel train and two flights—just in case—were booked out of Heathrow around two in the morning on Saturday. Last-minute decisions based on available information meant I'd take one of the flights.

The plane landed at the Charles de Gaulle airport in France—the second busiest airport in Europe—around nine in the morning. The long immigration line wasn't moving. The wait was estimated to be two hours.

Immigration officers were going through everyone's credentials from top to bottom. Around two hundred people were packed into a small area. Cell phone service was spotty.

Time was ticking. "I'm having trouble getting to a camera," I emailed to NBC.

"Do you think you can do a report from the immigration line?" the executive producer asked. Though video phone calls were not encouraged in the immigration line, I called in and filed a live phone report for our early morning show on NBC News.

After seventy-five minutes, I finally made it through the line, found a taxi, and headed into Paris. On my way to the city center, I was delayed at several lockdown areas close to the six attack locations. Before I arrived, producers and crew had already staked out our broadcast location. It was closest to and had the best angle of the Bataclan theatre, where ninety young people were killed while enjoying a rock concert. In the confusion of loud music, concertgoers initially thought the gunfire was special effects. They had no idea that people had been mowed down in the concert hall.

Our network's European correspondent and I were the first correspondents at the site. Our location was good because of the proximity to the crime scene, but it also was the one location where all the cars and traffic were funneling through because of multiple road closings. Every car had to turn down the one-way street where I stood. For those driving down that one-way road, the first camera crew they'd see would be ours, and then ninety-nine more in a straight line.

"This is going to be a long one," the field producer on-site told me. "We're six hours ahead of 30 Rock." I'd been awake for twenty-four hours at this point, and the breaking news adrenaline was in charge.

"Is this location safe?" I asked the security personnel and my producer. The terrorists were still at large. They had killed people in an asymmetric pattern of attacks in different locations. The producer peered carefully at the cars driving by. The terrorists could easily get into a van, wait in traffic, make a left turn, open the van door, and spray the journalists with bullets. Such an attack would be consistent with what they had already done. No rules.

I reported live every hour on the hour for our network. After thirty-six hours of being awake, I knew there was more to come. My hotel room was five minutes away, and I took several strategic breaks for a hit of sleep, no more than twenty minutes at a time. I had no real sleep for almost two days. Adrenaline kept me going—even though once in a while I might have seen a nonexistent spider.

The news as it developed included a growing death toll. The terrorist cell killed 131 people across six locations, including the Bataclan theatre. Several had been shot at a restaurant. At the national stadium, Stade de France, explosions occurred. It seemed the terrorists were everywhere. Tensions were high, as the suspects were still at large and could be planning another wave. But where?

The next day, we had to relocate. As good as our first spot was, we lost it when we packed up for the night. Along with most other networks, our secondary setup was at Place de la République, a plaza where Parisians and tourists spent nice afternoons in normal times. Even though officials had told people to stay inside because the terrorists were still at large, people wanted to gather at the square to mourn, place flowers, and express their solidarity in rejecting terror.

I was standing on an equipment case to get a little elevation for the broadcast, facing the camera, with the crowd and vigil behind me. In my earpiece I heard, "Live in thirty seconds."

Then the entire crowd started running. People screamed and charged toward us. Nobody saw them coming, and I was pushed over and fell to the ground thirty seconds before going on air. I felt a foot on my leg, and another on my back. I had run with the bulls in Spain, but this was no exotic adventure vacation. When the realization of the real danger of death by trampling hit me, I knew I had to get up. I was confused, not knowing what had caused the stampede.

"Get out, get out, get out!" team members yelled. I fell into line with the crowd. It was harder than you might think to run in a large group—people had fallen; camera crews and equipment were everywhere; and rows of parked cars slowed the flow of people trying to escape. Once they cleared the cars, people sprinted.

"Do you know what caused the stampede?" I asked somebody next to me.

"A gunshot," came the panicked response.

So I turned back. I hadn't seen the cameraman and had only seen a couple members of our team. In the worst-case scenario, I worried they were injured. In a better scenario, I figured they were already heading back to our location and I would need to join them.

I made it back to our location, and our cameraman was there. He had been trampled but stayed down and moved closer to the alleged shooting location. He had filmed in conflict and war zones and knew that a low position was safer in case of a gunfight.

We began to set up again. Producers in New York wanted us back on air, and of course we were worried about what had just happened. Although viewers couldn't see the chaos, the control room could as they prepared us to go live. Yet they had no idea what was going on. "Where's Richard? He's not there? What happened?"

I stood in front of the camera.

"I got it," my cameraman told me. "I didn't stop rolling."

Soon after, we went live to the United States. We fed the taped footage directly from the camera—a hot roll, not footage loaded to servers in New York and edited. I narrated as the video streamed.

"No shots have been fired," the police told us after they investigated. "We're all clear." As it turned out, the noise was reported to have been firecrackers that had been set off.

The next hour, as I once again stood on an equipment case doing my hit, I noticed a woman out of the corner of my eye. She looked to be in her sixties, had a large purse slung over her arm, and was standing alone. After I finished, I looked over and made eye contact.

"May I speak to you?" she asked. I walked over. People are often curious about the lights and television crews. They hover around the edges in an unobtrusive way. Other times, people hang around because they're angry and want to express displeasure. This woman was neither. She was patiently waiting for me to notice her.

"My name is Anita. My daughter told me I'm supposed to be in my apartment right now because of what the officials say. I live just a block and a half away," she said as she turned to point. "My daughter is in the United States, where you are from, and she's worried. I wanted you to let people know we Parisians are strong. It's important we remain strong together and accept each other and work together. It's the only way we will solve problems."

© Tak Toyoshima

Anita had come down from her apartment—undoubtedly afraid, but not afraid—to send the world a message of defiance. Then she grabbed my elbow and said she wanted to show me something. She escorted me to one corner of the eight-acre square and pointed to a mural, which read, "FLUCTUAT NEC MERGITUR."

"See?" Anita asked. "In Latin, it means, 'Tossed but not sunk.' The terrorists are not going to change our beliefs. This is Paris, France, and we're a democracy. We work together." The full translation of the Latin is, "She is tossed by the waves but does not sink." A perfect description of Anita.

• • • • • • • • • • •

In each of these scenarios, I met and interviewed ordinary people doing ordinary things. What struck me is that they did these ordinary things against an extraordinary backdrop. Though they might have made the decision at the time to drive in one direction on a highway instead of another, to keep a store open, or to make an effort to speak to a random stranger, these were accessible, simple acts of selflessness. Their "every fifteen minutes" of having to make a conscious choice happened to land at a very crucial time. They were confronted with unexpected, extraordinary circumstances, and they responded in simple ways that showed me the unexpected power of selflessness.

They beautifully demonstrate what "enough about me" can mean in even the direst circumstances. What little decisions can make all the difference for you?

Section Two

SHOULD I?

Chapter Four

GOODNESS MEETS GORGEOUS

I have always been a little self-conscious about my looks, but being surrounded by people who are paid to evaluate how I look (agents, style consultants, Chicago hot dog stand vendors) has definitely heightened my anxiety.

"Are you going gray? Better keep your hair shorter, but not *that* short."

"Can we go with more makeup overall? You have uneven skin tone."

"Your ties need to be skinnier."

These daily issues of appearance in my profession may or may not have made me semi-neurotic. Just the teensiest bit preoccupied with how good-looking I am, or am not. And maybe even a smidge paranoid that there could be a link between how good I look and how good of a person I am. Would a particularly bad blackhead spell the end of my career?

Crazy, right? We'd probably all argue that appearance and character are two separate things. What someone looks like does not determine how good a person he or she might be. But maybe there is a link between the two when it comes to how we are perceived by others—especially when we reverse the correlation. Then the question becomes, "Do nonphysical attributes such as selflessness affect the way others assess our appearance? Specifically, would selflessness make us appear *more* attractive to others?"

That's the question I posed to social psychologist and researcher Pelin Kesebir from the University of Wisconsin. To find out, she agreed to do a study. And to save a couple of shekels, Kesebir volunteered me as the test subject. Kesebir surveyed three hundred people, each of whom were randomly shown a card that included my picture and one of the following three sets of bullet points. Note that the three titles (such as "Neutral Richard") were not seen by the respondents.

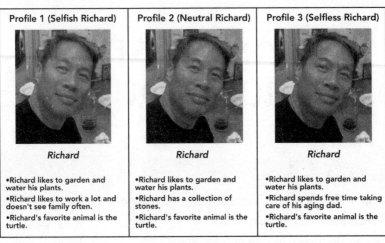

Profile 1 (Selfish Richard)	Profile 2 (Neutral Richard)	Profile 3 (Selfless Richard)
Richard	*Richard*	*Richard*
•Richard likes to garden and water his plants. •Richard likes to work a lot and doesn't see family often. •Richard's favorite animal is the turtle.	•Richard likes to garden and water his plants. •Richard has a collection of stones. •Richard's favorite animal is the turtle.	•Richard likes to garden and water his plants. •Richard spends free time taking care of his aging dad. •Richard's favorite animal is the turtle.

Pelin Kesebir

You'll notice the only difference in the three descriptions is the second bullet, which we subtly changed to reflect the three research demo profiles—selfish, neutral, and selfless. (You'll also notice that Neutral Richard is a pretty good name for a '90s indie band.)

After reviewing one of the three profiles, respondents were asked the following question: "In your view, how good-looking is Richard on a scale from 0 to 9?"*

Wait, wait, wait, I thought. *What did I sign up for?* It's bad enough to not get many Likes on social media for what I thought was a good post. Now I'm going to know exactly—numerically—how attractive a bunch of random strangers think I am? Hey, anything for science, I guess.

Here are the results:

- Selfish Richard: 6.6
- Neutral Richard: 6.8
- Selfless Richard: 7.1

---

* The survey language read "0 to 9," which is here adjusted to a "1 to 10" scale.

My first reaction: I didn't want to know this after all. But I did learn some interesting things from the three hundred respondents. For example, all of the Richards got ratings of "1." I'm consistent that way. Selfless Richard received triple the number of "9s" and "10s" as Selfish Richard. In fact, 9 was the second most frequent rating for Selfless Richard.

Let's look at a similar approach in a study of photographs from high school yearbooks. Sounds creepy, but bear with me. The researchers assembled two different groups—the actual classmates of people pictured in the yearbooks, and strangers who were of the same gender and roughly same age as the classmates. They asked all of the participants to rate the people in the yearbook photographs for physical attractiveness.

If ratings of physical attractiveness were entirely objective and independent of nonphysical traits, the ratings of classmates and strangers shouldn't differ much. However, this turned out not to be the case. Although some photographs were judged similarly by the classmates and strangers, a gap existed between the two ratings for many other photos. In those cases, how much a person was liked and respected by their classmates made a significant difference.

The conclusion? Nonphysical factors have a notable influence on perceptions of physical attractiveness.[1] Also, the participants in the yearbook study were middle-aged at the time of the study, which means perceptions of selflessness last for decades in the eye of the beholder. Notably, this effect was stronger for women. Character had more power to shape perceptions of attractiveness for women than it did for men.

On a transactional basis, if I'm asking myself whether I should try to be more selfless based on what's in it for me, this study shows there is a payoff. It seems a bit shallow and hypocritical to want to be more selfless so people will think I'm more attractive overall. On the flip side, it appears to be a win-win. And in the case of my low scores, I need all the help I can get.

ATTRACTIVENESS CAN CHANGE

Guess what, we can work to change how "attractive" we are. And I don't mean saving up for that big eyebrow microblading procedure. Here's the scenario from another fascinating study. Summer archaeology students were asked on the first day of class to rate each other on the following factors:

- familiarity (how well you know the person)
- intelligence (how smart they appear to you)
- effort (how hard you think they'll work on course activities)
- liking (how much you like them)
- physical attractiveness (how physically attractive you find them)

Fast-forward to the end of the summer after the students had spent six weeks working together on a dig site. Researchers asked students to rate their classmates on the same five factors. Again, nonphysical traits—how likable or hardworking they appeared—contributed to how physically attractive the students were rated. Some students clearly increased in their attractiveness over the course of the class, whereas others clearly dropped. As with the yearbook study, how likable and respectable a student turned out to be had a significant impact on their attractiveness ratings.[2]

For instance, one woman received a below average rating on the first day of class. However, over the course of the summer, she proved herself to be intelligent, well-liked, and hardworking. (Even the mummies liked her.) She started with a mean of 3.25 on the first day of class and then doubled to a mean of 7.00 by the last day of class. That's a real glow-up. Researchers said her appearance remained pretty much the same throughout the six-week class. (I wonder if she also wore a brown fedora, carried a whip, and was nicknamed "Indy.")

"Among people who actually know and interact with each other, the perception of physical attractiveness is based largely on traits that cannot be detected from physical appearance alone, either from photographs or from actually observing the person before forming a relationship," the researchers noted.[3] In other words, being seen as a selfless person has the potential to double how attractive the people around us see us without changing anything at all about our appearance.

This offers a bit of comfort, because most of the attributes typically associated with "beautiful people" are not achievable things—no matter how much we spend, how much we fuss, and how many skin creams we order from Goop.

THE BEAUTIFUL BOOGER

It was a hot day. My sister was perched on the seat of the boat, fidgeting with her life jacket. I had thrown my fishing line into the murky water and gotten a hit within ten seconds. She rolled her eyes as she watched me, over and over, pull in a flopping fish.

I loved fishing with my uncle and my buddies when I was a teen, but my sister didn't enjoy the outdoors. I could tell she regretted being dragged to the lake with us. She had caught nothing. (She was sadder to be in the boat than the fish were.)

Later in the afternoon, she tossed in a line and felt a tug. When she reeled it in, she was delighted to see a turtle—a big turtle, maybe seven inches long. It's not every day you get to look at a middle-aged turtle on the other end of a fishing line. We examined it, prodded it, and admired it. Then we gently removed the hook. The turtle's shell was seriously messed up though. He must've gotten mangled by something when he was young and his shell still malleable. Somehow he had survived and made his way to us.

"Well, he's not the best-looking," I said. Everyone nodded.

"How do you know it's a he?" my sister asked. I couldn't believe it—I'd gotten canceled on a fishing trip. There was something about this turtle that my sister and I both loved. We took him home and put him in an old aquarium in the living room. I named him "Booger," after a cat that had run away. Booger the turtle became part of our family. But each time I showed him off to friends and told the story about how we caught him, I got a less than enthusiastic response.

Friends did not use the most affectionate terms to describe Booger. So I became his defender and champion. He'd had no defenses as a little turtle when some inconsiderate creature took a bite out of his shell. Unlike some other mutant turtles, he didn't have a set of nunchucks. In a strange, "animal kingdom" sociological way, Booger was probably rejected by his turtle compadres. They no doubt considered him less able and "less than." Maybe he faced the same kind of rejection as Nemo, the little clown fish who had one smaller fin—and all the other fish in the school knew it. In an ironic way, Booger might have been thrown back by humans too. "That turtle looks odd," my uncle had said. But to me, Booger was a Galápagos 10.

Culture says beauty is an important attribute, even in pets. Pampered pets with outfits and the latest haircuts win "Best in Show" awards. Many of those well-coiffed dogs even have their own Instagram accounts. Then there are the owners of squished-face pugs and nearly hairless Chinese Crested Dogs. Their owners love them. They look beyond fur-deep and see the loyalty and sweet disposition in their pets—like those who gave Selfless Richard a higher rating in the research demo. I like the mutts because I, too, grow on people when they get to know me. When selfless, I'm a 7.1!

SEXUAL RELATIONSHIPS

All this talk about the impact of character on physical attractiveness sparks the question: "Are selfless people sexier?" One study went a step further than the one we described at the beginning of this chapter.

Using a scale of 1 to 9, two groups were asked to rank whether they'd like to have a short-term or a long-term sexual relationship with the individuals. Sure enough, when participants "met" the selfless folks first, they were more desirable on paper for short-term sexual relationships by as much as 3 percent. And for the long term, there was an even higher bump for the selfless folks—at 9 percent. If we're going for the long game, selflessness is the way to have longer-term sexual partners and maybe even stronger bonds of heart and mind.

Here's another interesting takeaway: women appeared to associate higher value with selflessness when considering men for a sexual relationship—almost twice as much as men did when considering sexual relations with women. This is consistent with the findings noted above: women's attractiveness ratings for men are more greatly influenced by personality factors than men's attractiveness ratings of women.[4]

Knowing this data, we may want to ask: "What is a good dating strategy for attracting a selfless and sexy mate?" People were shown the selfless card (Card A) first; two weeks later, the neutral card (Card N). The methodology was also done in reverse, with participants rating the neutral card first and then the selfless card two weeks later. Turns out, when the selfless card was shown first, it yielded a significantly higher net positive in desire to be a sexual partner and potential mate.

The world offers up a variety of ways we don't measure up—our hair is too thin, our thighs too thick, our wallets too empty. None of those deficiencies help in finding a forever partner. However, this study suggests that to treat others the way you would like to be treated is a very good thing indeed.

I read that in a book somewhere.[5]

DIGGING DEEPER

We've focused primarily on how we might become more attractive to others, but let's switch this around for a moment. How might things change if we made the effort to find *others* more attractive—first in character and personality, and then physically? How might we be intentional about looking for the beauty that's beyond skin-deep?

I'm guessing we've all had the experience of meeting people who become more attractive as we get to know them.

Oh, you volunteer with that charity? Maybe they start to look a little cuter.

And you ended up paying your way through college? Is that a dimple on your cheek when you smile?

Oooh, you donated at the blood bank last week? They must do CrossFit; I can tell.

That's so great you bring food to your uncle on weekends. This person slowly becomes more attractive to you on the outside simply because they are genuinely attractive on the inside.

You rescued a deformed baby turtle? A perfect 10!

Typically, we evaluate how attractive someone is and then hope their personality meshes with ours. What if we could swipe right on their personalities first before we ever saw their photos? Sounds like a *Black Mirror* episode, but the data suggests this is the better way. It's a way of determining whether our first impressions—those early red flags or green flags—are significant or superficial. And if the conversation goes on long enough and the green flags are indeed green, you might ask for a phone number, an email address, or an Instagram handle. (Or set up a time to meet at the blood bank.)

. . . .

Whenever we had a discussion in our house about appearance—whether my sister and I were talking about Booger, or even when we fretted about what to wear to school that day—it wasn't uncommon for one of my parents to go to this nugget of wisdom from the Bible: "Your beauty should not come from outward adornment, such as elaborate hairstyles and the wearing of gold jewelry or fine clothes. Rather, it should be that of your inner self, the unfading beauty of a gentle and quiet spirit."[6] In one of the most popular lines (and in fact the final line) in the musical rendition of Victor Hugo's *Les Misérables*, Jean Valjean says this: "To love another person is to see the face of God."

I was visiting my father recently. He can no longer walk, talk, or take food by mouth. But he has a deep peace about him. The caregivers at the nursing facility often say he has a kind spirit, though he can say nothing. He has a quiet spirit. We are very intuitive animals, able to pick up the smallest nuances of others' souls.

This chapter began with reflections on a study where the only difference was one sentence in describing Selfish and Selfless Richard. Yet there was a marked change in perception scoring. Goodness *does* meet gorgeous. Saying somebody is gorgeous may be a reaction to somebody's insides. And maybe that's the way we should reframe words like *attractive*, *lovely*, and *gorgeous*—using them to describe the inside, not the outside.

I've been challenged to do that. In seeing the way my father fights and remains positive, I know he has become that kind "angel on earth," as my sister likes to call him. As he smiles with his eyes, my whole family has learned to love his inner gorgeousness anew. As he changes, so do we.

I once again learn the same lesson: all of us are more than our shells.

Chapter Five

LONGEVITY AND YOUTH

Let's face it, we've been obsessed with youth and beauty from the beginning of time—or, more accurately, with keeping youth and beauty at all costs.

For more than a thousand years, the Balinese have told the story of a sacred spring found high on the slopes of Mount Batur. Their holy texts recount a battle between the gods and a wretched king.

The ruler of the gods was Indra, who led his armies to pursue a vile king. However, this king had a trick up his sleeve. Through sorcery, he turned a spring to poison and then tempted his enemy, Indra's soldiers, to drink from it. They died the moment their lips made contact with the poisoned water.

In his anguish, Indra pointed his spear at the poisoned spring, turning it into a fountain of immortality. Drink from it, and you live forever. The actual spring drips into a pool to this day. The water quenches, but nothing more.

Myths of life-extending elixirs span many cultures, from the Crusader's Holy Grail to Xu Fu's immortal island of Mount Penglai to Ponce de Léon's Fountain of Youth. These stories inspire and also reflect us. These days, we may not be searching for a literal fountain of youth, but we still pursue ways to prolong our days. Cook with more turmeric. Keep your mitochondria alive with this supplement. Sleep in an oxygen chamber. Inject your body with stuff from other humans (or even pigs). Though these remedies are promoted by "experts," they are, of course, too good to be true.

There is a strategy that not only adds years but also helps others: *selflessness.* You probably saw that coming. While we may do stuff for others because it's simply the right thing to do—and not to live longer, per se—the consideration exists.

LOWER MORTALITY

One of the surprising discoveries I encountered as I looked at longevity and selflessness was the physical benefits for those who needed it most. Stony Brook University professor Stephen Post found that the giving of oneself increases health benefits in people—even those with chronic illnesses such as HIV/AIDS and multiple sclerosis.[1] Best of all, it's free. In addition, it could quite possibly lengthen our life.

More Volunteering Means Longer Life

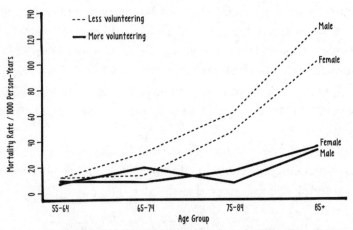

Doug Oman, Carl E. Thoresen, and Kay McMahon, "Volunteerism and Mortality among the Community-Dwelling Elderly," *Journal of Health Psychology* 4, no. 3 (1999): 301–16.

People who are fifty-five and older who volunteered for two or more organizations were 44 percent less likely to die over a five-year period than non-volunteers, according to a 1999 study led by Doug Oman of the University of California, Berkeley (Go, Bears!). And the more selfless the fifty-five-and-older group was, the fewer strokes they had; they also experienced better lung function. In comparison, going out to help others was even healthier than exercising four times a week. The only thing that reduced mortality rate more was quitting smoking (at 49 percent less likely to die than non-volunteers).[2]

It's not merely the *act* of volunteering that's beneficial; we also need to put our *heart* into it. If you volunteered for selfless reasons, you lived longer. Conversely, in that fifty-five-plus group, if you volunteered predominantly to enhance yourself or for similar self-oriented reasons, it had a negative impact.

Folks who gave a higher priority to motives for volunteering "that explicitly consider some personal reward such as improving one's mood or self-esteem, escaping one's problems, or learning a new skill" had an above-average likelihood of dying earlier—nearly four times the rate of others-oriented people.[3] It's okay to want to help others in part because you are getting something out of it; just make sure it's not the primary reason. By doing selfless things, we can do more of them because we'll be around for more years than we otherwise would have been.

Bottom line: get busy caring or get busy dying.

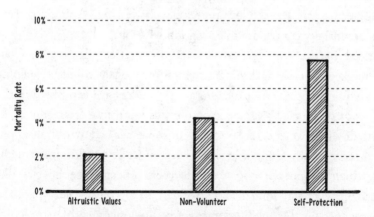

Volunteering Motivations

Sara Konrath et al., "Motives for Volunteering Are Associated with Mortality Risk in Older Adults, *Health Psychology* 31, no. 1 (2012): 87–96.

LOOKING YOUNGER

Back to the research demo with Pelin Kesebir (see chapter 4). One additional question asked of respondents was how old they estimated Selfish Richard to be in comparison with Selfless Richard. The same picture was shown for all three profiles—Selfish Richard, Neutral Richard, and Selfless Richard.

The lowest and highest 10 percent of age estimates for both Richards had some notable differences. Selfish Richard was seen as two years older on the low end of age estimates, and four years older on the high end of age estimates.

	Lowest 10 percent	*Highest 10 percent*
	Age Estimates	
Selfish Richard	32	57
Selfless Richard	30	53

In the study, age perception seems to be affected by perceptions of a person's selflessness. So we could say selflessness has an element of agelessness to it. And I thought it was just, "Asian don't raisin." (Or your pick. "Black don't crack" or "Brown don't frown" also work.) Different studies have shown the more selfless we are, the longer we live (see chapter 2), the happier we are, and the lower stress levels we have. And all of these factors potentially contribute to how good we look.

One thing that's in your favor if you do practice selflessness—your telomeres keep their length longer, which means you could be keeping that glowing complexion a bit longer. Telomeres are kind of like the plastic ends of shoelaces. They keep our chromosomes from fraying or wearing down as we age.[4] As our chromosomes wear down, so does our body. A recent study found that when we practice loving-kindness meditation, which is about opening up our hearts to others, those shoelace-like protective covers stay longer and stronger. In a twelve-week span, the group engaged in this meditation practice lost only a third as much of their telomere ends as the control group. They also had stronger chromosomes, which kept them looking like a fresh pair of Adidas a little longer.[5]

HALF-SMILES, WHOLE YEARS

Another way to look as fresh as a new pair of Stan Smiths is to be happier. The Declaration of Independence tells us that the "pursuit of happiness" is one of our core privileges. How each of us pursues happiness is up to us and is based on a lot of trial and error. My pursuit included trying fast cars—a souped-up, used Toyota Supra and a slammed Corvette. I gotta admit that winning a street drag race or two did put a smile on my face. Social scientists are now showing us there may be a trick to getting happy without having to buy fatter tires.

One way to be happier: do selfless things that de-stress our lives. A 2015 study of seventy-seven adults, ages eighteen to forty-four, asked participants to take a mental health questionnaire every night. They commented on potentially stressful aspects of their days—things like commuting, working, figuring out finances, and carrying out domestic responsibilities.

They kept track of the helpful things they did during the day—both big and small, from holding the door open for a stranger to asking someone if they needed help—and how they felt about doing these things. At the end of the day, the participants were asked to rate their mental health on a 0–100 scale.

The results showed that participants who performed more acts of kindness reported less stress. For each act of kindness performed, a participant's mental health improved by 1 percent on average. When they couldn't complete acts of kindness, they reported more stress.[6]

In other findings, higher blood pressure was also measured. Those who completed acts of kindness had lower readings. That's a big deal, since lower blood pressure has a myriad of benefits, such as lower risks of heart failure, aneurysms, and vision loss. When we give social support to others, we also get more back. Plus, we are less depressed and more productive.[7]

The National Institutes of Health looked at functional MRIs of subjects engaged in giving to others. The test subjects were given $100 and told that whatever money was left at the end of the experiment was theirs to keep. They then lay down in the fMRI scanner, where a computer screen prompted them to donate to a food bank. At times, the donations were voluntary; other times, they were made mandatory. The researchers watched the results in real time, as the fMRI scanner showed which parts of the brain were activated on a heat map.

To their surprise, regardless of whether the donation was voluntary or mandatory, they saw the "pleasure-related centers deep in the brain" light up like a Christmas tree (or Hanukkah menorah or Kwanzaa kinara).[8] Though voluntary donations produced a stronger effect, the study suggests that spending money toward a good cause makes us feel good. Neuroscientists believe it's because the reward center in the brain, or the mesolimbic pathway, releases endorphins. Quite possibly the Kenny Chesney of neurochemicals, endorphins are well known to create euphoria, commonly noticed after exercise. (Sorry, eating donuts does not have the same effect.) In addition, we secrete "feel-good" chemicals such as serotonin, dopamine, and oxytocin. That happy band of brain juices creates a sense of well-being, makes us feel bonded to others, mediates our mood, and creates compassion.[9] "Happy" experts describe this as a "helper's high."[10]

The high is expressed in many ways. We frame situations in balanced or positive ways. We set aside time to focus on the positive things in our lives and careers. Or we may just practice doing half-smiles to express the appreciation for things that make us happy. All of these expressions are indicators of our trying to be happier that can in the end add years to our calendar by reducing disease.[11]

Money affects happiness too. I can hear the "no, duh"s in my earpiece right now. That's why sociologists and scientists have been trying to figure out how to buy happiness for a long time. And if they could figure it out, they might be indirectly buying more years of life. Some smart folks from the University of Virginia and Purdue University cross-referenced the earnings and life satisfaction of 1.7 million people in 164 countries and came up with an answer. For individuals without kids, the level where income was believed to be ideal for "life satisfaction," the "Ah, that is all I need" point is $95,000. If you are targeting "emotional well-being" specifically, you get that for between $60,000 and $75,000.[12] Interestingly, when we make more money than the average satiation point of $95,000, no major increase in happiness (or sadness) occurs.

Based on that leveling-off point, there's an interesting debate about why we continue to stay on the hamster wheel so long every day. Here's one good reason: we want to make more money so we can help others. You know anyone who thinks this way? The ones who think about doing things for others instead of the next car to buy?

Researchers from Harvard Business School and the University of British Columbia conducted a study in which they investigated whether people are generally happier to spend money on themselves or to give it away. Most of us would have predicted that people would be happier if they were allowed to spend the money on themselves. But it was the opposite. The correlation to happiness when we spend money on ourselves is lower than when we spend money prosocially on others. Even spending as little as five dollars on somebody else was good enough to register gains in feelings of happiness.[13] We can be selfless for as little as the price of a cup of coffee. (Grande in a venti cup, twenty-pump vanilla, twenty-pump hazelnut, whole milk, 190-degree, whip and extra caramel drizzle latte.) At that price, we can buy happiness.

Then let the warm glow set in. By the way, the stuff that causes this "feeling happier" experience has a name—phenylethylamine. It's the same hormone triggered by eating chocolate, doing something selfless, or taking the methamphetamine Ecstasy. You experience euphoria, relaxation, energy, sociability—all of the things that are the opposite of the stuff that can lead to diseases, strokes, and heart attacks.

In many ways, if we can get that chocolate feeling, we could be extending our life. And because selflessness is well equipped to make us happy and healthy, it also may help us add on some extra years.

Chapter Six

CAREER PAYOFF

It's a common aphorism: "You gotta look out for number one." I imagine Charles Montgomery Burns, the greedy entrepreneur-billionaire of *The Simpsons* fame, agreeing as he deviously whispers, "Eeexcellent," while tapping his fingertips together.

In a me-first era, selflessness and career may not seem like they belong together in the same breath. We work to get ahead. We are employed primarily to make money. A boss is someone from whom we get our paycheck. Why can't we just keep our "earn a living" work in one column and our "do good" work in another? And doesn't it just make sense to earn my small fortune first and then give back? Or as Elmer J. Fudd of the firm *Looney Tunes* might say, "How can I decide which charity to donate to when I don't even have my first yacht? I'd have more to give later too." Makes sense.

The other option is to go for purpose first and compromise on income. My mother was a schoolteacher in the 1960s, which was one of the lower-paying jobs of her era. Teachers today make almost 50 percent more (inflation adjusted) but still fall behind non-teachers in earnings power.[1] She was offered promotions several times to become a vice principal with the potential of becoming a principal in her school district. She always said no. She just loved teaching her elementary school classes. She took joy in buying students their school supplies during recessions, driving kids home when parents didn't show up, taking calls from parents who were in jail, even teaching music and library classes when the music teacher and librarian were furloughed. A vice principal job would have pulled her away from directly changing these kids' futures.

My father started out working as a youth pastor but eventually had to change jobs because his annual salary was the equivalent today of about $15,000. Since my mom had taken a break from teaching to stay at home to care for the four kids, there was no way to stretch Dad's salary far enough to pay the bills. That's when he became a social worker. It was a good job for who he was and what he could do, though not for money. Finances were still tight. So although he spent his day job approving food stamps for his general assistance clients at the Department of Social Services for the city and county of San Francisco, one day he needed to apply for that same social aid for himself. Only he couldn't approve himself, so he asked one of his coworkers to take his case. He told me many times how this was a tough moment for him. Circumstances required him to swallow his pride so his family could swallow food.

While some choose income first, and others, such as my parents, choose passion first, still others find a way to choose both. They make enough money at their day job to pursue their real passions outside of work. Admirable as well. The challenge is to not exclude what we do for a living from our social obligation to help one another. Because a large portion of my days is spent at work, a large portion of my *life* is spent at work.

Although the all-consuming nature of work may appear to be exhibit A for why we can't both work and volunteer, it's the primary reason we can't have a bifurcated life. Consider what the great philosopher (Canadian rock band) Loverboy said: "Everybody's Working for the Weekend." The lyrics never mention balance. (Actually, it's possible they do. I only have their greatest hits.) Some, like Bill Gates, have been successful at first making their fortune and then doing the good stuff later in life. (At this point, the Gates Foundation's malaria eradication program is running more smoothly than the latest version of Windows and is way better at stopping viruses.)

While I'd love to be a bajillionaire like Gates, I don't see any pickup trucks with money stopping by my house anytime soon. All I know is what I've seen bring happiness in a work life and in retirement days. Be like Rose and Stephen Lui. Do a little bit every day in your career and life—not separate, but together. It may feel tough early on, as it did for them when they'd argue about the food and clothing budgets for the family. I realize the frustration was more than not having enough money. It may have been that they wanted to do more. But they kept it simple and just kept at it every day.

Tuna sandwiches. Each weeknight, it was just my dad and me at the dinner table. He liked to eat whatever the rest of the family didn't. I ate slowly. He'd do the dishes. I'd put the leftovers away. Then he'd start to prepare lunch for the next workday. Clean the lettuce. Dry it with towels. Toast the bread. Open the Bumble Bee tuna. (This must be where my anchoring warm-up inspiration comes from.) Mix in mayonnaise. Assemble sandwich and place in a plastic bag. Every workday for thirty years, it seemed. Tuna was affordable. Not so tasty by year fifteen.

In retirement and even as he lived through Alzheimer's, my dad began to buy tuna subs again, up to three times a week. What was a sometimes monotonous work meal he had grown tired of became something he savored. Working every day in a low-paying, tough job that served the city's neediest population was the same: something he savored years later.

THE DAILY ROUTINE

Speaking of lunches, I was out working on a film project, and we had just wrapped up for the day. The crew and I were sitting down to grab a bite to eat. As we relaxed and talked about the day, I noticed a team member demand something from the server. Over the course of the next hour or so, he demanded more of this or that, refusing to even acknowledge the server when she returned with the requested items.

"Here are your creamers," the server said, but my colleague didn't even make eye contact with her or make a space on the table for the new plate. I don't think anyone noticed—his dismissiveness wasn't particularly dramatic. However, you can tell a lot about people by how they treat those they have power over. If you don't think tipping holds power over a server, you haven't worked in the food and beverage or hospitality industry. Anyone who has ever had a job in those industries knows what it is like to wait for a tip from a difficult customer. Sometimes the tip isn't worth the effort. (It seems to me that if servers ran the United Nations, there would be no wars. Countries would simply say, "I'm sorry you didn't like that. Let's see what we can do to fix it.")

Though I had worked with this person for long hours, day after day, I learned more about him during the course of one meal than in all the previous hours combined. "How others treat the CEO says nothing," wrote Del Jones in *USA Today*. "But how others treat the waiter is like a magical window into the soul."[2] From my vantage point across the table, I learned that my coworker's kindness was conditional on whether or not it benefited him. He didn't understand that everything matters—that who he is in the routine moments with everyday people is, in fact, who he really is.

At 30 Rockefeller Plaza, we have kitchenettes on each floor, complete with a fridge, a sink, and a coffee maker. One of the things I try to remember to do is clean up not only my messes but also other people's. There's no reason to leave the kitchen dirty until the cleaning service arrives.

We've all seen the messes—dried-up coffee spilled on the floor, splatters in the microwave, cups scattered everywhere. As we rush from one meeting to another with a cup of coffee and a laptop, we can inadvertently spill. It happens. But it only takes a moment to clean up after ourselves. Quickly wipe the microwave after your overheated lunch splatters inside. And please don't ever microwave tuna. (I'm looking at you, Seth Meyers.) These little things help keep spirits up at work. Hold the door open (regardless of the person's gender), say thank you in person instead of by email, avoid participating in office gossip (even if it's about Seth Meyers's tuna issue), and, when appropriate, write letters of recommendation if someone asks. (Or bring in donuts. Then I will write a stellar recommendation for you.)

During the heart of the pandemic at 30 Rock, our staff was reduced to 5 percent of our normal occupancy in the building—an amazing feat given that we're in television. Fortunately, technology allows us to operate even teleprompters remotely. Even so, not everything could be done from a distance, so I still had to go in three days a week. Tom was my floor director for two of those days each week. Before coming to work, he'd call in a donut order at his New Jersey neighborhood bakery. He picked up a dozen each day and brought them in for the few colleagues who came into the office. And he went first-class, ordering all the fancy donuts and then offering them to every person he encountered.

"Hey, want a donut? They're great, and I ordered a lot of the special ones with sprinkles and Oreos on top," he'd say. The way Tom saw it, donuts were a win-win. He was helping his favorite hometown bakery stay in business, and he was doing something nice for his coworkers. Each chocolate old-fashioned I ate reinforced the value of *we*. Thanks, Tom!

CASHING IN ON OTHERISHNESS

If pop culture is any indication, Tom's generosity won't get him very far when it comes to payday. The lifestyles of most pop culture icons seem to show that focusing on *me* rather than *we* is what pays off in greater wealth. Think about it. Most evil villains are wealthy, right? Even heroes can be wealthy people who have at least some selfish tendencies. Think of Tony Stark, the billionaire industrialist and alter ego of Iron Man. He does good deeds, but he is also quite fond of himself. In other words, his selfishness pays off.

In contrast to pop culture are the morality tales from folklore that encourage us to strive for goodness and selflessness by using the "happy ending" approach. Do good, and good things happen—black-and-white. But even here, Stark remains a good example. As he becomes more selfless, at least in the movies, he strengthens his ability to create social bonds and to collaborate with his fellow superheroes, the Avengers. In the end, they're able to work together to save the world.

For us non-superheroes, it turns out that the payoffs for a "we over me" mindset are both socially and financially rewarding. As we do selfless things—saving the world little by little, if you will—we also create stronger social ties, team strength, and positive relationships. As a result, says a recent study in the *Journal of Personality and Social Psychology*, we actually become more marketable to higher-paying positions that require such skills.[3]

Researchers tracked income over fourteen years of families in the United States—4,017 respondents in all. They asked such questions as whether respondents agreed that "people need to look after themselves and not overly worry about others" and how many times they had offered their seat to someone on the bus. These questions helped quantify selfless motivations and behaviors. When each person's selfless level was compared with incomes, a trend formed. The selfless (or "otherish," as the researchers put it) category had the highest income of all groups at the end of the fourteen years. They started higher to begin with as well, roughly $10,000 higher income per year than the "selfish" group, or about 33 percent higher. That gap only widened as selfless incomes increased at a greater rate. At the end of the study, the otherish group was making over $20,000 more than the selfish group, or almost 50 percent more. The researchers found similar results in European countries.

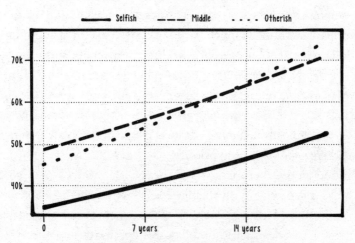

Otherishness Grows Income
Estimated growth trajectories for labor income conditioned on selfish/otherish behavior in GBP

——— Selfish   — — — Middle   · · · · Otherish

Kimmo Eriksson et al., "Generosity Pays: Selfish People Have
Fewer Children and Earn Less Money," *Journal of Personality
and Social Psychology,* https://doi.org/10.1037/pspp0000213.

Here's another interesting lesson to take from this: those who were moderately selfless also did quite well. The small things count. Trying works. We don't have to go all out or have superpowers to see positive outcomes economically when we make it a practice to help others.

SELFLESSNESS IS GOOD BUSINESS

As I mentioned in chapter 1, I felt apprehensive about telling my boss, Yvette, about my dad's Alzheimer's disease, which meant I needed to reduce my time on air. After NBC responded in such an accommodating way, many of my coworkers shared about their own caregiving journeys. I was surprised at the time by the sheer number of people who were caregivers. Caregivers at work seemed so prevalent that I decided to do some research to learn more about the impact of having caregivers in the workplace. As it turns out, selflessness benefits not only the caregiver and the care recipient but also the caregiver's employer.

Harvard Business School published a report that explains the benefits to companies that cultivate an environment supportive of its employees' need to care for their family members.[4] One of the findings was that employers who choose not to support caregivers pay hidden costs related to higher turnover, rehiring, presenteeism, and absenteeism. Instead of letting workers quit when their obligations at home become too great to bear, companies would be much better off if they retained and improved the productivity of their current workforce, especially since the workers most affected by caregiving responsibilities are disproportionately top earners and therefore harder to replace. Since many workers in the "sandwich" stage of life—people who care for both children and aging parents—are typically at a more advanced stage in their career, retaining these workers should be a top priority.

"Productive workers who have proven themselves in a specific employer's workplace are invaluable assets," write the article's authors Joseph Fuller and Manjari Raman. "Enabling them to become even more productive, more consistently, is obviously beneficial to a company's performance." Not only is it the right thing to do; the numbers work to their advantage. "In addition to maintaining continuity in operations, employee retention allows a company to avoid the substantial and indirect costs incurred when replacing a worker."[5]

After learning about this study and hearing my coworkers' stories, I asked if I could develop a Business Resource Group or Employee Resource Group (BRG/ERG) that would benefit caregivers. After speaking with representatives of AARP and Alzheimer's Association, with whom I've worked during the last five years to get out the word on the needs of the country's 53 million family caregivers, I found that caregiver ERG/BRGs are uncommon. The idea was not to change company policies or start some sort of office mutiny so much as it was to allow employees to share their journeys of caring for a family member and the stresses we were living out. And then to start the office mutiny. My bosses said to go for it—to put together a proposal to see what it would look like.

Caregiving is costly for employers in many ways. A 2013 AARP study found that eldercare costs US employers $6.6 billion to replace employees who quit or retire early, and this is on top of $6.3 billion in workday interruptions (arriving late, leaving early, taking time off during the day, or spending work time on eldercare matters). Thirteen billion dollars annually is nothing to sneeze at.

As part of that loss, research shows that caregivers of dementia patients lose between 2.5 and 3.5 hours of sleep each week.[6] This means employers lose significant productivity over the course of years. Companies are now realizing "selflessness" by supporting team members who are caregivers is good for business (and is good business, as the saying goes). It costs less to support caregivers and set new, reasonable expectations on productivity than it is to lose them altogether. So businesses are now creating caregiver employee resource groups, offering counseling and sensitivity training, as well as training HR managers to help caregiver employees.

MENTORING

I had no idea until recently that the practice of mentoring originated in the ancient Greek myths with a character named Mentor. Mentor was supposed to protect and guide a royal son while his father, the king, was away fighting in the Trojan War. Mentor's failure to give proper guidance left the family vulnerable to attack. I guess Mentor wasn't a good mentor. That's why the goddess of wisdom, Athena, stepped in and guided the son. (So technically, mentoring should be called "Athena-ing" because a goddess had to step in where a mortal guy failed. Classic case of a guy getting credit for a woman's work.) The ancient Greeks knew what we now know—the truest form of mentoring is divine intervention from Wisdom *herself*.

All of us could use a little divine inspiration in our occupational lives. A survey by the American Society for Training and Development reveals that 75 percent of executives believe mentoring has been critical to their career development.[7]

My mentor was Mike Breslin. I met Mike when I was an undergrad at UC Berkeley in the '90s. I responded to a flier advertising a marketing intern position for a small manufacturer called Clean Environment Engineers. Even though I was a little bleary-eyed from studying rhetoric (also known as a BA in BS), I knew this was a perfect part-time job for me. I had interest in advertising, having worked the previous summer at DDB Needham, one of the big agencies.

I met Mike when I went for my first interview. He was a mechanical engineer who gave off a nerdy, fun vibe. He was tall, maybe six foot two. Wore glasses. During the interview, he looked me straight in the eye, squinting as though what I was saying was blindingly interesting. He listened intently. All of a sudden, his seat dropped six inches, the chair finishing its descent with a comic jiggle. I knew it wasn't an accident—he'd had his hand on the height adjustment lever beneath his seat the whole time. Throughout that move, we never stopped talking or lost eye contact. Was this a strange game of concentration? Was it some kind of test? Would he laugh hysterically or start a series of eye twitches to see what I would do? Did he buy his chair at IKEA?

I wasn't about to give in on this game of chicken, and I made it through the interview. If the chair drop issue was a test, fortunately I passed. I got the job.

It was twenty minutes by bicycle to Emeryville three times a week. I worked with ten people and didn't make a lot of money, but we made good stuff. We were a small manufacturer, and I liked that. After working there during the summer and fall, I spent the first semester of my senior year studying abroad in Spain. I wanted to work on my Spanish. (And drink sangria. I'd need sangria, because while there, a recession hit, and unemployment in the United States reached almost 7 percent in 1993.) Even though I emailed Mike to ask if there might be an opening for me when I returned, I felt certain he wouldn't be able to hire me back.

I got Mike's reply in the form of a fax. (First, he had used a flier, now a fax—stone tablets were sure to be next.) That day, I was sitting in class at the Universidad de Alicante when my teacher walked in and handed me an envelope. Mike had faxed me an offer from Emeryville. I was shocked. I read it several times, unable to believe I had gotten a solid job offer in the middle of the recession from a company I actually liked. My classmates couldn't believe the news either.

When I returned, Mike had me start the process of putting together the company's global advertising and public relations efforts. He pushed me to be creative, even to the point of changing the name of his company. He asked, "What do you think?" and listened and lowered his chair each time we talked. I asked to increase the budget to $200,000 per year, a huge amount of money for our small company and a young marketer. Mike's response: "Why and how?" not "No." He saw every person as an equal, regardless of age, background, or experience. He knew that his employees were dynamic and growing, just like he was. He also asked everyone for their input on big decisions—the secretary, the service manager, and even Sangria Lui, the fresh-out-of-college marketer.

My first year there, the recession hit us harder than many other businesses. We made underground oil spill cleanup products used at gas stations and refineries. Since hazardous cleanups became less of a priority during the recession as businesses and the government focused on keeping jobs, the recession was an especially hard blow. And as a manufacturer, it hurt more. We had to put product on shelves, and we would lose money the longer the product sat there.

One day, Mike gave us the bad news. We'd have to take a pay cut of roughly 20 percent. What Mike didn't say was that he would get a different deal. He'd get zero pay. *Zero!* He didn't tell anyone about his sacrifice. He made the decision and stayed later and worked harder. Throughout those lean years and in the period after that, I watched Mike talk to many different people in his office, and without fail, he'd lower his chair with the subtlety of a falling piano.

"Why do you do that?" I finally asked him one day. Turns out, it was a purposeful effort to talk to people eye to eye. It's the same reason Mike Bloomberg sits on a phonebook during a meeting. To be equal. It wasn't a mind game; it was Mike Breslin simply and selflessly deciding to embrace what others thought by engaging them at eye level—literally. Remember the old Michael Jordan commercials with the slogan "I want to be like Mike"? That's how I've always felt about Mike Breslin. His servant leadership still inspires me. He is a hero of zero. Zero pay, zero arrogance, zero selfishness.

Years later, he retired and sold the business for a sum that had a fair number of zeroes in it. He ended up doing very well.

. . . .

In 2020, I found myself on Mike's side of the table. I may not possess the wisdom of Athena, but I had learned a few things from Mike and others over the ensuing years and had achieved my dream of being a television news anchor and producing and directing a documentary film.

I met Alex when he was a student of mine at a high school journalism class I taught years ago. Each day, he came to class wearing a suit—the kind that a mother would look at and say, "Just wait. You'll grow into it someday." To be honest, at that point in time, I didn't think he'd "grow into" broadcast journalism. His story instinct didn't seem to be there. But boy was I wrong.

While he was in college, Alex reached out for tips on navigating the formidable internship application process at 30 Rock. I mentioned off-handedly that I was working on a not-for-profit documentary film called *Sky Blossom*, which featured young caregivers across America. It was no blockbuster, though caregiving does sometimes feel like it's a "mission: impossible." He wanted in, because like so many others, his family had cared for his grandparents.

Alex got the internship at NBC. He spent his summer at 30 Rock—thirteen hours a day, three days a week—and his remaining four "days off" as a volunteer producer for *Sky Blossom*. I appreciated his work ethic, skills, and willing attitude, especially since he was doing it pro bono. He believed he had been given a potentially career-changing opportunity, and he wasn't going to let it pass him by.

Almost a year later, and a few months before his graduation, he asked for some mentoring advice. "Now that the coronavirus is shaking up the economy, do you think my career in journalism might be over before it's even started?"

"Don't worry, this is a strong industry," I assured him. "Several of the key products our company creates remain in demand, and that means producers will remain in demand." A month later, when he was just a few days away from officially being hired, he received an email saying that hiring was frozen. Where was Athena when I needed her?

I had just reviewed the budget line for donations for *Sky Blossom*, so I knew what we needed to complete the project. I offered Alex a position on that not-for-profit project, but now I could pay him a salary.

"You've been volunteering for a year and a half, recently doing more than forty hours a week," I said. "The film project will hire you for three months to start or until you find the job you'd like in journalism. The film will also pay you above-market wages." My hope was to help Alex well beyond the three months so he could go back to the workforce with proof that he is marketable—even in the midst of a pandemic recession.

Until that moment, I didn't realize how much Mike Breslin's mentorship affected the way I would later make decisions. I didn't send Alex a fax, but I knew how to pay it forward. During a recession, Mike was willing to sacrifice for my sake, to give me a solid base on which to start my career. In 2020, the coronavirus-induced financial meltdown made the 1990s recession look like an economic boom.

I have hired dozens of employees in my various jobs, but never one quite like this. My rather sudden decision to hire Alex was clearly influenced by the instincts I had gained working with Mike. He helped me develop the muscle memory I needed to make the right decisions selflessly. I didn't owe Mike or the universe some debt I needed to repay. I had simply seen Mike live graciously and selflessly. Deep down, the kindness shown to me all those years ago bubbled to the surface unexpectedly.

WATERING THREE PLANTS

Long before I worked with Mike, I was at a California start-up selling cookies. Is there a better gig for a recent high school grad? At eighteen, a year into my job, I became the youngest manager of a regional training center at Mrs. Fields Cookies. I also ran the Pier 39 Mrs. Fields in San Francisco, while Debbi Fields (yes, there is an actual Mrs. Fields) was in Park City, Utah. I loved the job and raised the store's sales rank from number ten of five hundred stores to number one. At the peak, I was working maybe a hundred hours a week. And I did that, and nothing else—for years. No volunteer work. No family. No church. No friends.

Then the day came when I was pulled aside. "Richard, you're not performing well." During my fourth year, I was fired.

Now what?

You remember that high school scenario, right? Good friend gets a girlfriend or boyfriend. Good friend disappears. Doesn't talk with anybody. Then the inevitable breakup happens. All of a sudden, good friend wants to be your friend again and doesn't understand why you moved on to other friends.

That was me after I was fired. I had nothing. All of a sudden, the cupboards were empty. Only it wasn't all of a sudden. The cupboards of my life had been emptied long ago. By me.

So began a crash course in learning not to put all my marbles in one jar, all my eggs in one basket, all my sangria in one pitcher. I later came up with my own metaphor for maintaining diversity and balance in life, which was to "water three plants." It occurred to me that most things that matter in life are like plants, which means they require the essentials of growth—fertilization, sunlight, and daily watering.

In my Mrs. Fields days, I had just one plant. Something like that happens to many of us. We give all of ourselves to one thing, such as a job, a relationship, a cause. Then we wake up one day to discover that our one thing is gone, and we have no other plants in the garden. It's okay to prioritize some plants over others—career, sports, volunteering, family, what have you—but I found I had to have at least three healthy plants to maintain a diversified, balanced life.

Watering three plants keeps alive what's important to me while also recognizing that my resources—my daily supply of time and energy—are limited. I only have so much "water" to give, and so I have to be intentional with it. For example, this is what I could do with my daily watering can:

- pour 75 percent of my water on work
- pour 15 percent of my water on sports and working out at the gym
- pour 10 percent of my water on volunteering at the food pantry

On any given day, we have at least three parts of our lives we are nurturing and growing—some more and some less than the others. And should any one of them go away or die, we still have two others cultivated and growing.

"Who'd I miss?..."

© Tak Toyoshima

Who knows—one of our two smaller plants (side gigs) could someday become our main plant. And to that point, sometimes nurturing a small plant makes the main plant more successful, and at some point the small plant will have its day and be the main plant. Just like PayPal was for eBay. It was first the side business they needed so they could run the main business. eBay was the digital sales hub, and it needed a digital payment hub. Then PayPal became a fintech darling, and eBay became a bit of a sideshow. Their tight relationship has since loosened, as PayPal's revenue almost doubles eBay's. The point is that small plants can help the big plant, and at some point they can even become the big plant in our business and personal lives.

Why three plants and not two? Or four? Or seven? When I'm asked this, I think of the scene in *Monty Python and the Holy Grail* in which the monks call out God's instructions on how to use the Holy Hand Grenade of Antioch:

"First shalt thou take out the Holy Pin. Then, shalt thou count to three, no more, no less. Three shalt be the number thou shalt count, and the number of the counting shalt be three. Four shalt thou not count, neither count thou two, excepting that thou then proceed to three. Five is right out. Once the number three, being the third number, be reached, then lobbest thou thy Holy Hand Grenade of Antioch towards thou foe, who being naughty in my sight, shall snuff it."[8]

So the answer, I suggest, is three. (Just wait until I get to Mel Brooks's explanation of the Ten Commandments.)

Seriously, this is not a scientific formula, but a general guideline. However, the principle of cultivating a diversified and balanced life is one that has been adapted by many successful people. Kabir Sehgal, founder and CEO of Tiger Turn Productions, wrote an article in the *Harvard Business Review* titled "Why You Should Have (at Least) Two Careers." He wrote:

It's not uncommon to meet a lawyer who'd like to work in renewable energy, or an app developer who'd like to write a novel, or an editor who fantasizes about becoming a landscape designer. Maybe you also dream about switching to a career that's drastically different from your current job. But in my experience, it's rare for such people to actually make the leap. The costs of switching seem too high, and the possibility of success seems too remote.[9]

Sehgal says having more than one "plant" gives people the chance to express themselves in different areas, creatively and occupationally, and prevents people from getting locked into one area and feeling trapped. Pursuing diverse interests also provides advantages in all areas of life, making it more likely you'll end up doing at least some of what pleases you, acquire skill sets in various areas, and make friends through diverse contacts. Plus, it allows you to see where these various areas could—or ideally should—interrelate.

As Apple cofounder Steve Jobs pointed out, "It's technology married with liberal arts, married with the humanities, that yields us the result that makes our heart sing."[10]

ABOUT MONEY

When I was working at home during the first few months of the coronavirus pandemic, a *Wall Street Journal* article caught my eye because it was about my workplace. The article stated that NBCUniversal had to cut salaries to offset the negative financial impact of the pandemic. It indicated that emails would be going out to employees in short order. I hadn't received any memos about a pay cut, so this was a surprise. Since the coronavirus had taken hold of my city, I'd spent most of my time on the Upper West Side, staring out my living room window while typing away on my laptop. I was still able to go in to work, but the office was 95 percent empty. I felt out of touch with coworkers and out of the loop.

The reporter said NBCUniversal was cutting senior management salaries by 20 percent, and employees making more than $100,000 would have their salaries reduced by 3 percent. Comcast owns NBCUniversal, which in turn owns the NBC broadcast network, the cable channels CNBC, USA network, MSNBC (where I work), and Universal Pictures movie studio and theme parks (which had to shut their gates and were sitting empty), to name a few. I'm no genius, but I knew as the virus raged, that ads were harder to sell, television and movie production was stalled, and the billion-dollar Summer Olympic Games (which would have aired on NBC) were postponed.

I doubted my pay cut would put even a dent in what the conglomerate was losing, but I also remembered Mike Breslin's lesson. All of the employees were in this together. I emailed my agent. "I hear a 3 percent pay cut is coming our way," I wrote. "I'm open to giving up 3 percent, but I'm also willing to give 20 percent, regardless of what salary bracket I'm in. MSNBC has been generous to me since I arrived, especially when it came to helping me care for my dad. I want to do this because I appreciate that they've treated me like family."

When I pressed "Send," I imagined his reaction on receiving my message. My agent would probably think I had hit my head on the kitchen cupboard. But this company helped me reduce my work schedule so I could care for my dad. They had given me so much. I could be selfless, too, and I needed to be. Mike had done the same when he accepted a zero salary to keep his staff employed. Tom had brought in donuts. Alex had worked pro bono for months.

At work, small choices of selflessness count. They make larger, sometimes more sacrificial choices obvious and easier to make. And given that we make a conscious choice every fifteen minutes, cultivating selflessness at work is not a postscript to daily living; it's at the core of it. With tangible career payoffs.

Looking out for number one doesn't have to be what it used to be.

Lower your chair.

Chapter Seven

PERSONAL RELATIONSHIPS

My mother was the primary caregiver for my father at home for four years as his Alzheimer's increased in severity. She remained positive throughout. When I spoke to her on the phone, she was her usual congenial, calm self, despite the demands and stresses of taking care of my father—and it *was* stressful. At one point, he was getting up a dozen times each night to take a shower. He tried to leave the house every fifteen minutes, despite the doors being locked. He wanted to eat all the time. Mom hid the food and moved the refrigerator into the locked garage so he couldn't get to it. Even then, he tried to open canned food with a knife.

After Dad started to fall more frequently, my siblings and I installed cloud cameras so we could keep an eye on things in case my parents needed help. We also wanted to see how and why Dad was falling. That's how we heard someone screaming at the top of their lungs—the kind of scream you hear in movies when people are thrown over cliffs or running away in terror. Except this scream came from my mom and was directed at my father after he tried to open a locked door. She was so distressed, and the only person she could express it to was my father. He didn't know she was angry, sad, and stressed, all at the same time, but her scream clearly told me she was.

The camera also showed how chaotic my mother's life was, constantly

71

trying to chase Dad down. Trying to keep both herself and him safe from his behaviors. Trying to cook meals he'd grab before she was even done preparing them.

On the phone or when I was visiting, she was calm. No screams. No expressions of resentment. She had never complained, never asked for help from us directly. Everything she had done her entire life was for the benefit of our family. When the family budget was tight, she would buy me the new pair of jeans I needed instead of buying anything for herself. But *this* was too much. My father's disease demanded too much of her. And she still kept on giving. She never let us know how stressed she felt. That's why her screams, her cries for help, surprised us.

The day my father was moved to a care facility, I saw how conflicted my mom was. Her faith and her values were leading her to resist letting him go. She thought that caring for him herself was the best way to help him navigate the disease. But the fact that Dad needed to move to a place where he could get the additional care he needed wasn't an indictment of her care for him. The disease was too big for this eighty-year-old retired teacher. It had deceived her into giving up her life too.

In the first few months after my father had moved to the care facility, it became even more apparent Mom had been giving more than she could handle. She moved more slowly and looked more tired than I had ever seen her. A musician for her whole life, she could no longer remember the violin and piano pieces she had once played by heart. All of us were committed to caring for my father, but we had neglected to care for my mother, and her body had become weak.

There are limits to selflessness. We cannot and should not *always* be selfless. (In fact, if you're acting selfless for more than four hours or experience dizziness, call your doctor and don't operate any heavy machinery.) Most often, this "too selfless" point manifests itself in our relationships—with our spouse, partner, family, and close friends. When the needs of those we love are extensive, trying to meet their needs can push us to the point where acting selflessly is no longer productive and healthy. Though most of us have deficits in selflessness, there are also times when too much of a good thing does more harm than good.

UNMITIGATED SELFLESSNESS

My mother wasn't sleeping or eating in a healthy manner. She often ate only a hot dog or got takeout food so she didn't have to cook. She wasn't playing music daily, like she used to. Making it to Friday exercise class was impossible. Sometimes we don't know when we've passed into the "too selfless" zone. There are no billboards or street signs. Because of this, it can be important to talk with others about our relationships. When I talked to my mom about how her care for my father had become too much for her, it opened the door for her to accept that idea. A few months after he moved out, she was finally able to acknowledge it *was* too much for her—which was a huge admission for my mom.

What about you? Ever wonder whether you could be falling into the "too selfless" category? Below is an adaptation of a short question-naire that may help. Put together by researchers Heidi Fritz and Vicki Helgeson, the assessment scores how likely you may be to experience too much selflessness.[1]

Are You Too Selfless?

For each statement, write the number that describes how true the statement is.

5 = always true of me	2 = rarely true of me
4 = frequently true of me	1 = never true of me
3 = occasionally true of me	

_____ 1. I always place the needs of others above my own.

_____ 2. I routinely find myself getting overly involved in problems of others.

_____ 3. For me to be happy, I need others to be happy.

_____ 4. I worry about how other people get along without me when I'm not there.

➤

_____ 5. I often have trouble sleeping at night when other people are upset.

_____ 6. It is impossible for me to satisfy my own needs when they interfere with the needs of others.

_____ 7. I can't say no when someone asks me for help.

_____ 8. Even when exhausted, I will always help other people.

_____ 9. I often worry about others' problems.

_____ Total

Now add up your scores. The range of possible scores is 9 to 45. The closer your score is to 45, the greater the likelihood that you may be too selfless.

When we support others to the detriment of our own well-being, researchers call this behavior "unmitigated selflessness." That's what happened to my mom, though she is far from alone in this regard. A broad study reviewing one hundred different pieces of research and twenty-six thousand participants showed it is common to fall into unmitigated selflessness. When we compromise our own needs to such a high degree, our relationships and our well-being inevitably suffer.

Gender role stereotypes are part of this too. A sort of quiet chauvinism lurks within many dating, partner, and married relationships. Who moves and quits their job for the mutual benefit of the couple? Who stays home to care for the newborn? Who takes paternity/maternity leave? Who cooks, cleans, and does the laundry? Who cleans up the baby? Who breastfeeds the dishes? (Oops, I got that switched around.) We often default to gender role stereotypes when it comes to these and other questions. However, such role limitations also have the potential to decrease our well-being. One researcher discovered that we so strongly want to adhere to our gender role stereotypes that we'd even accept an unequal relationship simply to stay in the preferred role.[2] There are generational and geographic variations of this (whether it's housecleaning or yurtcleaning), but we agree more than we differ about what we want in personal relationships, regardless of gender identification.[3]

I am a caregiver. I take care of my dad. Over the course of four years, I cleaned him and cooked for him. Such caregiving is widely considered a female gender role, one that, to this way of thinking, my sister and mom—rather than my brothers and I—should carry out. But such traditional values don't make me feel any less of a man for doing it. (Nor does the fact that my father calls me his favorite daughter.) Had I chosen to strictly adhere to gender roles, it would have been at the expense of Dad's health. The thing is, 39 percent of family caregivers are men.[4] And the demands of family caregiving pose one of the biggest challenges to personal relationships today. Fifty-three million of us are caring for an ailing family member or close friend.[5] Gender roles should not stand in the way of providing the necessary care.

If you're curious about how good you are at selflessness in personal relationships, you can take this brief assessment that is adapted from the selflessness "communal strength measure" developed by social psychologist Judson Mills and his team.[6] Your answers to the ten questions give you a benchmark of how strong your selflessness is with one person from your inner circle.

What Is Your Selflessness Strength in Personal Relationships?

Put the same name in the blank at the end of each question. In the blank at the beginning of the question, write the number that best describes your response, from 1 to 5, with 1 being "not at all" and 5 being "a lot."

_____ 1. How many hours would you be willing to travel to visit _____?

_____ 2. How happy do you feel when doing something that helps _____?

➤

_____ 3. How much would you be willing to change for _____?

_____ 4. How large a cost would you incur to meet a need of _____?

_____ 5. How difficult is it to put the needs of _____ out of your thoughts?

_____ 6. How high a priority for you is meeting the needs of _____?

_____ 7. How willing would you be to sacrifice for _____?

_____ 8. How much would you be willing to give up to benefit _____?

_____ 9. How far would you go out of your way to do something for _____?

_____ 10. How difficult would it be to not help _____?

_____ Total

Now add up your responses. The range of possible total scores is 10 to 50. Again, too close to 50 and you might be too selfless, to the point of not taking care of yourself. How'd you do?

INNER CIRCLES

I've heard it said, "If you want to change the world, go home and love your family." This statement points out something important about human nature: (1) we often look far afield to do selfless things, and (2) it's better to start showing true love and kindness to the people closest to us. We all know people who want peace in the Middle East but will scream at their neighbor across an untrimmed hedge. Or people who want to help those in a faraway land but refuse to help Aunt Cindy (who doesn't drive) run some errands.

Ecological systems theory (EST), developed by Urie Bronfenbrenner, has had significant influence in the study of childhood development over the last twenty years. EST posits that children develop within a complex system of relationships affected by multiple levels of the surrounding environment. The innermost ring of the closest people is the most important ring in childhood development.[7]

As we grow older, we stay in these sorts of systems that determine our happiness and sense of fulfillment. So if we want to live our best lives and achieve the highest societal good, we should invest in the microlocal by caring first for those closest to us. To attempt to change the world while ignoring the microlocal is like planning a cross-country road trip without putting gas in your car. You'll never get started, never mind making it to your destination.

Take poverty, for example. Everyone wants to get rid of it. Helping the poor is a core principle of most major religions. Interestingly, the Bible suggests a triage system for poverty—going close before going far. Moses, in a speech to his people on the verge of reaching the Promised Land, proclaimed, "There will always be poor people in the land."[8] That seems sort of coldhearted, no? But let's back that truck up. Was this an offhanded way to dismiss the efforts of poverty eradication? Was Moses throwing up his hands and saying, "Whatcha gonna do? Let's go grab a falafel?" Was he saying some people are destined to live in the bad hoods of ancient Egypt? No. Right after his comment about the perpetual poor in the land, he said, "I command you to be openhanded toward your fellow Israelites who are poor and needy in your land." Moses was consistent that way. The poor were near in proximity.

Some sociologists have gone so far as to suggest that communal closeness is essential to any religious activity. The early twentieth-century sociologist Émile Durkheim was studying Australian Aboriginals when he observed that their spiritual rites produced a "collective effervescence" as the group came together to worship animal totems.[9] We've all felt the sensation of collective effervescence before—think of the electric outpouring of emotion you feel as part of a screaming crowd at a concert, while singing a hymn with fellow parishioners at church, or doing the wave at a football game. Collective effervescence is absent without a crowd. Or as Durkheim put it, "Religion is something eminently social."[10] Spirituality asks us to embrace this sense of closeness and to care for those gathered closest to us, our innermost community. Because when we do—whether it's high-fiving the fans behind you at a game or joining together in prayer—we become a part of something so much larger than ourselves.

LIFE PARTNERS

Let's suppose for a moment you *can* buy love. And where you go to buy it is the supermarket of love. (Let's call it Whole-Hearted Foods or, if you prefer, Trader Joy's.) It's where you get to choose your mate's qualities. Head to aisle 3 for creativity, which is next to physical attractiveness, and then come good financial prospects, the desire to have children, and humor. In the back of the store are kindness, religiosity, and chastity. How much would you spend on each of these qualities?

Some folks were asked to do exactly that in a hypothetical study.[11] And as it turns out, when the budget is generous, the top qualities that both men and women spend the most on are creativity and humor. Interestingly, when the budget is low, things shift. People decide to spend the most on kindness, at more than double the percentage of a high-budget scenario. The traits that are seen as luxuries are creativity and humor—the 1,200-thread-count sheets when we only need cheap sheets. In addition, the Supermarket of Love experiment, which was conducted globally, found that Western women and men saw humor as a necessity, while Eastern men and women considered it a luxury. Sure is! The staples of mates—the characteristics they consider essential—are kindness and physical attractiveness. This is true for both men and women and helps us understand an important aspect of selecting our mates.

For your friend who is all about ROI, compromising and growing together with their loved one pay off. Jay Zagorsky, a research scientist at The Ohio State University, found that couples who got married and stayed married had statistically four times the wealth of a single person.[12] (It's the monthly gym membership dues and paying for dates that do us single folks in.)

Whether single, married, or partnered, the one thing that's true when it comes to close personal relationships is that we don't have many of them. At any given point, we typically only have five people in our inner circle.[13] That's five close friends out of as many as 150 total connections (casual friends). But the acid test is this: Would any of the 150 ever help you move? Five out of 150 is a small percentage; a mere 3.3 percent of our total connections represent close personal relationships.

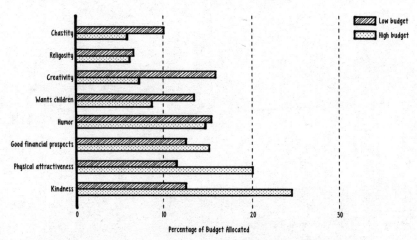

How We Value Our Mate's Traits

Percentage of Budget Allocated

Andrew G. Thomas et al., "Mate Preference Priorities in the East and West: A Cross-Cultural Test of the Mate Preference Priority Model," *Journal of Personality* (2020), 606–20.

Whether it's the 3.3 or the 96.7 percent, in all of these we can find opportunities to invest in the well-being of others—but at different levels and with different impacts. We can't do it all, and we shouldn't think we have to. But we should try to whenever and wherever we can. We have to be healthy to be able to help.

Section Three

WHAT'S IN IT
FOR WE?

Chapter Eight

A MEISM ERA

At ten years old, I was quite the social misfit. My love of not show-ering notwithstanding, I spent my days worrying about my friends' salvation. I'd judge people for wearing brand-name clothes or showing off their wealth. (I don't know why fashion made me angry. *Project Runway* was still a twinkle in Heidi Klum's eye.) I could just tell there was something wrong with those fancy Jordache jeans. Most of the time, my sermons about materialism landed awkwardly, and folks changed the subject.

My best buddy from elementary to middle school was a good guy named Jason. Though he wasn't concerned with Hermès scarves, his main problem—as far as my ten-year-old self could diagnose—was his parents' Buddhism. For Asian Americans in my era, Buddhism was base-line religion, our default screensaver—you were Buddhist even when you weren't Buddhist.

Jason and I were in the garage working on some contraption, maybe one of our remote-control boats or cars, trying to jury-rig the engine so it'd go faster. Sometimes we'd overdo it and blow out the motor. Clearly, this "connect battery to wire" moment was the perfect time to share my spiritual wisdom. I was racking my brain about how best to share the Good Book without freaking him out. I took a deep breath and plunged ahead.

"Hey, if we reverse the polarity, maybe it will work better. Speaking of which, have you ever thought about what happens after you die?" (Billy

Graham had nothing on me.) "God is kind of cool." As I was speaking, I planned for radical success. Once Jason accepted the gospel, I'd lead him in a prayer right there in the garage. Then maybe my dad could baptize him in the bathtub.

Instead of an ecstatic buy-in to eternal life, he looked at me blankly. (It was so quiet I'm pretty sure I heard Jesus whisper, "Pssst, hey kid. You're bombing.") Then after a second, Jason looked down and continued tinkering on the car.

"Ma'am, I'd like to share the good news..."

© Tak Toyoshima

My mind raced. *Should I incorporate threats? Should I throw out an "infidel"?* I hadn't game-planned utter silence. I stayed for another half hour, which seemed like a week, and then left.

84

Afterward, in our occasional conversations, awkwardness hung between Jason and me like a disease. My mom had taught me the "rule of three." Say what you think—try three times—and if the other person doesn't understand or accept it, move on. And it's okay to move on. With Jason, I think I followed the "rule of two," as I remember bringing it up one more time. My second effort was equally stunning.

Eventually, we hung out more, pretending those uneasy conversations had never happened. That was my "junior apostle" phase, and boy was I bad at it. You'd think failure would have given me some vital information about my strengths and weaknesses. But no. I must have turned at least thirty classmates into stone-cold atheists. *On the fence about God? Let me tip you over to complete nihilism.* I have never been a good salesperson.

In college, I sold used cars. I was not good. I didn't just suck; I sucked in several different ways, depending on the occasion. One time, as I made a pitch for a GMC pickup, I was met by the gaze of an uncomfortable-looking customer. I looked down, and there was a giant booger on my tie. Another time, I pushed a Subaru, only to realize that my fly was open.

Over the course of two years, I sold a total of 1.5 cars. *How could that be?* you ask. When you're that bad at things, yes, you can be given credit for selling only half of a car. And if you're counting, that's 1.5 cars and zero salvations from all of my evangelism as a kid.

Since then, I've had a lot of ebbs and flows with what Christianity means for me. And I am far from the mindset of that kid back in the garage. I don't feel nervous if my friends don't openly "believe." Your faith is your faith; mine is mine. You won't see me bring it up on first or even tenth conversations. I'm fully aware that my approach isn't necessarily the right way, nor will it be my forever way, if my past zigging and zagging in life is any indication. The fact that I am even openly discussing my faith is new.

Looking back, I realize I had a skewed sense of what selflessness was. By espousing the Good Book, I wasn't helping my classmates; I was just doing it for myself, trying to check a box on my evangelism to-do list. There was so much more *me* than *we* in my efforts. I was like a used car dealer trying to hit his daily quota of Ford Pintos. (Well, let's keep in mind that selling someone a Pinto, at any price, is one of the least altruistic things you can do.)

WORLD RELIGIONS AGREE
ON SELFLESSNESS

Since sixth grade, I've heard much about "common grace." As my dad would remind me, "Every good and perfect gift is from above, coming down from the Father of the heavenly lights."[1] He'd also remind me that Christians share views with others on values like honesty, love, justice, and selflessness. And that many of the world's major religions emphasize giving to others in selfless ways.

One of the Five Pillars of Islam is the mandate to give alms to the poor. Muslims are supposed to donate a certain amount of their property—depending on one's wealth—to the less fortunate every year. In most Muslim-majority countries today, these contributions are voluntary, but in some countries, this generosity is collected and distributed by the government. Muslims worldwide are encouraged to volunteer at soup kitchens, hospitals, schools, mosques, and libraries.

In the Hindu scriptures—the Bhagavad Gita—the essence of karma yoga is revealed. You guessed it; the basis of all existence is selfless action. The Sanskrit word *dāna* is the practice of cultivating generosity, and it can be traced back to ancient Indian texts and the oldest Hindu scriptures.

Buddhism also promotes altruism. One of this religion's ancient teachings is that something that doesn't benefit others isn't worth doing. The monk credited with founding Zen and kung fu monasteries (yes, the ones from which I consider myself to have been a mini-graduate) was named Bodhidharma, or sometimes Daruma. Dating back to the fifth or sixth century, he was South Asian, but he made his name in another country—China. He later had a wide influence in Japan. He is quoted as having said, "To give up yourself without regret is the greatest charity."[2]

Sikhism also encourages giving oneself charitably and helping people in distress—the oppressed and needy. Sikhs are encouraged to use their skills to help others, enabling the less fortunate to grow into more active members of their community. Their word *seva* means "selfless service for altruistic purposes on behalf of, and for the betterment of a community."[3]

Judaism has the concept of *tikkun olam*, which refers to the responsibility to repair what is broken in this world. Jews believe they are responsible not only for their own spiritual and material welfare but also for that of others. The Torah teaches that human beings are made *b'tzelem Elohim*—in the image of God. This suggests that when we mistreat anyone, we are essentially mistreating God—something all religions would agree is "not cool." Therefore, selfless service is necessary when we encounter the suffering of others.

This is by no means an attempt to establish a hierarchy of religions. To try to do so would be way above my pay grade. Rather, I'm talking about an understanding of selflessness that most of the world's religions affirm. Yet meism today has never been stronger. For long-simmering reasons, we can't see what's in it for we.

"I'M OK—YOU'RE OK"

I lived through the 1980s, when pink suits and feathered hair were in. Not too long before that neon epoch, the book *I'm OK—You're OK* by Thomas Anthony Harris shot up to the number one position on the *New York Times* bestseller list and stayed there for a couple of years. In fact, the book is still in print, and according to its latest cover, it has sold more than fifteen million copies to date. Harris argued that people can't flourish without the proper "I'm okay" mindset. It served as the stage for the self-esteem movement of the 1980s and 1990s, which started in my home state of California with state assemblyman John Vasconcellos Jr.

After reading a hundred self-help books, Vasconcellos decided that self-esteem could be our missing cultural ingredient for success. Since a lack of self-esteem was associated with many bad behaviors—poor academic performance, drug use, teen pregnancy, athletic inability, bad relationships, wishing that you had Jessie's girl,[4] and more—he thought that increasing people's self-esteem could improve society in unprecedented ways.

In 1986, Vasconcellos created a California task force to figure out how self-esteem is "nurtured, harmed, rehabilitated,"[5] an initiative that cost more than $735,000.[6] That was rapper money.

Also, in the 1980s, boasting about materialism was first becoming fashionable, as demonstrated by the emergence of designer jeans and Robin Leach's *Lifestyles of the Rich and Famous*—the *MTV Cribs* of its day. It was a perfect stew of "meism." What started in the '80s in Leach's circles spread nationally and became accepted as common practice.

Self-esteem had a few critics. Cartoonist Garry Trudeau mocked the concept for three straight weeks in his super popular *Doonesbury* strip by naming his ditzy character Boopsie as a member of the fictionalized self-esteem task force. This pleased Vasconcellos, who believed that Trudeau helped draw more attention to the self-esteem movement than he could ever have done alone. Vasconcellos turned out to be correct about the public's embrace. *Doonesbury* did for self-esteem what *Garfield* did for lasagna.

Everyone jumped on the bandwagon. The promise was alluring. What if all sorts of bad social outcomes were caused directly by low self-esteem? That would suggest an easy fix—one that could appeal not only to liberals but to conservatives too. "This bipartisanship was key to the idea's success and widespread adoption," wrote Jesse Singal in *The CUT*.[7] Some politicians even believed that self-esteem could somehow reduce pollution. (Just believe in yourself, Mother Nature!) It was like a diet pill that promised results without hard work. We didn't have to look at systemic racism, poverty, or educational failings. It was much easier to get people to believe in themselves. You were late to the game, Instagram. The "me" era started in the '80s. Meism's peak, near or far—nobody would know its future height.

There I was, in California as meism began to take hold in the schools. "Hundreds of school districts have added self-esteem motivational materials to their curriculums," wrote reporter Lena Williams in the *New York Times* in 1990.[8] Schools began pushing the idea that children should never feel bad about anything. I could have flunked out of trigonometry, and my teachers would have told my parents, "Richard's triangles are just 'different' triangles."

I was also told I was special, unique, different from everyone else. "You just need to believe in yourself"; "you gotta believe anything is possible"; and "you have to love yourself first before you can love someone else." These phrases are common today on T-shirts and inspirational posters. They are modern extrapolations of the self-esteem movement. This sort of advice is now given as ordinary and frequent encouragement.

As it turns out, John Vasconcellos may *not* have been "on to something" after all. In his obituary, he was described as a "famously rumpled bear-of-a-man" who was "colorful, witty, brilliant, angry, intellectual and elegantly foul of mouth."[9] He was also known for his unscientific approach to issues. *Why believe in science when you can simply believe in yourself?* a good "meist" might ask.

In 1984, after suffering a heart attack, Vasconcellos asked a group of friends to, at the same time every day, visualize themselves as tiny brushes scrubbing his veins while he visualized them scrubbing. Four weeks of this rather unorthodox treatment—and his health further deteriorated. He needed to undergo bypass surgery, begin a more healthful diet, and quit smoking.[10] Self-esteem may feel good, but it's no substitute for thirty minutes of cardio.

In the end, the self-esteem movement had as much scientific basis as the "vein-scrubbing visualization" technique. Vasconcellos had failed to ask these important questions: What if self-esteem is a correlation, not a causation? What if high-achieving people have lots of self-esteem because of their success? What if self-esteem is a natural by-product, not a cause? (Oh, and what if my triangles were actually circles?)

Decades later, social researchers couldn't find evidence to back up the claims of the self-esteem era, and the much-touted results of increased self-esteem simply didn't happen. In fact, they were shocked to learn that prisoners were one of the demographics that had the most self-esteem. Apparently, you shouldn't tell potential bank robbers they can do anything if they put their minds to it. By then, the movement had grown into a billion-dollar industry.

One thing's for sure, the "believe in yourself" industry benefited from believing in itself.

CYCLICAL, GENERATIONAL MEISM

The psychologist Jean Twenge is an expert on the long-term impact of the focus on self-esteem on millennials. She says, "The self-esteem movement is at least one factor in explaining why millennials have higher self-esteem, are more likely to see themselves as above average, and in general have more positive self-views than previous generations did at the same age. I also think it may explain why they score higher in measures of narcissistic personality traits."[11] Other generations have said this of the generations before them. I'm sure my parents said the same of my generation. (Go back far enough, and there's a Chinese farmer shaking his head at his good-for-nothing son for telling his own reflection in the river he's worthwhile. This was before selfie sticks.) It may not be about our age, but more about a phase we all go through. I'm living in one, but so have Gen Y, Gen Z, Boomers, and the Silent and Greatest Generations. We all pass through the meism gauntlet.

We can be pretty obsessed with ourselves. You know this if you've ever read a newspaper or watched the news or—I don't know—been on social media. I have, unfortunately, had to report on too many stories of humanity's selfishness. The prism of pop culture has layers of this too. Today's reality shows could be considered both a window into and a playbook for dominant cultural norms. One such popular reality Netflix series about Gen Z set in Japan—*Terrace House: Tokyo 2019–2020*—has an international cast from the United States, Japan, Russia, and more. This was a conversation two twentysomething members of the *Real World*–like cast had:

Tupas: You wouldn't know how to love someone else if you didn't know what it was like to be loved.
Vivi: You're saying if you never receive love, you'll never be able to love?
Tupas: Of course that's the case.
Vivi: But it's not . . .
Tupas: You've got it backwards.
Vivi: You first have to discover love within yourself.
Tupas: That's not possible.
Vivi: Why?
Tupas: For example, your parents . . . They show you love for the first time and you learn what it is. Then you can exemplify that for others.
Vivi: That's not true. What if you grew up without your parents?
Tupas: How is someone supposed to understand love out of thin air?
Vivi: You first focus on nourishing yourself.
Tupas: Well, that's a beautiful theory.[12]

When I used to take my ailing dad on walks, I was worried he would lose his balance or get lost. Once, when he was out on a walk by himself, someone pushed him, which caused him to fall to the ground. The person left my dad there. A dispatcher at the 911 call center dialed my mother. Why would anyone want to push my elderly father to the ground? Nothing justifies that kind of act. His dementia had given him nothing but more kindness and friendliness . . . and unfortunately weakness too.

We are better than this, right? You know the answer if you've spent any amount of time around children, where the most frequently heard word is *mine*! Children love themselves and naturally take care of number one, to the detriment of their playmates.

A Swiss study examined children's willingness to share candy with a friend.[13] (Leave it to the Swiss to potentially want everyone to have their own Toblerone. I'm only assuming it was Toblerone because the palates of Swiss children are probably far too refined for an Almond Joy or a Whatchamacallit.) The researchers gave each child two pieces of candy and gave them two options: split the pieces of candy evenly or take it all for themselves.

The study found that at age three and four, only 8.7 percent of children chose to share. "Three-year-olds will use the language of fairness, but mainly to their own advantage and to support their egoism," lead researcher Ernst Fehr told *Nature*.[14] But by ages seven and eight, 45 percent of the kids chose to share. The fivefold increase suggests that our understanding of selflessness and equality evolves as we grow—at least when it comes to chocolate. Though we start with caring for ourselves first, we eventually grow into more selfless beings. (Maybe we realize if we were to get all the chocolate, we might never see our toes again.)

Other evidence suggests we may even be born with a sense of selflessness. Yale's Infant Cognition Center (a.k.a. the Baby Lab) found a difference between what babies do and what they aspire to do. In their study, pre-verbal six- to ten-month-olds watched a puppet show of a selfless yellow triangle (clearly not drawn by me) push a red ball up a hill. On the other side of the red ball, a selfish blue square was pushing it down the hill.[15]

Modern studies of babies observe eye movements to gauge their interest. Psychologists at the Baby Lab call this "looking time." When babies see something they like, they look at it.

After watching the puppet show, more than 80 percent of the children chose the selfless yellow triangle by staring at it admiringly when prompted to pick a character. One side of their brains wants to guard their chocolate, while the other wants to find equality and perhaps learn how to be more giving. One infant in the study went a step further and took justice into his own tiny hands, smacking the selfish blue square upside the head.[16]

Paul Bloom, one of the psychologists who ran the experiment, suggests it is a misguided assumption that children must be "civilized" and taught by parents to "override selfish impulses." Even in infants, "you can see glimmers of moral thought, moral judgment, and moral feeling," Bloom argues.[17] It seems we want to be selfless, even if we can't live up to it quite yet.[18]

So which are we born to be? Which part of the struggle are we inherently set up to be in—the yellow triangle, the blue square, or the red ball? Interestingly, whether we're driven by self-regard or by self-loathing, our energy is still focused on the "self" part of the condition. Is it possible to be both self-focused and selfless? Consider Pastor Rick Warren's definition of humility: "Humility is not thinking less of yourself; it is thinking of yourself less."[19]

I'm reminded of the city I work in. There was a building in New York City after World War II that had super slow elevators. I encounter this phenomenon all the time—especially on Saturday nights, when 30 Rock is filled with the lucky dozens who got tickets and are running late to get to their seats to see *Saturday Night Live*. Normally, I use different elevators to get out of the building. (I don't mind the hullabaloo because *SNL* was *the* show for me growing up.)

It was different for some impatient tenants in the 1940s. They threatened to move out if the landlord didn't fix the elevator delay. The building owners tried to figure out how to speed up the lifts, but because the building was old, they couldn't find a cost-effective fix.

Instead, the owner installed mirrors next to every elevator bank. Now, instead of fuming over the slow elevators, the tenants could look at themselves without appearing to be vain. They were so obsessed with their own image that the complaints dropped to nearly zero.[20] (How can you be mad about an elevator when you're busy pulling spinach out of your teeth?)

Even today, you may notice how frequently mirrors are placed next to elevators.[21] They are there for a reason. No matter if we like or dislike what we see in the mirror, we'll gaze at ourselves for a long time. We're not only obsessed with our appearance; we're obsessed with our comfort too. (Otherwise we'd take the stairs.) To borrow from Carly Simon, we really are "so vain."[22]

Though the era of self-care and self-love had its benefits, after many decades of perfecting the art of meism, we've become too good at it. Part of this expert meism is the immediacy with which we can satisfy our meist cravings. Just download it—anytime anywhere. When I'm feeling down, there's nothing like some on-demand social media ♥ ♥ ♥ and, to perk me up 👍👍👍, a double espresso of self-affirmation to get me through lunch. And it's free.

That is, until we explore what's in it for we.

Chapter Nine

COMMUNITIES
OF OTHER

Remember the "helper's high" from doing random acts of kindness? Remember how people's brain MRIs lit up like a Christmas tree and released endorphins when they did random acts of kindness? How could I maximize the endorphins I was getting each time I put on my rubber gloves to pick up trash in the park?

Back to Pelin Kesebir, my "selfless" scientist. "There are actually many studies suggesting random acts of kindness can quite significantly increase well-being, especially if you do around five acts or more in a day," she told me. "Try seeing how many small acts of kindness you can fit into an afternoon, and see how you feel."

To make a long story short, I took Pelin's advice, and I did feel better when I had a higher concentration of acts of kindness. I spent the afternoon trying to do small things. Picking up trash in Central Park meant being patient, since New Yorkers aren't especially used to seeing everyday folks pick up the trash. (If anything, they're probably going to think it's a reaction to a fever.) At the takeout window of the coffee boutique (not a lot of Dunkins on the Upper West Side), the barista thought maybe he was on *Candid Camera* when I told him I wanted to pay for the order of the person behind me—but then he got that it was a good idea. Donating the suits I had barely worn to the neighborhood Salvation Army was easy. It felt strange but satisfying that what kept me warm was going to do that for someone else. (Being a former suit salesman, I wanted to be the one who showed the next owner how to best wear the one I was donating.)

Helping my community be a better community, little by little, was something I had failed to do in the years I had lived in this city. As I walked around my neighborhood, this thought made me wistful. There was a time when the communities I lived in felt more cohesive. We all used to do more together with our neighborhoods.

I'm far from the first to take note of the trend. In 2000, Robert Putnam published his seminal work titled *Bowling Alone: The Collapse and Revival of American Community*, in which he described a strange phenomenon. Even though America had more bowlers per capita, fewer people were bowling in leagues. The activities that had once connected us—bowling leagues, front-porch conversations, card playing, attending houses of worship, parent-teacher associations, community groups, garden clubs, and so forth—were becoming less and less popular.

"Community has warred incessantly with individualism," Putnam wrote. "For the first two-thirds of the twentieth century a powerful tide bore Americans into ever deeper engagement in the life of their communities, but a few decades ago—silently, without warning—that tide reversed and we were overtaken by a treacherous rip current. Without at first noticing, we have been pulled apart from one another and from our communities over the last third of the century."[1]

Putnam wrote his book when Netflix was renting DVDs. Imagine how he would approach the subject now that every pocket has a smartphone and everything a person needs to stay alive can be delivered by Amazon. It's pretty easy these days to live an isolated life. We see signs around us of how community has broken down. We don't trust each other because we don't know each other. We no longer instinctively give strangers the benefit of the doubt.

Studies show there's a greater sense of community when we live near enough to walk to parks and schools. One study found that living more than five minutes from a park lowered a sense of community by about 5 percent; living more than half a mile from a school drops it another 3.4 percent.[2] A sense of community increases when we have more face-to-face interactions that result from living within walking distance of public spaces.

In Manhattan, we are surrounded by 4 million strangers, and we get to know people because we're not commuting in cars or having plenty of space between dwellings. We live elbow to elbow, pressed up next to each other in bodegas, subways, coffee shops, and elevators. We can identify our neighbors by their BO.

It was slightly different growing up in San Francisco. Though my home was a beige, two-story San Francisco row house with a front-facing garage and a stoop, it wasn't nearly as compact as New York City.

I shared my bedroom with one or two of my three siblings at any given time. All six of us in the family shared one bathroom. The stoop was a nice perk because I could walk outside and see if my friends were home, sometimes tossing a rock to get their attention. To the right of my house lived a kid from a first-generation Japanese family. Across the street lived a boy from a first-generation French family and kids from a Filipino family. A White family lived next to them.

Every day, my friends and I rode our bikes, roller-skated, and played baseball until our moms rang dinner bells and called us home at dusk. We could tell by the different accents which family was about to eat.

In the mornings, my siblings and I hauled ourselves out of bed and walked to Argonne Elementary two-and-a-half blocks away. My brother and I frequently ran to school, though not because of my incredible enthusiasm for education. Rather, I liked to compete.

One morning, we had made it only one block when I blurted out, "Beat you to the corner!" and put my little legs on overdrive. I dashed across the street like I was late for Free Cone Day at Ben & Jerry's. However, right after I entered the crosswalk, I didn't see this coming . . .

I was hit by a car.

My brother wasn't sure what had happened. After seeing me on the ground, he ran to me as the car drove off. A hit-and-run.

My brother turned around and ran back in the other direction. "Richard got hit by a car!" he yelled as he ran into the house. "Richard got hit by a car!" he said repeatedly, as if he were some sort of mini–Paul Revere.

My mother hurried down the stoop and ran up the block to where I lay near the crosswalk. This was a tight-knit community. My neighbors huddled around me after a couple of them had called the ambulance.

One had seen the car drive away and gave the police a description of the car and driver. They knew who I was, where I lived, and what I needed. By the time my mother got there moments later, I was already surrounded by people who were caring for me.

While in my first ambulance ride—which certainly wasn't going to be my last—I looked down and saw the white bone of my ankle. Fortunately, that was the worst of my injuries. Had I been one step faster into the intersection, I would've been killed.

A few months later, my neighbor's description of the car and driver led to the driver's arrest. My mother decided not to press charges. She forgave him. I was bewildered. I wanted to put this joker behind bars. I felt like Starsky and Hutch all rolled up into one, with a serious case of the Hill Street Blues.

My old neighborhood has changed a lot since then. Groups of kids no longer play in the streets. Neighbors don't congregate and talk to each other. There are no moms with accents calling kids home for supper. My neighborhood of today may not have been there to care for the Richard of yesterday.

DESIGNING "OTHER" SPACES

Over the course of the last century, city planners have attempted to create good neighborhoods that mix different types of people. The planners carried out the organic city growth approach with good intentions, which resulted in both wins and losses. Many cities that formed organically were haphazardly laid out, which often gave them character and charm—think Boston (definitely laid out by planners in a bar), London (in a pub), Seoul (while singing karaoke), Sydney (well, anywhere). Locals come to love it—but also to hate it. It takes forever to get ten blocks crosstown, so we just stay home!

Of course, this can lead to an undesired extreme. Isolation exacts a physical toll on the brain, increasing our vulnerability to disease, even among people who likely wouldn't have otherwise gotten sick. Loneliness can trigger high blood pressure, increase inflammation, and raise heart rates and levels of stress hormones.

An analysis of seventy studies found that over time—no matter the subject's gender, age, location, or culture—social isolation, loneliness, and living alone had a significant negative impact on lifespan. Among the findings:

- Loneliness increased the likelihood of death by 26 percent.
- Social isolation increased the likelihood of death by 29 percent.
- Living alone increased the likelihood of death by 32 percent.[3]

So in contemporary urban design, planners are increasingly seeking to reduce the sense of loneliness and balance the infrastructure needs of the community with layouts that not only encourage gathering and foster a shared sense of identity but also promote political objectives.

When India gained its independence from Britain in 1947, the country was divided, and 14 million Hindus, Sikhs, and Muslims were displaced. Ethnic tensions ran high. More than a million people were murdered in the ensuing violence. The new dividing lines placed the old capital in the country of Pakistan, so India's leaders created a new one.

In 1949, they established Chandigarh as the new capital of Indian Punjab and—with the help of renowned Swiss-French architect Le Corbusier—designed the new city with the hope of promoting peace, democracy, unity, and equality. That's a lot of pressure to put on a city planner. Yet Chandigarh was a success. Its architecture is interesting. The city has more trees than most Indian cities and has a grid of well-planned, self-contained neighborhoods that encourage, well, neighborliness. City services such as parks and shopping areas are strategically placed so all residents are afforded equal access.[4]

Such purposeful design has also been used on college campuses. The University of California, Berkeley has traditionally been considered a hotbed of free-speech activities. Perhaps it's not surprising that it was designed with common spaces that encourage gatherings of all types of people. When I was a student there, it was common for students to gather and have spontaneous public debates about everything from peace in the Middle East to abortion and taxes. In Sproul Plaza, students often hovered around the Free Speech Monument, a six-foot-wide granite disk with a six-inch hole in the middle filled with soil. Most monuments are tall, not flat to the ground, but there's a reason this one is different—the

...he inscription reads, "This soil and
...be a part of any nation and shall
... So instead of looking up at
...k at each other to engage.

...uth of Berkeley was
...ning a new school
...a, San Diego admin-
...activism. An oppressive,
eight-story... ...d as the school's library. The
planners also... ...pus to be especially compact as a
way to discoura... ...gs. Perhaps they took their inspiration
from those who de... ...ty of Lights. Paris, which was rebuilt after
the 1789–1799 Frenc... ...volution, was designed to prevent gatherings.
Emperor Napoleon III asked Georges-Eugène Haussmann to bulldoze
entire neighborhoods to execute his plan. Critics accused Haussmann of
widening boulevards so the French army could more easily maneuver on
its way to confront armed uprisings in the streets.

Space—and its use—have the power to dictate how people live and
get along.

Interestingly, some neighborhoods in the United States are now being
designed to encourage people to be selfless, to reach out to their neighbors. In Seaside, Florida, a town built from the ground up in the 1980s,
there are white picket fences galore. A little post office sits proudly in
the town square. (Things could be a bit *too* perfect here though. You may
have seen Seaside before—the town was cast as the home of the titular
character in *The Truman Show*.)

What makes towns like Seaside feel perfect? The developers put
homes on small lots and included pedestrian-friendly streets where
everyone, whether on foot, riding a bike, or driving a car, could get
around easily. It was one of the first new communities since the 1920s to
accommodate pedestrians. This meant businesses could exist within the
community, because city planners hadn't zoned everything for housing.
This approach created a nice combination of places to go—for work, exercise, shopping, and play—that are all within walking distance, allowing
neighbors to greet each other along the way.

Additionally, the developers incorporated more affordable housing—small houses and apartments located on top of businesses—which meant everyone could walk to the town center in about fifteen minutes. This new neighborhood was built to include the qualities we love about older neighborhoods. Other similarly strategic communities soon sprang up around the nation.

I wish you could see my one-bedroom apartment. Although it's tiny compared to the average American home, I'm blessed to have it. On a good day, it's 450 square feet. I have room for just one bookshelf and have to make sure I purposefully select the books to put on it. I have a Murphy bed so I can fold it up into a space in the wall and have a workout area. Some urban designers believe apartment buildings should have a communal space for residents to gather. Think dorm life. In Manhattan, it would be an expensive proposition to leave any apartment building space empty for common use, but the richness of the random connections with a diverse group of people would be worth it.

Libraries—a traditional space if there ever was one—are following this approach. Instead of the dusty shelves and solitary study booths of days gone by, new libraries have more group spaces where students can help each other and people can engage with members of their community they haven't met yet. Through social interaction, we learn to help others, respond to selfless opportunities, and accept differences in order to find commonality. Given that we spend 90 percent of our time indoors, designing indoor spaces conducive to interaction is important.[6] Bowling anyone?

COMMUNITIES WITHIN COMMUNITIES

I've had trouble my whole life knowing what Asian American means. *Doesn't Asian equal Chinese?* That's what I passively assumed as a kid. Nope. Asia has more than fifty different countries—such as India, Micronesia, Macronesia (made that up for false equivalency), Kazakhstan, and others. Indeed, *Asian American* means a ton of different things.

If the United States were a pizza cut into twelve slices, Asian Americans would be represented by one slice. The Asian Americans who live in that slice speak more than a hundred different languages, and two-thirds are foreign-born. Divide that one slice of pizza into fifty smaller pieces (especially if prone to ethnic heartburn), and I'd be part of one bite-sized piece.

As a teen, I wasn't exactly welcoming when I encountered new Asian folks arriving from another country. I was American. In fact, I was a sixth-generation American on one side of my family. By Asian American standards, that was as good as coming over on the Mayflower. I didn't dress like these new Asians. I didn't eat what they ate. I didn't smell like they smelled. I was *authentically* American. That meant I was better. Which meant I became an "ugly" sixteen-year-old American.

One of the unique qualities of the United States is that it represents all communities of communities. Like mine. At least thirty-seven diasporas make up the Asian American population. There are some twenty countries of origin that make up the African American community, and at least thirty-two diasporas that make up the Latino American community. In the United States, there are 574 Native American tribes and 120-plus origin countries represented within our borders.[7] Nationally, we are a community of communities.

Perhaps one of the most inspirational stories of what it means to live out this value took place several decades ago in college sports. Robert "Bobby" Grier was an average American kid who loved playing football. In 1952, he earned a spot on the team at the University of Pittsburgh as the team's star fullback. He was the only Black man on the team. He and his team did so well in 1955 that they were invited to play Georgia Tech in the Sugar Bowl. Only Georgia's governor was opposed to having any African American players in the Sugar Bowl, and he petitioned the board of regents to boycott the game. The regents declined to do so, and Grier would become the first-ever Black man at the championship series game.

Many years later, it was my privilege to interview Grier, who related the rest of the story. "All the players got together without me to talk and decided that if I didn't play, they wouldn't play," Grier said. His White teammates started saying, "No Grier, no game." In the end, Grier traveled with his team to play in the Sugar Bowl, effectively breaking the color barrier in college football. Football history was changed on January 2, 1956, because a team made up of many members became united as one.

• • • • • • • • • •

Not long ago, legislative bodies in France did something similar to what Grier's teammates had done. Male council members, legislative representatives, and European representatives risked their own political futures by insisting that their legislative bodies needed more women in them. Up until the 1990s, the rates of French women who held elected office were among the lowest in Europe. And based on the built-in political dynamics, both formal and informal, this reality didn't seem to be changing anytime soon. So legislators passed a parity law that required each party's ballot slate to have equal numbers of men and women. Parties that did not adhere to this law were subject to fines totaling as much as $4 million and would lose election eligibility.

In 2001, the first year the law was in effect, the number of women elected to town councils more than doubled. One of the women who made her first foray into politics that year was Anne Hidalgo, who later became the first woman to be elected mayor of Paris. France's National Assembly, made up of 12 percent women in 2002, rose to 39 percent in 2017.[8]

Before the parity law, male legislators dominated at a ratio of nine to one. They routinely voted to replace themselves with other men. But then they voted to make their country stronger and better. Such an approach may not be replicated en masse anytime soon by parliaments and congresses globally, but France has thrown down the proverbial gauntlet with its parity law. In France, various political communities demonstrated it is possible to set aside self-serving and short-term interests for the long-term benefit of the community as a whole.

There could have been multiple reasons these male politicians decided to lean in to say equity and equality are parliamentary priorities. And one reason may have been something not so obvious: *Brains are wired to focus on others.* Sleep makes us more otherish. Yes, we more or less spend a third of our lives asleep, as the ads for mattress companies often remind us. Since our brains are optimized to help us survive, whatever happens during sleep must be something important.

Using MRIs to study the brain at rest, UCLA professor Matthew

Lieberman and his colleagues found that we are biologically designed to be social and think of others, and our brains are wired to connect with one another.[9] So it makes sense that when the brain is at rest, it's focused on thinking about, mulling over, and processing our interactions with other people.

© Tak Toyoshima

The dorsomedial prefrontal cortex (the "CEO of the social brain," according to Lieberman) lights up when we're at rest, as well as when we're explicitly thinking about others.[10] (The French politicians must have been getting more rest.) Why would our brains—which consume 20 percent of all our energy—expend that much effort thinking about other people and social interactions? According to Lieberman, "Evolution has made a bet that the best thing for our brain to do in any spare moment is to get ready for what comes next in social terms."[11]

All of us have left a conversation wondering whether a friend or date really understood what we said or even liked us. We may review their words, wondering what they meant. What did they *really* mean by, "Richard, please leave this dinner party before we call the police"? *Did we connect or not?* the brain wants to know. And it's natural. Our "thinking of others" brain is one of the more important aspects of our cognition.

The human brain constantly processes recent experiences with other people and updates our assumptions. It's getting us ready to make sense of the world in terms of other people's thoughts, feelings, and goals. We walk around with our brains trying to reset themselves to start thinking about other people.

We do it quickly too. Though snap judgments of others are a specialty of dating apps, in evolutionary terms, such assessments could have resulted in life or death. In the old days, we'd have to make a quick decision about who among us was going to help us cook the deer we killed or who was going to steal it. Our survival depended on our interactions with a number of people.

Though most of us no longer have to hunt the food we eat, attaining it does require a great number of people. I couldn't drink my morning cup of coffee without the help of the Ethiopian farmers, the roasters, the shippers, the grocery store cashiers, the city of New York's water supply, the electricity grid, and the people in China who made my coffeepot. (That's just my coffee. I could also detail the supply chain for my donut, but that's a whole other chapter.)

For the vast majority of us, life requires getting along and cooperating with others, so our brains are fixated on processing and developing social skills. And get this—the brain even has the potential to get bigger as we get better at this task. The size of the neocortex (the outermost layer of our brain) relative to the rest of the brain varies according to the size of one's community or social group.

In a study of monkeys, the ones that hung around with about five other monkeys had a brain size ratio of about 2.3. Monkeys that spent time with about forty other monkeys had a brain size ratio of around 3.8.[12] (The only downside was found in the monkeys that hung out at a dive bar drinking Natty Lights; their brain size ratio dipped to -0.3.) In most cases, the relative size of the neocortex got bigger as social groups did. I guess we can conclude that as we increase our community, we also get smarter.

OATH TO STRANGERS

Paul Cary spent his career around people from various communities. After three decades as a fireman and paramedic, he decided to retire. A colleague described him as a "really, really dependable gentleman."[13] When Paul watched the news and saw fellow Americans in distress, he instinctively wanted to pitch in to help. On the day that New York 911 dispatchers got a volume of calls not seen since 9/11, he knew he had to go. Instead of a terrorist attack, the world was being attacked by a virus.

It was Thursday, March 28, 2020, when he got in his car and drove from Aurora, Colorado, to New York City. Eighteen hundred miles later, he showed up to help. For the next three weeks, he drove an ambulance up and down the streets of New York City to get the sick to the hospital. Trip after trip, hour after hour, he shuttled people who were struggling to live. He was about to finish his first thirty-day emergency stint. He told friends he was going to sign up for another. This wasn't his hometown, but he knew this faraway city needed him.

Paul didn't make it to the second stint.

He started to feel sick. Eleven days later, after decades of saving lives, Paul lost his own to COVID-19—in the process of helping strangers. He left behind two sons and four grandchildren. He was sixty-six years old. As the coffin made its way to the airport, local stations covered Paul's story—as they certainly should have. He received a hero's send-off. Colorado's son was on his way home.

Every evening, around seven o'clock, a little bit of Paul's spirit got an embrace. Along with thousands of other New Yorkers, I stepped onto my balcony to pound a pot lid with a spoon, rap on the railing, or just cheer into the air. *Hey, Paul, this is for you.* In the middle of a global pandemic that had all of us sheltering in place, it was the one thing we could do to thank our frontline heroes, all the medical caregivers, all our CareHeroes. During that surreal three minutes every night, windows popped open. People crawled onto rusty fire escapes. The city remembered to give thanks for those who cared for us.

At the beginning of the pandemic, many medical facilities lacked sufficient protective gear, and many frontline staff ended up contracting the disease. At one point, health care workers accounted for as many as 20 percent of known COVID-19 cases. Many of them died. It's difficult to track the number. And yet time and time again, they kept showing up, selflessly doing their job to save us.

Medical students even graduated early to rush to the 2020 pandemic frontlines. Julia Probert, whose story is told in the *Wall Street Journal*, graduated early from medical school to rush to Bellevue Hospital in New York. Her badge read "COVID-19 junior physician."[14] Prior to her deployment to the frontlines, she, along with many other medical students who had also been sent out, recited the Hippocratic Oath by video conferencing—an oath that truly does inspire.

A Modern Hippocratic Oath

I swear to fulfill, to the best of my ability and judgment, this covenant:

I will respect the hard-won scientific gains of those physicians in whose steps I walk, and gladly share such knowledge as is mine with those who are to follow.

I will apply, for the benefit of the sick, all measures [that] are required, avoiding those twin traps of overtreatment and therapeutic nihilism.

I will remember that there is art to medicine as well as science, and that warmth, sympathy, and understanding may outweigh the surgeon's knife or the chemist's drug.

I will not be ashamed to say "I know not," nor will I fail to call in my colleagues when the skills of another are needed for a patient's recovery.

I will respect the privacy of my patients, for their problems are not disclosed to me that the world may know. Most especially must I tread with care in matters of life and death. If it is given me to save a life, all thanks. But it may also be within my power to take a life; this awesome responsibility

---

must be faced with great humbleness and awareness of my own frailty. Above all, I must not play at God.

I will remember that I do not treat a fever chart, a cancerous growth, but a sick human being, whose illness may affect the person's family and economic stability. My responsibility includes these related problems, if I am to care adequately for the sick.

I will prevent disease whenever I can, for prevention is preferable to cure.

I will remember that I remain a member of society, with special obligations to all my fellow human beings, those sound of mind and body as well as the infirm.

If I do not violate this oath, may I enjoy life and art, respected while I live and remembered with affection thereafter. May I always act so as to preserve the finest traditions of my calling and may I long experience the joy of healing those who seek my help.[15]

Modernized version, written by Louis Lasagna, academic dean of the School of Medicine at Tufts University, 1964

The oath inspires us to try a little of what the members of this medical community swear to do for their careers and for their lives—to help others who are often strangers to them.

The unknown. Communities of others—of color, of origin, of economics, of profession, of politics, and more—are these "unknown." It's important for us to see how not knowing hurts society. Like medical professionals and the designers of cities, we are stronger when we strive to learn about and fully embrace communities of other.

Chapter Ten

REPUBLICANS
AND DEMOCRATS

A s a kid, I watched with fascination as the wooden collection plate on Sunday mornings went by. I sat on a pew as it passed from hand to hand, brimming with folded checks, coins, and some actual paper money. I was filled with wonder: *What is stopping someone from reaching in and pulling out the greenbacks? Who gave what? How much does the church bring in? Who counts it?*

Every time I saw my parents' folded check drop into the offering plate, I thought to myself, *Why give when we have so little?* Christians are taught to tithe—to give 10 percent of their income to the church, which distributes the money to people in need, supports outreach programs and missions, and keeps the lights on. (Communion wafers don't buy themselves.) Muslims have *zakat*, which is a 2.5 percent giving threshold of their total wealth. Buddhism has *dāna*, which is money that is mostly given to monks. And in Hinduism, it is customary to donate a portion of one's salary to religious work. As you can see, most of the world's major religions foster giving oneself—a giving not only of mind, heart, and spirit, but also of time and money.

Which takes us to another modern religion—namely, politics. It's omnipresent and almost omnipotent, given the way many pay homage to it. It dominates dinner tables, provokes arguments, affects marriages, and sometimes precipitates divorces. Televisions are swamped with channel choices for content about Republicans, Democrats, Libertarians, and politicians of any other persuasion. No matter your flavor, there's a channel on which you can satisfy your hunger for getting the scoop on all the latest topics.

So when considering giving and selflessness, does something we spend so much time and energy on serve as an indicator? How do the "bleeding heart liberals" (who are perceived to be generous) compare to the "hard-hearted conservatives" (who are perceived to be stingy)? Who is more selfless—the Democrats or the Republicans?

PRESIDENTS

"My mother's gonna kill me," Laetitia Thompson said as she got up the nerve to pose a question to the president of the United States in front of two hundred college and high school students. It was 1994, and Bill Clinton was speaking at MTV's forum on youth and violence. Seventeen-year-old Laetitia's question was of the more personal variety. "The world is dying to know," she said. "Is it boxers or briefs?"

"Usually briefs," came the reply. The audience erupted into cheers, wondering if "usually" meant sometimes briefs and sometimes nothing.[1]

That was not the first (or last) time the country had reason to wonder about Bill Clinton's underwear. The first occasion was a lesser-known, arguably stranger moment when Bill was the governor of Arkansas. The Clintons circled the house and collected used items they no longer wanted. They took them to the Salvation Army, Goodwill, and other places that accept donations. When they released their tax returns, Governor Clinton had made an itemized list in his own handwriting of each donated item, with dollar amounts indicating their value. On the list—an old shower curtain, shoes, jogging shorts, and Bill's used underwear. (Thanks to Laetitia—or not—for determining they were probably tighty-whities.) How does the saying go—one man's used underwear is another man's treasure?

What really raised eyebrows—other than the idea of a bunch of Arkansas Goodwill customers buying Clinton's used underwear—is that they claimed these as "charitable donations" at values well above their actual worth. They claimed that the underwear was worth $2 per pair.[2]

(In 1980s money, $2 was the price of two gallons of gas or ten pounds of potatoes.[3]) They claimed a "gabardine suit—ripped pants" was worth $75, and a "salmon sports coat" was worth $75. (Somebody wanted to look like *Miami Vice* in the '90s.)

All of this personal information bandied about by pundits might make you wonder, *Why do politicians put themselves through the financial version of a public colonoscopy by releasing tax returns?*

It started in 1952. Critics accused Richard Nixon of allowing political backers to pay for his campaign for Dwight Eisenhower's vice president slot. Nixon admitted to taking a gift from a political donor. A donor had shipped a cocker spaniel to his family in a crate. The Nixons immediately fell in love with the dog they named Checkers. They weren't about to give him up, no matter the political ramifications. Now referred to as the "Checkers speech," President Nixon said, "The kids, like all kids, love the dog, and I just want to say this, right now, that regardless of what they say about it, we're gonna keep it." Then he challenged the Democrat candidates to "make a complete financial statement as to their financial history" unless, he suggested, "they have something to hide."[4]

Democrat challenger Adlai Stevenson and his running mate, Alabama Senator John Sparkman, apparently weren't hiding. They released ten years of tax returns. Eisenhower released a summary of his taxes too. Nixon did not at that point, but twenty-one years later, the IRS audited Nixon. A suspicious charitable donation caused people to speculate he had gamed the tax system. "People have got to know whether or not their president is a crook," Nixon said on November 17, 1973—lines that would come to define his presidency. "Well, I'm not a crook."[5] In December 1973, a congressional investigation found Nixon owed $476,431 (about $2.5 million in today's dollars) in unpaid taxes and accrued interest.[6] From that day forward, presidential candidates released their tax returns. (And had cute dogs. The only exception to the "cute dog" standard in a hundred years is President Donald Trump. The "First Dog" felt phony to him—like a political prop. Plus, he said he didn't have time for animals.[7])

The tax release tradition *does* help keep politicians honest. The public gets to explore potential conflicts of interest and to see if the candidates are paying taxes and if they are charitable.

Years after the "charitable underwear scandal," Hillary Clinton ran for president against Donald Trump. She released a decade's worth of tax returns, hoping to prompt Trump to keep his promise to do the same. Her taxes revealed she and her husband gave between 8 and 15 percent of their income to charity. Most of it was to the Clinton Family Foundation. Critics questioned whether Hillary's donations to the Clinton Foundation were offered as an act of true charity or one of selfishness.

The generosity of politicians is fascinating. It's a peek into their inner lives. President George H. W. Bush's 1991 tax returns revealed he was an unusually altruistic man. The History Channel said he was one of the most generous presidents the country has ever had. He gave away almost 62 percent of his $1.3 million income.[8] His son was generous too. In 1999, George W. Bush's tax returns showed he gave away more than $210,000.[9] That was around 15 percent of his income and puts W well above the national average of giving, which is roughly 2 percent.[10]

Mitt Romney, the Republican party's presidential nominee in 2012, released his tax returns that year. He and his wife, Ann, gave away almost 30 percent of their income in one year, totaling $4,020,772 out of $13,696,951 earnings.[11] In modern times, he is the most financially generous of any presidential candidate or US president in absolute dollars.

The Obamas were also charitable, with an upward trajectory as their income grew. According to *The Chronicle of Philanthropy*, from 2000 to 2004, they donated about 1 percent of their income; in 2005, they donated 5 percent. In 2006, they donated 6 percent. In 2007, they donated 5.7 percent.[12] As White House inhabitants in 2010, they donated 14 percent,[13] and in 2011, they donated nearly 22 percent.[14]

For Romney and Obama, there were no itemizations for undies. After the early '90s, perhaps the White House chief of protocol added a paragraph or two of guidance to the official policy. Whatever the case, these returns show that POTUSes have wanted to be selfless and donate. And voters want the same—namely, a selfless president.

VOTERS

Speaking of voters, according to Michael LaBossiere from Florida A&M University, Republicans and Democrats actually have some important similarities. Since the country's founding, both progressives and conservatives have agreed on a fundamental principle: government by the people, for the people. He says, "Democrats and Republicans are united in the once radical view that government exists for the good of the people."[15] And yet what we focus on most is not what unites the two but what defines their differences. So what are the differences when it comes to selflessness and governing for the good of the people?

Some say, "Democrats care more but do less; Republicans care less but do more. Republicans care more about the individual; Democrats care more about the masses."

These are, of course, broad stereotypes about how one group may or may not be more selfless than the other. Going back to the way our country started, whether Democrat, Republican, Independent, Libertarian, or Green, most agree the government should guard life and liberty. Based on party and many other variables, we differ on how to implement this task. Except when it comes to the act of voting, on which all parties seem to agree: it's important to vote. But is it?

More than 150 million Americans cast their ballots in the 2020 presidential election. With so many ballots cast, in the grand scheme of things, we could say that one vote really doesn't matter. It's not likely to turn a large-scale election. Even the state of Florida in 2000—a memorably close race—had a 537-vote margin. But here's another way to think about it: the fact that one vote doesn't matter is what makes the act of voting selfless.

Political scientists call this idea "the altruism theory of voting." Put simply, if voters were entirely selfish, they wouldn't turn out to vote. They'd stay at home and eat tortilla chips while watching reruns of *The Office*. A selfish person may think voting is a waste of time because their individual vote is unlikely to affect the outcome.

And yet we vote, and we feel good about it when we do. According to Professor James H. Fowler at UC Davis, "Although the probability that a single vote affects the outcome of an election is quite small, the number of people who enjoy the benefit when the preferred alternative wins is large. As a result, people who care about benefits to others and who think one of the alternatives makes others better off are more likely to vote."[16] Regardless of the side you pick, heading to the polls is a key part of being a selfless member of your community.

Fowler also found this not quite intuitive nugget. If you raise your hand as a Republican or a Democrat, identifying with a party, you tend to vote more as you become more altruistic. When looking at altruists as a group, the reverse also seemed to be true. The more that altruists identified as a Democrat or Republican, the more likely they were to vote. So identifying with a party and going to the voting booth mean you are more likely a selfless person who thinks of others as the outcome of politics and voting.

The correlation between selflessness and voting may be explained by how compassionate we are, collectively and individually. When we look at compassion by party as one measurement, some interesting findings emerge.

University of Pittsburgh lecturer Meri Long says, "Compassion is defined by many psychology researchers as concern for others in need and a desire to see others' welfare improved."[17] Her research looked at the degree of compassion in voters of both parties by analyzing their agreement or disagreement with two statements:

- People should be willing to help others who are less fortunate.
- These days people need to look after themselves and not overly worry about others.

Complete agreement with the compassionate side of these statements would give a score of 1, and complete disagreement a score of 0. This would measure an intensity rating of compassion.

When we look at the chart, we see that Republicans had a broader range of compassion intensity, meaning they had a higher number of respondents measuring moderate as well as high levels of compassion. Republicans had a flatter, wider curve. In contrast, Democrats had higher numbers of respondents at higher compassion intensity levels. Democrats had a taller, skinnier curve.

In other words, you are more likely to find a Republican who is compassionate, but potentially at lower rates than Democrats. And you are more likely to find a Democrat at higher and lower extremes of compassion.

4444444444

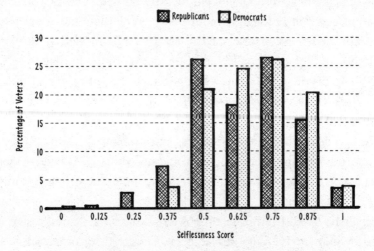

Republicans and Democrats Are Similarly Selfless

© 2012 by the General Social Survey (GSS), a project of the independent research organization NORC at the University of Chicago, with principal funding from the National Science Foundation.

That's splitting the data hairs. The researcher says both parties are similar: "Republicans score an average of 0.649, which is statistically indistinguishable from the Democrats' average of 0.687."[18] In addition, both sides are more likely to say compassion is very or extremely important in political candidates, with Democrats agreeing with that statement 73.3 percent of the time and Republicans at 66.8 percent of the time.[19]

Republican and Democrat brains also explain why they are both different and the same to some degree in their political outlet. MRI tests found that conservatives had larger amygdalas (excuse my language), the part of the brain linked to emotion, while progressives had bigger anterior cingulates (NSFW), the part of the brain linked to feelings of optimism.

But historian Larrie Ferreiro says it may be that each of us has competing forces in us: "Two competing forces are at work within the political organism: the 'Republican genotype,' which favors individualistic behaviors, and the 'Democratic genotype,' which favors altruism. Both forces are simultaneously at work at the individual and group levels."[20] Ferreiro says each of us has some Democrat and Republican in us. The proportions of those two ingredients, he says, is what makes us select one party or the other, or none at all.

Growing up, I saw both genotypes express themselves in my family, often at the dinner table. My family had both Republicans and Democrats passing me the spaghetti at dinner each night. (There were few food fights, though if we'd had a decibel meter handy during the Lui supper-time, I'm pretty sure it would have registered some red-zone level spikes.)

My father was a Republican before becoming a Democrat and then having no party at all. (A little "inside baseball" about a voting block that can swing most of the swing states—they're up for grabs.) He was your typical Asian American voter. He switched parties based on allegiance to what seemed best for his family. He was before his time, as few would change parties as easily as he would. Asian American voters today follow his pattern (unlike the average voter) and change parties similarly.

When my father switched parties, it was because he wanted to have a pastor in the White House—the Rev. Jesse Jackson. This made sense, according to Larrie Ferreiro and Meri Long—what your political leaders say and do to a great degree affects your political affiliations. In my father's case, it was his faith that led him. He proves out the theory that when it comes to the political leaders we support, their values significantly affect our choices.

There are broad disagreements today on both sides of the aisle when it comes to issues, values, and ethics. It's the heart of what I've reported on in the past ten years. Despite divergent "last mile" approaches, there are underlying motivations that are similar for most voters, specifically the compassion and drive to improve the lives of others.

A NATION OF DONATION

When it comes to voters' wallets and donations, researchers who have studied which party is more generous found that Republican counties tend to report higher charitable contributions than Democrat-dominated counties.[21] To put it in overly simplified language, Republicans are not fans of government intervention. They prefer local players to step in and step up. Researcher Rebecca Nesbit explains, "Their preference is to provide for the collective good through private institutions."[22]

On the flip side, one could say that residents living in liberal areas pay a great deal more taxes, which in turn helps support the poor. "The county you live in and the political ideology of that county affects the tax burden of the community," Nesbit said. This "involuntary giving" (commonly known as taxes) may not seem charitable in the classic sense of the word, but people live in these areas voluntarily. This means they are "opting in" to a system that allows them to be taxed at a higher rate to support others.

My parents donated to the church, and they volunteered at food pantries and schools. They are "all-American" when it comes to those things. The United States has been the most generous country for a very long time.[23] A recent survey conducted to better understand altruistic behavior of Americans made some interesting discoveries:

- Two-thirds of respondents made a charitable donation within the last year; 34 percent did so more than once.
- Gen Z has the most monthly donations to the same charity.
- Millennials are more likely to donate to crowdfunding campaigns such as GoFundMe.
- Democrats were more likely to donate to environmental and overseas causes; Republicans were more likely to donate to religious causes.[24]

Americans can do this for a reason. "The developed world's poor and middle classes are, by global standards, extraordinarily rich," wrote Yale scholar Gautam Nair in the *Washington Post*. "After adjusting for cost-of-living differences, a typical American still earns an income that is 10 times the income received by the typical person in the world. Do Americans understand this fact? In short, no."[25]

We're rich, yet we profoundly underestimate our wealth compared to the rest of the world. The Canadian Red Cross says, "If you have food in the refrigerator, clothes on your back, a roof over your head and a place to sleep, then you are richer than 75 percent of this world." And, "If you have money in the bank, in your wallet, and spare change in a dish someplace, then you are among the top 8 percent of the world's wealthy."[26]

It reminds me of the Bible verse frequently quoted by my father:

"From everyone who has been given much, much will be demanded."[27] Or as Peter Parker's uncle puts it in *Spider-Man*, "With great power comes great responsibility." That is a tap on the shoulder for us in the United States—both Democrats and Republicans.

So when the collection plate is passed down a row of Republicans and Democrats and some put money in and others don't, what we're seeing is not so much that selflessness is about which lever one pulls in the voting booth; it's that both Republicans and Democrats, by declaring a party (and for those who don't as well), are leaning in on the idea that politics is about helping others. About allocating scarce resources in a fairer way to meet others' needs, to say "enough about me." Let's help not one, but all.

Chapter Eleven

TIIREE LUNCHES

Following the contentious 2016 presidential election, a Reuters/Ipsos poll found that about one in seven Americans had ended a relationship with a family member or close friend due to insurmountable political differences.[1] Even before election day, the Pew Research Center found that Americans (both Donkeys and Elephants) believed that people who didn't share their same views were closed-minded, dishonest, immoral, and lazy.[2] They said that spending time with them made them feel angry, afraid, and frustrated.

Some of our nation's top pundits and leaders reaffirm the "us versus them" antipathy when they say "those people" are what's wrong with America. The divide is so deep that it has become countercultural to even be friends with anyone who disagrees with us politically. I get it. Sometimes we just have to draw the line. (That's why I once ended a friendship over pineapple on pizza.) And in some cases, we don't even like our "own people," so we sure as heck don't like the other team.

In the months leading up to the 2016 election, the Pew Research Center shared more findings:

- Ninety-one percent of Republicans had unfavorable or very unfavorable views of the Democratic Party. The rate of those holding very unfavorable views had more than doubled between 2000 and 2016, from 26 percent to 58 percent.

- Eighty-six percent of Democrats had unfavorable or very unfavorable views of the Republican Party. The Democrats' rate of very unfavorable views had more than doubled in the same time frame, from 23 percent to 56 percent.[3]

How are we to make sense of these numbers in a nation whose motto is *e pluribus unum*, or "out of many, one"?

On the plus side, there's definitely a benefit when different values and opinions come together to form a whole. In a fully functioning marketplace of ideas, we get closer to the truth, or to unity, through robust discussion. Thankfully, America's First Amendment provides a nationwide "safe space" for disagreement. But it's hard not to wonder if we have forgotten how to use our freedom of speech as a two-way conversation. Do we no longer affirm that as we speak, we should also listen? Talking to "those people" requires effort, and it appears we either no longer believe the effort is worth it, or we are no longer willing to *act* on our belief that it is.

Former Secretary of Defense James Mattis believes one of the biggest threats to our nation is not our ideological differences but our contempt for others, "the tone—the snarl, the scorn, the lacerating despair." He wrote:

> Lincoln warned that the greatest danger to the nation came from within. All the armies of the world could not crush us, he maintained, but we could still "die by suicide." And now, today, we look around. Our politics are paralyzing the country. We practice suspicion or contempt where trust is needed, imposing a sentence of anger and loneliness on others and ourselves. We scorch our opponents with language that precludes compromise. We brush aside the possibility that a person with whom we disagree might be right. We talk about what divides us and seldom acknowledge what unites us.[4]

There was a day when I thought the internet was something that would unite us, that it would usher in an era of coming together in which people from different backgrounds could connect to form better relationships. I even wrote my college honor's thesis on the topic—on how digital communications would make us work better as collaborators.

And sometimes worse. This was just before the twenty-first century—before social media. We had only email and AOL. Dial-up was so slow back then that people still had time to think before pressing "Send." But I also warned in that thesis how great were the pitfalls that awaited us if we failed to follow the tech warning signs.

So here we are. Warning signs are on full blast. Today we are the digital nouveau riche, blessed with our newfound wealth, but cursed because we haven't learned how to handle it—which means we have a surprisingly significant probability of ending up in digital poverty, sleeping in the back of our virtual Mercedes-Benz.

Here's how digitally rich we are. In 2016, we had access to 13 zettabytes of digital information. A zettabyte (no relation to Michael Douglas's wife) is one trillion gigabytes—which is enough data (at least half of which must be cat videos) to fill 15 billion 2016 iPhones. That's more than seven times the total number of iPhones ever sold as of 2020.

Speaking of 2020, we were even wealthier digital data millionaires in that year. The World Economic Forum estimated that at the dawn of 2020, there were 44 zettabytes of digital content floating around for us to click on at any time.[5] A 2018 white paper estimated that this number would grow to a planetary-sized 175 zettabytes of content within five years.[6] That's enough to fill 1.3 trillion 2020 iPhones.

With all this digital wealth, a social media muting or unfriending shouldn't be a big deal, right? If I offend one group or don't like a particular group in the digital space, I can just find another. So, in a way, the wealth of digital options lowers the investment required to establish and maintain personal bonds. It also fails to encourage a commitment to understanding what it means to make these bonds strong in the first place.

Furthermore, digital algorithms predispose us to friend or follow people who share our interests. And to get more of what we like as well. Amazon has been weaving an algorithmic web, a digital marketing holy grail, for two decades. But it's hard not to wonder how things might be different if there were also algorithms designed to show us feeds of what we don't like or what we don't yet know we like.

If you are a Latino American woman, it's unlikely that Instagram will show you hair care product ads formulated for your African American friend. If you donated to a Democrat, you're not going to see ads for

Republicans on Facebook. If you even mention, say, needing to buy a new pair of glasses, here come the ads for eyeglasses.

Consequently, we are increasingly experiencing self-segregation. Many of us watch only news channels that reflect our own politics, avoid places occupied by our political opponents, and live where people vote in a similar way. We stay in our own tribes.

As mentioned, we are digital data millionaires. We are also "connection millionaires" at costs that are cheaper in time, money, and personal sacrifice than any time before. The downside? The nouveau riche often swiftly become nouveau poor. I'm hoping there's a middle ground out there, a point where half the pizza can have pineapple, and the other half can be, well, the way it should be.

DEFENDING EACH OTHER

On Friday, February 17, 2012, I went to sleep at my then-normal bedtime of eight o'clock. I had to be up by 4:00 a.m. to work on the *TODAY Show* the next morning. When my phone alarm went off, I checked to see what news and texts I had missed while snoozing. One text pointed me to an ESPN article on New York Knicks guard Jeremy Lin's turnovers. The article title was "Chink in the Armor."

The slur "chink" is as deeply hurtful to Chinese Americans as the N-word is to African Americans. It didn't make sense. ESPN knew better. They had even received an "excellence in diversity" award two years earlier from the Asian American Journalists Association. Theoretically, therefore, ESPN had the journalistic and editorial checks and balances in place to catch something like this. But not that day. Instead, their headline sounded like a coarse one-liner overheard at a corner bar.

In a competitive and overcrowded digital space, online content outlets vie for clicks by crafting headlines designed to draw the most attention. Some articles are even simultaneously beta tested in different areas of the country with two different headlines. The headline receiving the most clicks then becomes the final headline when the article is released. One study found such testing resulted in 34 percent more views on average— and potentially 34 percent higher ad revenue.[7]

But the ESPN article was no beta test.

That morning, despite my belief that the opportunity cost for social media engagement was higher than the return (which meant I hadn't posted anything for years), I broke my vow of Twitter silence and posted about the Lin article.

I forwarded the story to the executive producer of *Weekend TODAY* and the executive editor of MSNBC. Over the next two days, we aired at least four in-depth segments on the ESPN story. And for the first time, despite working hard to remain a non-opinion broadcast journalist during a period when there was high demand for "opinion journalism" (in which one thoroughly researches only facts that support one's opinion), I did what I had tried to avoid doing and delivered an on-air op-ed in the final block of the show:

> He's being watched by Asian Americans fanatically. I'm one of them. But he's also being watched by everybody else. If this were to be a teachable moment, maybe it's that these American stories are inspirational and understandable alone. But all together, they transcend the world of sport. Misunderstandings may continue to come about. Bad puns are inevitable. But for Jeremy, it's only about the team, the game, and God. That's so extraordinary.[8]

My grandparents are from China. There's no doubt I would benefit from a society that directed fewer insulting stereotypes at Asian American men. Wouldn't it be great, however, if all Americans rallied against these insults when any one of us is denigrated? If the people who are victimized by racism didn't have to carry the burden alone?

It seems that this doesn't come naturally. We have to learn how to share responsibility for each other, says National Credit Union Administration chairman Rodney E. Hood in the *Wall Street Journal*. Hood was appointed by President Trump as the first African American to lead a federal banking regulatory agency. He suggested that healing America's divides requires a "commitment to having the difficult conversations about diversity, equity and inclusion needed to foster and nurture greater understanding."[9] These difficult conversations don't drive us apart; rather, in Hood's words, they are "the forces that bring us together and serve as sources of enrichment, strength and unity."

I like that. I want to have these difficult conversations. I want to reach out and develop relationships with people who are different and fight for them when things go wrong. How about at your next Thanksgiving gathering, when your uncle starts yapping, instead of yapping back, why not try to begin a dialogue?

SPENDING TIME WITH EACH OTHER

Overcoming the temptation to think of those who are different from us as "the other" rather than as part of "us" is the challenge we face. In today's "division is cool" culture, it's hard to form friendships with those who are different. I live in New York, where people from all over the globe squeeze onto the island of Manhattan to make a go of it. But I grew up in San Francisco and spent a lot of time in the city's famed Chinatown, where most people looked like me. In fact, most San Franciscans didn't live in ethnically diverse areas, but rather in enclaves of people who were similar to them. We self-segregate for many reasons—some good, some bad—but we need to figure out a way to overcome this tendency.

In his book *Love Your Enemies*, Arthur Brooks suggests a practical solution to our self-segregating tendencies: "Escape the bubble. Go where you're not invited."[10] No, this doesn't mean crashing your disagreeable neighbor's BBQ. Instead, Brooks pointed to a Stanford experiment that yielded promising results about combating feelings of racism.

In that experiment, the researchers assigned White and Latino college students to get acquainted with a same-gendered student of either the same ethnicity or a different ethnicity. They determined how anxious these participants were about hanging out with their partner by measuring levels of the hormone cortisol in saliva. They found that participants who had been assigned partners from a different ethnicity had high levels of stress. Some were afraid of rejection because of their ethnicity; others were anxious because they were prejudiced against their partner.

The researchers asked the pairs to get to know each other. After each of three different meetings of conversation and casual game playing, the researchers measured participants' cortisol again. Stress levels dropped each time. The people who had been afraid of rejection had the same cortisol levels as someone who had never felt anxious at all. The stress levels of the prejudiced people dropped to the same levels as those of unprejudiced people. After making a friend of a person of a different ethnicity, these participants also initiated more interactions with people of other ethnicities over the next few weeks. The stress of prejudice was gone after three face-to-face meetings.[11]

It's an interesting notion and not difficult to try—simply getting to know each other as an antidote to polarization. Every day, we hear of more racial strife or see the polls indicating that xenophobia is getting worse. But could those polls be mistaken?

Sociologist Richard LaPiere conducted a fascinating study in the early 1930s to get to the bottom of anti-Chinese rhetoric, beliefs, and practices in the United States. LaPiere asked a young Chinese couple to visit restaurants and hotels throughout the country. (Today this would be a hit food series called *Digs and Dumplings*.) After the couple returned, LaPiere sent a survey to each proprietor to measure their self-identified attitudes toward people of Chinese descent.

He discovered that the way the owners of the restaurants and hotels described their intended actions toward Chinese people differed from how they actually acted toward them. Out of 250 visits to hotels and restaurants, the young Chinese couple was denied service only once, and 40 percent of the time they received above average service. And yet when restaurant and hotel owners were later surveyed, 90 percent of them said they would not accommodate guests of Chinese descent.[12] Apparently, it's easy to dislike a certain group on paper, but it's harder to maintain discriminatory views when you encounter a real-life person who belongs to that group. For one thing, it's awkward.

So how do we begin to make the kind of cross-group connections that break down barriers and prejudice? Here's one idea: make a list of three people you'd never hang out with. Folks you don't often see in your circles, folks you don't much like, folks you want to avoid. Be honest with yourself. Don't be politically correct. Put these three people on a list. Now figure out a way to have lunch with them. Maybe they're a friend of a friend. Perhaps you can go to one of the events hosted at work that this person is attending. You know how we network when we have interest in the topic? Same thing. It may take time to invite a person from your list to lunch, but sometimes they're sitting next to you. When these three lunches have been completed, make a list of another three. Rinse and repeat.

As an additional side dish to the lunches, seek out the people with whom you disagree politically and follow them on social media. Reaching out to our political counterparts is a simple step toward reducing knee-jerk contempt (or maybe just jerk-jerk contempt) secretly lurking in plain sight in varying degrees. This is a tougher consideration, but one desperately needed today. If one group outreach doesn't work, it's time to move on. We can't always have good outcomes.

I have to admit that having interactions such as these is pretty much part of my job description as a journalist. I interview the most unlikely people every day. And because it's my job to listen to their stories, identify what makes them stand out, and then cogently tell their stories, I've become more understanding and accepting of others—especially of people I'd never see myself hanging out with but now do, in fact, hang out with.

DEVELOPING CURIOSITY ABOUT EACH OTHER

The yawning gaps developing between us are what psychologist Peter Coleman describes as "intractable conflicts," which happen when people's encounters with their perceived opponents are more and more charged.[13] The "us versus them" dynamic causes the brain to operate differently. When a person feels threatened, it's impossible for them to also feel curious. Their hypervigilant state makes it hard to process new information. During the threat, people feel the need to defend themselves and attack the others.

"Everyone loses," writes Eyal Rabinovitch, who specializes in facilitating conversation in the Middle East. His findings are becoming more applicable to polarization writ large as well. He says, "Such conflicts undermine the dignity and integrity of all involved and stand as obstacles to creative thinking and wise solutions."[14]

Remember the French woman, Anita, from chapter 3, who left her apartment during the lockdown to communicate a message of democracy, tolerance, and love for our fellow human beings? She was so inspirational that I talked about her on air the next day. She challenged me not to lump people into simplistic categories, not to generalize and take the easy way out. Her admonition struck me, probably because I needed to hear it.

At the time, many were using the phrase "no-go zones" for areas in France (and in other parts of Europe) where extremists, terrorists, and Muslims lived, where Sharia law was adhered to, where police refused to go, and where outsiders were unwelcome.

When I heard the term "no-go zone," my first thought was, *I'm gonna go there.* Journalists are the way we are because we have some, well, authority issues. The idea of zones was something I had reported on in the United States. The residents of various zones or neighborhoods are often defined in oversimplified and stereotyped terms. In the US, even descriptions of regions can be oversimplified and distorted—East, South, Midwest, and West—characterized by words such as *rude, boring, unintelligent, flaky.* Having lived in each of these regions, I guess I'm quite the mix. (It's no wonder I'm asked to leave dinner parties so often.) Bottom line—from my experiences, I've learned that all regions are far more complex than their stereotypes and that I should refuse to accept a simplistic descriptor like "no-go."

And so I made plans to go to Saint-Denis, the no-go zone outside of downtown Paris. My first step was to ask my producer for a camera crew. No crews were available for an enterprise piece, which means the no-go zone wasn't core to our coverage. Depending on traffic, Saint-Denis was a thirty- to forty-five-minute drive, and a crew wouldn't be able to quickly return to Paris if another attack were to happen downtown. Made sense, but I still wish I could have had a crew. (I hear my producer buddies saying, "What correspondent doesn't wish he always had a crew?" So true. That, and a makeup team because my skin doesn't always look this flawless.) Instead, I had to make do with my phone's camera. I had the afternoon off, so it was a good time to pursue this. Inspired by Anita's example, I knew I needed to see the no-go zone with my own eyes. I hopped into a rideshare.

"I understand that where we're going is called a no-go zone," I said to the driver. He looked at me blankly. He couldn't speak English, and I couldn't speak French. This was going to be challenging, as I was planning to wander through the neighborhood and make last-minute audibles—in English. My years of Spanish might work? Probably not. I speak like a nine-year-old in Spanish, which means I double my volume and energetically wave my hand.

The driver smiled. His name was Amir. He put up his finger, pointed to his phone, and pulled up an app to translate from French to English. And so began an almost three-hour tour in which we used an app to communicate. I moved to the front passenger seat, and off we went.

"I want to go to this neighborhood," I said into the phone.

"Je veux aller dans ce quartier," the phone said out loud after three seconds. This was cool. Slow, but cool.

Using the translation app, Amir told me he had immigrated to France six years ago from a Middle Eastern country. He was Muslim and had once lived in the area we were driving to. Then he asked, "Are you sure you want to go there?" On that very day, French authorities were furiously trying to locate Abdelhamid Abaaoud, who had planned the attacks that killed 130 people. Still, I nodded. And so Amir took me on a tour of the area. The neighborhood was still nervous, since the terrorists were at large and believed to be planning more attacks.

I peered through the car window, as any tourist would, as we drove past areas where people were selling drugs, but I gazed with equal interest at shopping centers full of families buying groceries. Saint-Denis's facades looked different from those of downtown Paris, but the city also had much in common with every other metropolitan area. Amir took me to the French halal equivalent of McDonald's, where I ordered six sandwiches—again using the app to ask Amir for his culinary advice. He raised an amused eyebrow at all the sandwiches I ordered, but I wanted to truly experience this moment. I was curious about everything.

Amir gave me a quick tour of this no-go neighborhood on foot, and then we went to a café across the street, where I bought a coffee to go with my bulging paper bag of sandwiches. He told me he and his wife shopped in the area. I'm sure the two of us stuck out like the proverbial sore thumb, sitting in a café together and using our phones to talk to each other.

"When our curiosity is triggered, we are less likely to fall prey to confirmation bias (looking for information that supports our beliefs rather than for evidence suggesting we are wrong) and to stereotyping people," wrote behavioral scientist Francesca Gino in the *Harvard Business Review*. "Curiosity has these positive effects because it leads us to generate alternatives."[15]

I'm much more interested in finding alternatives than I am in cultivating constant contempt for others. I want to be a curious cat, not a xenophobic ferret. (That's right, all ferrets are xenophobic. It's the one generalization I'm comfortable making.) We tend to quickly demonize political opponents, throwing around accusations and labels in the hope that they'll stick so we don't have to argue our points, much less examine them critically. "Tidy narratives succumb to this urge to simplify, gently warping reality until one side looks good and the other looks evil," wrote journalist Amanda Ripley. "We soothe ourselves with the knowledge that all Republicans are racist rednecks—or all Democrats are precious snowflakes who hate America."[16] However, if we label all conservatives as "Nazis" and all liberals as "socialists," it's easy to overlook the complexities of our political differences and even easier to obscure our many similarities.

Was the no-go zone, Saint-Denis, a place that fosters jihadism and terror? During my tour, Amir told me he had lived in a neighborhood condo complex there for a couple of years. He pointed to the apartment where his two children were raised. And he showed me the area that reminded me of the Tenderloin district in San Francisco, a neighborhood with similar no-go stereotypes attached to it over the decades. So which was it—an area that harbored terrorists or a place where families lived their lives? The answer can be both. Extremism can coexist with delicious halal lunch sandwiches. That doesn't make for a good political attack ad, but it's true.

Below you'll see a photo of my rideshare receipt. I saved it, and not just for tax purposes, but also because it's an apt metaphor for what it means to be curious as a way to overcome the kind of stereotyping that leads to contempt. There were risks involved in traveling to a no-go zone. The trip was long and took many twists and turns. And it took time, patience, and a translation app to help Amir and me understand each other. It also took a lot of effort to understand the complexities of what I had seen and experienced there.

€71.93   Thanks for choosing **Uber**, Richard

FARE BREAKDOWN

Base Fare	1,00
Distance	29,55
Time	41,38
Subtotal	**€71.93**

CHARGED
Business •••• 7734   **€71.93**

Visit the trip page for more information, including invoices (where available)

04:01pm
2-6 Avenue de la République, 75011 Paris, France

06:46pm
10 Place de la République, 75011 Paris, France

CAR	KILOMETERS	TRIP TIME
uberX	29.55	02:45:32

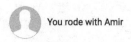 You rode with Amir   RATE YOUR DRIVER ⭐ ⭐ ⭐ ⭐ ⭐

As it turned out, the terrorist planner Abaaoud *was* in that neighborhood, even as I meandered around in my rideshare. Three days before, two women had run into him by his roadside hiding place. One of the women, his cousin, met him warmly. The other woman was horrified. She recognized him from police videos that had showed him dragging dead bodies behind a truck. She secretly went to authorities, risking her own life to turn him in. In the hours after I left Saint-Denis, police raided his apartment. Abaaoud and his cousin were killed.

"It's important the world knows that I am Muslim myself," the informant told the *Washington Post*.[17] In an attack that left people fearful of Islam, she wanted the world to know that the planner of the attacks was thwarted by a Muslim woman who had the courage to do the right thing.

The news teaches us that regions have layers—lots of them. And we can't afford to oversimplify our characterizations of groups. That's why

I'm thankful I had the chance to spend my day in Saint-Denis instead of touring the Eiffel Tower or feasting on haute cuisine. I figured out that I have to go into the no-go zones to learn that there should be no such thing as a no-go zone. When Amir dropped me off that afternoon, I was thankful for him, that he cared to share his life with me so much that he pulled up an app to try to help this fumbling journalist. His very actions allowed me to understand what a no-go zone meant for him—and for me as well.

My no-go zones have often been people I have judged to not be like me. Don't go to church—no go. Not from California—no go. Graduated from Ohio State—no go. When it comes to getting to know no-go folks, "three lunches" is an easy reminder of how accessible the road is to changing no-go to go. I am lucky I went to get lunch with Amir.

Section Four

FINDING THE POWER

Chapter Twelve

MUSCLE MEMORY

O n the first day of class, the ceramics teacher divided his students into two different groups. The students on the left would be graded on the *quantity* of the art they produced. At the end of the semester, the teacher would simply weigh their copious amount of art pieces to determine their grade. The students on the right would be graded on *quality*. To get an A, they simply had to make one perfect pot.

On the last day of class, the teacher surprised the class by evaluating the quality of work produced by both groups of students. To everyone's surprise, the highest quality works were made by students in the quantity group. How did this happen?

"It seems that while the 'quantity' group was busily churning out piles of work—and learning from their mistakes—the 'quality' group had sat theorizing about perfection, and in the end had little more to show for their efforts than grandiose theories and a pile of dead clay," wrote David Bayles and Ted Orland in their book about optimizing artistic creation.[1]

Students in the quantity group had unknowingly developed creative "muscles." They practiced, made intentional decisions that ended up as mistakes, readjusted, created a new plan, and tried again. Students in the quality group were so focused on getting everything right that they had fewer "reps"—and therefore smaller creative muscles.

In essence, what the quality group failed to develop is a kind of muscle memory. Muscle memory is what enables you to get on a bike and ride without thinking; your body just knows what to do. (Like when you're at a wedding and the Macarena starts playing. Your hips are like, "We got this!") However, according to Oxford neuroscientist Ainslie Johnstone, the scientific reality of muscle memory is a little different: "The processes that are important for learning and memory of new skills occur mainly in the brain, not in the muscles."[2] Put simply, when we train our muscles, we are actually training our brains. The brain, or more specifically the motor cortex, strengthens its connections to the neurons responsible for the motions, learning exactly when each needs to fire. The stronger these connections, the stronger the memory, and the easier it is to access.[3]

It is these frequent actions that lead to bigger things—muscles. Muscle memory increases the probability that we will be capable of doing even bigger things. When life blocks our path with a chasm that seems too big to cross, we will be ready to leap over it rather than be swallowed up by it. In fact, we may even do something heroic.

If muscle memory is all about training our brains rather than our limbs, maybe we can train ourselves to have selfless muscles. Actually, it turns out this isn't a new idea. The idea has been around since ancient times, when people first started making pots and using crocodile dung as skin cream.

The ancient Greek philosopher Aristotle, born in 384 BC, believed that morality was a craft much like art making. People had to learn it, practice it, and get better at it over time. (Think of it as push-ups for principles, burpees for brotherhood, Kegels for consideration.) Morality, Aristotle argued, was about finding a balance between excess and deficiency. (Aristotle came before another philosopher, Goldilocks—known for her "not too hot, not too cold, but just right" approach to life.) Similar to the way a skilled potter learns through practice to avoid using too much or too little pressure when shaping a pot, Aristotle suggested that his students could be "morally virtuous" by learning to find a balance.

In *Nicomachean Ethics*, Aristotle told the story of three different people facing a dangerous situation.[4] The first, a rash person, declares the ancient Greek equivalent of, "You only live once," and does not fear danger. The second, a cowardly person, essentially says, "Heck no!" and runs away. The third, a moral person, courageously decides whether or not the danger is worth facing. Not many of us are born to be like the courageous person—the Aegean James Bond, if you will—but we can become more courageous by practicing courage in small ways until it becomes part of us.

Creativity and morality "muscles"? Well, if these are possible, how about selflessness muscles? By doing many smaller selfless things, can we get stronger, allowing us to work up to bigger selfless acts? This presumes there are smaller and bigger acts—on a continuum, if you will. Perhaps there are more bite-size or snackable selfless acts. (How did I start with muscles and end up talking about snacks?)

One of my passions is investing in better communities through volunteer work. It's something I started doing when I was thirteen, thanks to my parents and mentors. I didn't have selfless muscles back then, just philanthropy flab. I've made many mistakes as I've embraced learning how to live selflessly. The church camp newsletter I wrote offended campers because of my off-kilter view of church camp. The human trafficking story I wrote failed to adequately consider the fragility of identity exposure of a survivor. The forty-page strategy slide presentation I volunteered to do in my free time (who does that?) was way too long, and I got reprimanded for doing something that wasn't in my job description. These are just a few of the things I did—thinking I was being selfless— that didn't end well. I had to let these things go.

But I'll never let go of working on my selfless muscles. You see, exercising these muscles changed everything for me.

• • • • • • • • •

The mythology of selflessness often conjures up images of dramatic or extreme proportion—traveling to another country to build a clinic, rescuing a teen girl from a brothel, helping a homeless person find shelter. These are certainly great outcomes, but the less dramatic moments of altruism are good too—providing a meal for a sick friend, buying a coffee for the person in line behind me, asking a person a question that shows I care about them.

It took time for me to open up to that possibility. And when it arrived, it ramped up quickly. My father needed more and more help. From visiting once every three months to three times every month. From cooking and cleaning to showering him, and more. His experience of the devastating impact of Alzheimer's was making the small bigger.

I was watching my father progressively decline in front of me. My traveling from New York to San Francisco three times a month was a ten-hour door-to-door endeavor. I saw in his smiling face how the disease had taken away a lot of things each month. At one point, he forgot how to shave—something he had previously enjoyed doing. So I became his yeoman barber.

I took out his electric razor and turned it on . . . zzzzzzzz. Even the noise made him smile. Then I put the razor on his face, and he smiled wider. He liked the tickling. A daily onerous chore for many men, this was his happy habit. Each time I shaved his stubble, his eyes opened wide. He stared right at me, grabbed my hand warmly, and squealed with kidlike joy. It was my dad who had first taught me how to shave all those years ago. The role reversal was painful. I squeezed his hand, trying to convey that it was okay. For him and for me.

Shaving didn't slow the disease, nor was it the only personal habit my father now needed help with. "I have to poop," he said to me after developing a need for adult diapers. Those four words gave me pause each time. Cleaning up my father's poop and helping with diapers—not my idea of a fun Saturday. (It made me nostalgic for the halcyon days of earthquake and tsunami reporting and my coworker's tuna microwaving habit.) I can't say I felt selfless. Actor John Wayne is reported to have famously said, "Courage is being scared to death, but saddling up anyway." My equivalent of "saddling up" was to prepare myself mentally and emotionally.

Eventually, I got used to cleaning his poop, even when he forgot he needed to use his diaper. It never got easy, but I did get used to wanting to help him, no matter what. So as my siblings and I did more of these things for my father, we began to joke around the way we had when we were kids. I started using the poop emoji in our group texts when we took turns watching him. 💩 meant a small bowel movement. A healthy day was 💩💩. An above average delivery was 💩💩💩. And 💩💩💩💩 was a five-alarm code brown—take cover! So went our days caring for our father. "Hungry yet?" was our favorite postscript we added to our poop reports. Selfless doesn't mean no laughter.

As the pastor of a Presbyterian church, my father wasn't innately drawn to exuberance. He was a stressed-out guy in his middle-age years.

He took home the problems of the people he was trying to help as a social worker and a pastor—so much so that he started to do daily calming exercises, practice meditation, and take medicine to help reduce stress. However, when his Alzheimer's hit, it took from him his worry and concern for the things of this world. He began to wave and smile at everyone as he told them, "You're so good!"

In the middle stages of his disease, children were his weakness. He would innocently wave and be fixated on them, wanting to squeeze their cheeks, even though he was a complete stranger. It seemed as if he wanted to give them something.

If life is a stack of pancakes, Alzheimer's takes the top pancakes, one by one, until all that's left is an empty plate. Even when the disease stripped away many of his memories—like those pancakes, for example—the values he learned and lived as a person of faith stayed strong. He has lived so happily in these later years. The one benefit of the disease is that the worry and stress are now gone.

I'm no expert. But this "gym" that my father has brought me into has trained me in profoundly important ways.

HANGING WITH SELFLESS FOLKS

If he were alive today, Benjamin Franklin, one of our most quotable Founding Fathers, would be killing it on Twitter. In 1733, he wrote in *Poor Richard's* [no relation] *Almanack* a message about how friends affect our lives: "He that lieth down with dogs, shall rise up with fleas."[5] I take his point to be less about avoiding bad company and more about hanging out with those who represent the kind of person you want to be.

As my move toward selflessness evolved over the years, I've volunteered to develop my muscularity in each phase. Amazingly, I've found community-based organizations (CBOs) everywhere. In fact, some estimates show as many as 7.5 to 9.5 million grassroots CBOs across every state. This includes more than 1.5 million registered nonprofits that represent every sector and service you can imagine.[6]

Volunteer clearinghouses (somehow that category doesn't quite fit, but you get what I mean) such as VOMO (vomo.org)—the volunteer scheduling, engagement, and management platform—have seen recent jumps in people wanting to be selfless by *doing* something. VOMO founder and CEO Rob Peabody told me in 2020, "Eighty-two percent of Americans say they would like to volunteer, but typically only 18 percent of them actually make it from talk to action."

COVID-19 changed all that—in a positive way. There was a jump of 12 percentage points to 30 percent of folks wanting to volunteer. "That's a huge jump," Rob said. "Right now, the idea of being selfless is at an all-time high, but we must make it as easy as possible for people to engage with the least number of hurdles to get them into the funnel of service."

Good news: virtual volunteering is a new SOP (standard operating procedure). Peabody went on to tell me the younger you are, the greater the desire to be selfless and volunteer: 96 percent of millennials say they would like to volunteer. (Shout out to the remaining 4 percent for their honesty.) Looks like the Me Generation is about more "we" than we might have expected.

When I speak on human trafficking, I'm sometimes asked how one can pitch in. "Should I drive up and down the streets and look for those who appear to be trafficked and then call the police?" While this may seem like a good idea, tackling human trafficking on your own, especially without safety precautions and training, is dangerous.

Instead, find a CBO that is focused on stopping human trafficking or violence against women. The best bite-size step is to volunteer for a CBO for five hours a month. If it's a good fit, increase it to seven hours and then ten a month. It's a good way to meet others who share your kind of selflessness while also learning more about the complex social/legal/cultural/moral issues, but little by little instead of all at once. Remember, your goal is selflessness strength training—building up your altruistic muscles over time.

Another thing the old sage Aristotle promoted was learning from moral mentors, advising that we seek out virtuous exemplars and learn their ways. Aristotle was himself a great mentor, and he had been mentored by Plato, who was in turn mentored by Socrates. And you might have heard of Aristotle's "greatest" student, a young Macedonian prince named Alexander. Aristotle might have taught the future king how "we can contemplate our neighbours better than ourselves," as he writes in his *Ethics*.[7] Seeking out moral mentors to spend time with is a key part of growing muscle memory. Moral mentors set a selfless example. In following their lead, we find our own selfless path to follow, like navigating for goodness on a Google map.

· · · · · · · · · ·

Let's hypothesize that our selflessness muscles can get stronger, get bigger.

Uncle Donald was my dad's older brother. He loaned money to my parents for some home improvements when I was a teen. Up to that point in my life, we had lived in a house without heat. We huddled in front of the oven to keep warm, like a scene from the all-Asian production of *A Christmas Carol* (coming soon to a theater near you). So my uncle Donald bought us a house heater. Lending money in my parents' families essentially meant giving money.

A couple of years later, Uncle Donald helped us remodel the bathroom. My dad wasn't good at simple construction. Uncle Donald was the oldest son in my dad's family and took care of his twelve siblings after his parents—my grandparents—died. He'd always make sure I ate a lot and then say, "You eat like a bird."

This uncle, however, didn't eat like a bird when it came to selflessness. He lived a long life of giving. He died early, at the age of fifty-four, of a heart attack. It wasn't until his funeral, where there was a gun salute and an American flag draped over his coffin, that I learned he had received a Purple Heart for his service during the Korean War. He had put his life on the line to save his fellow soldiers.

It's folks like my uncle—the ones who live a life of giving, of quiet strength—who show that we can be selfless, and do so without a lot of hullabaloo.

WORKOUT PLAN

After my Michigan Ross MBA (Go, Blue!—that's obligatory, like saying "Gesundheit" after a sneeze), I had to figure out a way to pay off my student loans. In other words, I needed to get a job. I talked to friends, contacts, mentors, and family, each time laying out the options and the pros and cons. I took notes to keep all of the ideas in order. I realized I spent a lot of time talking about various career options but wasn't documenting my process properly so I could reflect, make adjustments, and build on what I was learning. For all the time I spent writing emails, reports, and grocery lists, why was I unable to write down my rough plans for the future?

I made the first entry in what I called my "career log" in 2001. Yes, kiddies, .docx hadn't even been invented yet. I took a four-step approach annually:

1. Where do I want to be in my career in two years?
2. What steps do I need to take to achieve each option? (the major six steps)
3. What steps are common across all career options I've been identifying?
4. What steps can I take first that apply to the steps in all options so I can kill two or three birds with one stone?

I've used this approach twenty times over the past twenty years. When I look back, I find the annual entries to be an interesting review of my career thoughts. Sometimes I hit my target, but most often I've missed it or, much like a struggling stand-up comic, got the timing wrong. For example, I wrote that I wanted to become a news anchor in the United States by 2003, but it didn't happen until 2005. Then I got my own show in 2007 on CNN Headline News. In 2013, I wrote, "I want to write my first book." Here you go, almost a decade later.

I've followed this process for volunteer work too. I laid out the years I was able to help Habitat for Humanity build houses in three countries, and I evaluated ways to use my platform to help UN Women grow their HeForShe social movement campaign in the US and abroad through being a global ambassador for Plan International's Because I am a Girl campaign. An important part of the career log exercise is to ask, *If I could do anything in the world right now, what would it be? When I reach the end of my life and look back on this season, is there anything I'd regret not doing?* These questions help me identify and be intentional about the selfless stuff too.

My career log is currently 150 pages long, filled with notes from me to me. This is how I dream on paper.

Life has a way of crowding out "nonessential activity," so I have to be purposeful about not letting selflessness be shoved out of the way for what I think are more pressing concerns. A plan helps. As you can tell, my career log includes philanthropic work goals. Career and volunteering are different activities, but the same principles are involved when it comes to the way we make life choices.

Want to adopt a child, give a large amount to charity, donate a kidney, grow out your hair for "Locks of Love," or anything else you decide fits into your desire to be selfless? Start small or start big—but write/type/ dictate it out. This will be your selflessness workout plan.

PAIN BUILDS TONE

When I lived in Atlanta, I emceed an event honoring businesses that subcontract to diverse businesses. I stepped to the podium, welcomed the audience, and introduced the main speaker. Pretty standard stuff. This man was older than the other speakers, and I watched with some concern as the octogenarian rose unsteadily from his seat and used a cane to amble to the podium. Event staff rushed to place a riser behind the lectern for him to stand on. I hadn't been able to do research on any of the speakers, so I stuck to my script. At the rostrum, he spoke slowly and quietly. I leaned in to hear.

His voice had the occasional but well-placed flourish. His pace and volume rose and fell, depending on the points he emphasized. Then he reached his resonance. His crescendo bowled me over. Then he hit an even higher note of a rapturous point. And then another. It was like watching Muhammad Ali sitting back, dancing, and then, *Whammo!* This speaker was a sleeper who had come to play. I was supposed to be the artful one, the master of ceremonies. Ha! I was the pupil. This was a true master working the room. I was schooled in a way I've never forgotten. (Which is impressive because, again, I hate school.)

The speaker that day was Joseph E. Lowery, one of the great preachers of the civil rights movement and the cofounder (with Martin Luther King Jr.) of the Southern Christian Leadership Conference.

Lowery's speech brought to mind Martin Luther King Jr.'s famous "I Have a Dream" speech. As a Chinese American man, my dad identified with the Southern-born Dr. King's eloquent and passionate call to pursue the dream of justice and freedom for all. I'm sure my dad thought, *Hey, there's a pastor of color, so I guess Asians can do it too.* About ten years ago, San Francisco community leader Cecil Williams's Glide Memorial Church awarded the "Spirit of Martin Luther King" trophy to my father. The trophy read, "Rev. Stephen Lui exemplified the spirit of Dr. Martin Luther King Jr. in empowering the community and public officials towards equitable and nondiscriminatory treatment and delivery of services to the public." He kept the award smack-dab in the middle of the mantle.[8]

I didn't just casually listen to Lowery that day long ago. No, I was *mesmerized* by his stories of pain in America's community. Of his early beginnings doing the little things that led to him being able to do the big things. Then 2014 and 2015 happened—Michael Brown, Eric Garner, Freddie Gray, and more killed—and a 1960s historical racial flash point was back. As Chinua Achebe would say, just when everything looks okay, "things fall apart."[9] The Rev. Lowery said during that time, "I'm with the kids."[10] And not only the Black kids who were dying, but also the kids who wanted to see major change take place. Lowery had lived through pain. It made him stronger. He died at the age of ninety-eight in 2020.

He didn't get to see the kids. They were protesting across the globe after George Floyd's killing in Minneapolis on May 25, 2020. As had happened many times before, heated debate simmered over the idea of "systemic racism." Some Whites were offended by the term, saying they never personally witness racism, while many Black people pointed out example after example of mistreatment that never would have happened had they been White.

The country reached a new milestone of awareness and progress, potentially maybe even a new level of solidarity for action not seen since the 1960s. It seemed that the horror of so many Black men and women dying at the hands of bad police officers—the rotten apples—had pushed people of all backgrounds to look outside themselves. It's as if, for a moment, the world finally understood and shared the enormity of what it meant to be George Floyd, suffocated as he cried out to his deceased mother in some of his final words.

This "headline news" moment of what it's like to be Black in America does not negate what it means to be White, Latino, Hispanic, Asian, or Native American. The moment is about including and understanding how the Black experience is also an American experience and, most important, a human experience. A human experience we cannot accept, one that falls to the east, west, north, south, to the left and to the right of us. It's a wall-to-wall problem that both afflicts and defines the collective soul of our country.

Reporting on such stories of race over the last fifteen years has helped me develop a new selflessness muscle—and a new language to give voice to it. In 2014, when an amateur Seattle theatre group selected the 130-year-old comic operetta *The Mikado*, I listened. The play contained exaggerated Asian singsong names (of the "Ching Chong" variety), simplistic Orientalist stereotypes (think gongs and single-string instruments), and slapstick gestures that fit the unsavory stereotypes of the early 1900s of Asians in America. In addition, all forty Asian roles were played by White actors, with the exception of two Latino actors. To make the White actors more Asian in appearance, they wore white face paint to mimic typical theatre makeup used in Asia in their traditional plays.

"It's yellowface, in your face," wrote Sharon Pian Chan of the *Seattle Times*, referring to the practice of Caucasian actors dressing in stereotypical Asian costumes and makeup with overwrought mannerisms. "The caricature of Japanese people as strange and barbarous was used to justify the internment of Japanese Americans during World War II . . . *The Mikado* opens old wounds and resurrects pejorative stereotypes."[11] Chan was pretty clear in her op-ed, but I still had to rethink both sides of it—as an Asian and as a journalist. What were the two sides?

Then I remembered blackface—Al Jolson putting black shoe polish on his face to portray racist-era roles in film. Nobody would do blackface in the theatre today. So why should they do yellowface? Lowery's lessons, Freddie Gray's lessons, Rodney King's lessons—they all taught me. Their stories helped me see why this performance of *The Mikado* was not right.

I pitched the story to my boss in the same way: blackface is alive today, but now it's yellowface in the Seattle Asian community. The key was to show both the differences and similarities at the same time. My boss saw the story immediately, and I was off to Seattle.

The pain of the tragic reporting I've had to do about the many decades of people who have been beaten or killed—in many cases, only because they looked different—has helped me see others better. With more nuance and layers. I still have much to learn, but I couldn't avoid the pain of these stories. It became the story.

* * * * * * * * * *

Caring for my dad has been a constant test of my selfless muscles.

I was standing in my parents' kitchen one day, trying to make my own version of turnip soup. (Who makes turnip soup if you're Asian? It's inevitably going to be a disaster, like a Russian trying to make Peking Duck.) Doubling the cultural mishap, I was also perfecting my home-made Bolognese at the same time. I may as well have been throwing a quinceañera. Since my mom was busy taking care of my dad, I had taught myself to cook. I thought my attempts were better than eating fried chicken or a BLT from the diner every night. Or maybe not.

So on one of my weekly visits, I was cutting turnips. I didn't even know which part to use—the root or the leaf. Deep into trying not to cut my fingers, I looked up. There was my naked Presbyterian minister dad, coming at me with his arms out for a hug. He wanted me to turn on the water for the shower. We had turned off the water line to the shower, because he was taking twenty showers a day, each time forgetting all the others he had taken before. He was so clean you could have eaten turnip soup off of him. So his ploy was to come over to hug us, tell us he loved us, and then ask us to turn on the water. A tried-and-true move perfected by toddlers around the world.

Here's what I learned as I was hugging my naked father, pajama pants at his ankles as I stood by the dishwasher with half-cut turnips at the ready. *I didn't sign up for this. I didn't want to do this. Yet I did sign up for this. I did want to do this.* Like a never-ending mental seesaw. This test of selflessness was right in front of me. I did not have to look for it; it found me. I wasn't ready to give my selflessness muscles this kind of workout. All of my talk in the past about doing the right thing was now coming home to roost. *Could my muscles grow fast enough to help my father?*

The days grew longer, and the demands heavier. Same with the decisions. The grand experiment of selflessness arrived, and I wasn't sure how it would end.

I'm still not.

"Time to test those giving glutes."

© Tak Toyoshima

Chapter Thirteen

ONE WORD
AT A TIME

I remember my first script for *NBC Nightly News*. It was the year 2010. As part of my training, I had the great pleasure of shadowing some of our network correspondents. That night it was Rehema Ellis. She is one of the network's superstars, with Emmy awards, Edward R. Murrow awards, and Associated Press awards. She has covered presidential elections, Hurricane Katrina, the September 11 attacks, and more. I remember her kindness and warmth in showing me the ropes.

The deal was, I would spend the day watching the way she filed a report, worked with the package producer, and wrote and then prepared for her live hit at 6:30 p.m. She told me to be ready for everything and nothing, that from the time the morning editorial meeting ended, she might have six hours to put a story together, which could change an hour before broadcast, when she'd have to get a different breaking story done.

It was a quiet Saturday. Never describe a day that way in the newsroom, because it is one of the much-derided jinxes. Sure enough, things changed about two hours before broadcast. The pace switched into high gear. I was watching Rehema calmly strategize with the executive producer and package producer. "What kind of pictures do we have?" she asked. A rule of thumb for broadcast journalists is to lead with your best pictures when possible, so it's a natural question to ask. Rehema sat down and began to pen a rough script with the limited details we had. This was going to be a perfect lesson to see her in action and to understand the way the team calmly put together an award-winning news broadcast each night—and make late-breaking stories like this look like they'd had all day to put them together.

Then the executive producer walked over. "Richard, we'd like you to do the story. Rehema can help you and guide you." Remember that sweaty CNN audition I told you about? Here I was again. I'd just started at 30 Rock and wasn't sure exactly how they did things at *NBC Nightly News*! I mean, this was the gold standard, and this was my first report. Rehema told me not to worry, that everything would be okay.

It wasn't. My script was bad. Illogical order. Too long. Not using the best pictures. Not using the best interview choices. I wasn't good at this script-writing thing. I couldn't put words together. After five major reworks by the editors and producers, we finally had a script. Each version was a reminder of my lack of skill. I have no doubt they were less than happy with my inability to hit the ground running. Admittedly, after five years in the profession, I thought I was familiar with what to do.

So began my long journey to figure out how to make better use of words. How to select the ones that fit and resonated. Jabs and uppercuts. Muscular verbs.[1] Every syllable counts. Every preposition builds the story. Each word conveys tone and intent. I'm still on the road that pros like Rehema Ellis have paved. (I wish Rehema didn't do it so effortlessly! It's inconsiderate of her to be that talented.) Indeed, there was a reason I needed to shadow her and others.

WE ARE WHAT WE READ

How I came to the point where I needed so much writing training work is probably because of my reading choices: cartoons and picture books on how to reshingle roofs. Plus self-help books. My choices are in keeping with recent trends in the sorts of words used in books. There has been a major change. Have you noticed? Authors are choosing:

- more words about personal choice, property accumulation, and individual-centeredness—*selfish words*
- fewer words about other people, respect, and duty—*selfless words*

When studied over the course of decades and centuries, books show us snapshots of our value sets at different points in time. Books are also better snapshots of word choices than other media—such as newspapers or magazines—because they are heavily curated content, which means the word choices are more intentional. Before they're published, books pass through a gauntlet that includes writing a proposal, shopping the idea to agents, pitching it to publishers, and then having the narrative shaped by various editors—part of a process that might unfold over the course of years. Therefore, what the words used in books reveal about society is worth paying attention to, especially when it comes to our language choices related to selflessness. Unfortunately, today's snapshot indicates we're heading downhill when it comes to selfless words.

Vocabulary Changes Over Time

Frequency of the words "give" and "get" in the Google corpus of American English books from the years 1800 to 2000

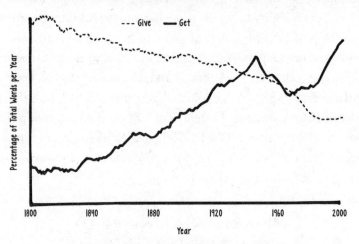

Patricia M. Greenfield, "The Changing Psychology of Culture from 1800 through 2000," *Psychology Science* (2013), 6.

Looking at more than 1.5 million books written in the United States and Britain from 1800 to 2000, researchers discovered some interesting things about changes in language choice. Patricia Greenfield, a psychologist and a professor at UCLA, analyzed all of these books. (She had Kindle Unlimited.) Using established sociological and psychological tools, she looked for words that indicated selflessness. In one test, she looked for the words *give*, which signified selflessness, and *get*, which signified the opposite. Broken down by the year in which books were released, she found that we're reading more about getting and less about giving. Since 1800, the use of *get* increased by almost 400 percent, while the use of *give* decreased by almost 50 percent. Words such as *obedience, authority, belong,* and *pray* were also in decline, while words such as *individual, self, unique,* and *child* were on the rise.[2] (Possible correlation to rising baby names such as Jayden and Brooklyn.)

Pelin Kesebir and Selin Kesebir, who are twin sisters as well as scholars, documented a century's worth of word choices in American books. Here's their conclusion: "Morality- and virtue-related words have for the most part been diminishing from the American vocabulary," particularly as evidenced by selfless words such as *generosity, thoughtfulness,* and *sacrifice,* whose usage fell by more than 45 percent each.[3] If the words we use reflect our changing values, and those values are degrading, we could be facing some serious consequences. In fact, according to the Kesebirs, the declining importance of words denoting virtue "may be partly responsible for this confused moral outlook of young Americans— they have not been socialized to think about issues of right and wrong, and they simply lack the vocabulary for it." (It may be time to introduce an empathy emoji.)

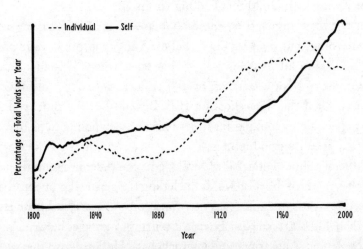

Vocabulary Has Become More Selfish

Patricia M. Greenfield, "The Changing Psychology of Culture from 1800 through 2000," *Psychology Science* (2013), 6.

I guess I read a lot of books about me, myself, and I. The score before we go to break:

- selfless: mentioned 200 times so far in the book
- me, myself, and I, and look at me: mentioned 1,000 times

ENOUGH ABOUT "I"

As rhetoric students in college, we were taught to make cases on facts, not our opinion. Because who were *we* after all? Just a bunch of rhetors, as the lingo goes. Not the sexiest title, certainly. *Hi, I'm Richard Lui. I'm a rhetor. Are you? Sorry, that was rhetorical.* Yeah, I put people to sleep like the best of them.

Take this sentence, for example. "I believe Kentucky taxes are too high." See the opinion lurking in there? To say, "I believe" or "I think" or "I prefer"—unsolicited—weakens the argument. Such phrases, which are referred to as "subjective qualifiers" or "function words," don't help in making a point, even if it's a hot topic of debate, such as taxes. Instead, effective rhetors (still a weird word) focus on facts by making declarations: "Kentucky taxes are higher than in the four surrounding states; therefore, Kentucky taxes might be considered too high in absolute terms." That statement, if it were to be true, conveys your thought but without having to lean only on the "I" opinion. By the way, there were three states that border Kentucky in 2020 that had higher taxes.[4]

In everyday language, it's common to use "I" as part of making a case for something, but does saying "I believe" help you prove your point? Who is "I" after all? It potentially makes sense when "I" is an authority on the topic of Kentucky taxes, or if "I" is a tax researcher or other tax authority. Or if the "I" is short for IRS. But most of the time, you'd be more persuasive by looking for other relevant viewpoints to justify why Kentucky taxes are too high.

Professor James Pennebaker developed a computer program that analyzed these sorts of function words (including the personal pronoun "I"), as opposed to words that refer to content and convey meaning. He reviewed more than 400,000 texts, college essays, romantic messages between lovers, press conference transcripts, and internet chats. He concluded that certain function words reveal a great deal about the speaker.

Take this sentence, for example: "I don't think I buy it." This could've been, more simply: "I don't buy it." Or even, "That's absurd."

"Pronouns tell us where people focus their attention. If someone uses the pronoun 'I,' it's a sign of self-focus," Dr. Pennebaker explained. "Say someone asks, 'What's the weather outside?' You could answer, 'It's hot' or 'I think it's hot.' The 'I think' may seem insignificant, but it's quite meaningful. It shows you're more focused on yourself."[5] His research also revealed that people who are depressed use the word "I" more frequently—"I" makes up 6.5 percent of their words, compared with 4 percent for those who aren't depressed. And when he analyzed military communication, he found that people who have a lower rank use "I" more frequently than those with higher ranks. (Makes sense. No general ever says, "I'd appreciate it if you'd drop and give me twenty.")

Even presidents face this "I" problem. An analysis of State of the Union addresses reveals a lot about the degree of meism evident in those who occupy the Oval Office. The address is especially telling because it is the most watched annual speech in the country and takes months of work by speechwriters, all branches of government, and various national organizations. Each word spoken by a president in a State of the Union address is the curated equivalent of book editing times ten.

Let's look at the last forty years of State of the Union addresses, focusing on seven presidents who were up for reelection—Jimmy Carter in 1980, Ronald Reagan in 1984, George H. W. Bush in 1992, Bill Clinton in 1996, George W. Bush in 2004, Barack Obama in 2012, and Donald Trump in 2020—to determine how frequently they referred to themselves. APM Research Lab counted each "I," "me," and "my," as well as the plurals "we," "us," and "our."[6]

The most selfless speech was given by Jimmy Carter, who referred to himself only twenty-seven times. Next came George W. Bush and Ronald Reagan, at forty-six and forty-nine mentions of themselves, respectively. The least selfless three were George H. W. Bush (150 "me" mentions), Bill Clinton (109), and Barack Obama (108). President Trump was in the middle of the pack on mentioning himself in the State of the Union at eighty-four. Interestingly, for George H. W. Bush, history books describe him as humble and selfless, known for his heroic service in World War II. In addition, Carter, true to his selfless brand, didn't think he should talk too much and had the shortest speech at 3,448 words, almost half that of his peers, who averaged 6,321 words.

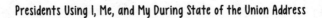

Presidents Using I, Me, and My During State of the Union Address

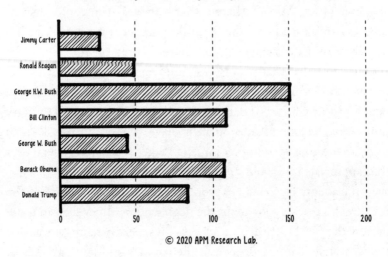

© 2020 APM Research Lab.

Determining which of these presidents was more popular or persuasive, based on how many times they referred to themselves in their State of the Union addresses, isn't a flawless measurement, given that this is based on only four speeches of their administrations. Over the course of four years, they make hundreds, if not thousands, of remarks. But this data does show that even the most well-prepared remarks in the world have a lot of meisms in them. Hard not to, given the power of the president of the United States. But since the president's authority is granted by "we the people," he or she should lead by example and refer to oneself less and refer to the facts and the hearts and minds of the country's citizens more. And we, in turn, can try to do the same.

MORE ABOUT "I"

After five months of the coronavirus quarantine, staying at home was getting long in the tooth. I went from routinely logging forty thousand frequent flyer miles a month to rarely venturing ten feet outside my apartment. My medallion status was in serious trouble. I could no longer fly back to San Francisco two or three times a month to care for my parents, as I had been doing for six years. While I was stuck in Manhattan, my dad was in a care facility whose COVID-19 case counts were rising in beds increasingly close to his room. When the disease finally took a respite from its grip on New York City and San Francisco, I grabbed some hand sanitizer, masked up, and got on a plane to visit. During the months I was away, my mother had fallen, and this was happening more often. Even though air travel still wasn't ideal, I wanted to get back to see what solutions we could put in place.

"Mom, I'm going to set up chairs in the backyard," I said. "You can sit eight feet away. I'll get the food, arrange it in a safe way, and then call you. While I'm here, I need to keep my distance, but I'll be upstairs only ten feet away." I was staying in an empty room above my mom's apartment. "I can't sit across from you face-to-face. I also won't be able to hug you. I know you feel lonely because you've been alone in your apartment for months. I know it's not good for an eighty-five-year-old."

Once I arranged the garden furniture eight feet apart, I called her. She opened the door almost like she was a bear emerging from months of hibernation—except that for people of her age, hibernation is generally not good. Walking in the fields is better; it keeps the joints flexible. Despite the awkwardness of social distancing, it was good to see her. One of the things I discovered during my visit was that her music lessons, which had always been a source of joy, no longer buoyed her spirits.

"How are classes?" I asked.

"Oh, they're going good, but I can't remember all the notes, and it's taking me longer to do my exercises. The teacher wants me to do these things that are so hard." She had always been an accomplished lover of music; now she was forgetting things she would have been able to recite and perform a year ago with aplomb.

I felt sad. I couldn't find the words. She'd always been so strong mentally and physically. And I felt she still could be, but this lockdown was wasting our precious time.

Sharing this story about my mom required me to refer to myself and my feelings more than I'm usually comfortable with. I allude to myself nearly thirty times in just 444 words. H. W. Bush and I are strange bedfellows on this metric.

But as many know, sharing vulnerability, in most cases, requires referring to oneself. More "I" is better here. If a statement is objective rather than subjective, it's not as vulnerable, not as honest. To communicate how difficult caregiving is, I have to talk about me rather than pointing to what the experts say or telling you what you should do in a similar situation.

I've shared personal stories in this book because I am indeed at halftime in my journey to be more selfless. And the first half of my journey involved a lot of inelegant, unsuccessful, and selfish moments. It's important to be honest about those moments too, because I am no better than my brothers or sister, my friends, or anyone else at trying to live a selfless life. But I've also made a surprising discovery in the process. As I became an advocate, highlighting the challenges faced by 53 million caregivers in the United States, I learned that sharing stories of weakness and vulnerability is a really good thing to do—that sharing these "me" stories is okay.

Admitting shortcomings and weaknesses feels uncomfortable and takes effort, but it has paid off for me in the form of increased trust and closeness in relationships, and healthier brains too. For example, good ways to use "I" include making statements such as, "I'm sorry" or "I miss you" or "I'm scared." Owning up to feelings first, and not waiting.

When researchers in Germany asked hundreds of participants to imagine themselves revealing a vulnerability, participants thought of themselves negatively as "weak" or "inadequate." However, when imagining others showing their vulnerability in the same scenarios, participants more often characterized the others positively—as "good" or "desirable."[7] Dr. Brené Brown says it's a paradox: "Vulnerability is the last thing I want you to see in me, but the first thing I look for in you."[8] (Brown's summary is also a great match.com bio.)

SAYING NAMES

We are vulnerable when we say names.

My business school classmates at Michigan Ross included more than thirty students from China. I participated in various international events and met a couple of them. The interesting thing is, they always introduced themselves using English first names. "Hi, my name is Joan Wei Chan." "Hi, my name is Davy Chingho Liu."

Wait, you were born and grew up in China, and your parents gave you those first names? Were your parents from a Western culture, hence the mixed English/Chinese name? Not usually. They had given themselves these names when they arrived in the United States so it'd be easier for folks like me who couldn't pronounce their Chinese names. There I was, calling them Jane and Michael when those weren't their names at all. There was no requirement at Michigan Ross that students change their names.

Recently I read about a student from Vietnam named Phuc Bui Diem Nguyen, who faced something more intimidating at Laney College. Her mathematics professor asked her to "Anglicize" her name. He said her name caused embarrassment to people who had to say it. He said it sounded like the "f-word" in English. After comparing her name to "f— boy," he explained that if he "lived in Vietnam and my name in your language sounded like Eat a D–, I would change it to avoid embarrassment both on my part and on the part of the people who had to say it."[9]

Dr. Rita Kohli, coauthor of a 2012 study on names and cultural disrespect,[10] explained why the professor's response to the student was one that was hardly made with her best interests in mind. Instead, Kohli said, "He was attempting to leverage his power to change who she is . . . When someone in a position of power, an educator for example, changes someone's name because they find it inconvenient or challenging to their comfort—through that interaction, they are disrespecting, devaluing who that person is."[11]

I appreciate people in various countries who do their best to pronounce my name. I don't have to give myself a Greek name like Ρίτσαρντ when I'm in Greece, or a Nepali name like रिचर्ड when I'm in Nepal. Pardon my languages. I'm Richard. It was the name I was given. And each time I travel to other countries, locals make an effort to pronounce my name as a way of respecting who I am, despite imperfect pronunciations that do not bother me but rather delight me. I, after all, experience the challenges of that name pronunciation thing too. It happens more with my last name than my first. Instead of Lui (sounds like "loo-eee"), I get a lot of "Loo."

That's when a conversation ensues that usually goes something like this:

Me: "Ah, it's no big deal at all. It's pronounced *loo-eee*, spelled L-U-I. Lots of folks don't recognize it."

Other Person: "How interesting! Where does that spelling come from?"

Me: "I'm not sure, but I know L-U-I is not common, and I get all sorts of pronunciations from folks."

Other Person: "Sorry again. I got it now. Great to meet you. I'll remember—Richard Loo." (Their hearts are clearly really in it.)

When I'm at work, I'll typically ask a guest for name pronunciations right before we go on air. I'll say it, get corrected, and then try again. Sometimes I'll call that person's or organization's voice mail. I'll YouTube their name. The Voice of America pronunciation guide (pronounce. voanews.com) is another great resource for learning how to pronounce non-English names. They list names you'd hear in the news. Making an effort to pronounce a name correctly shows respect to a person.

"Uh...and we're here with...T...Tiny K...Ke..."
© Tak Toyoshima

It's a way of saying, "Don't change your name for me or any other English speakers. Michael and Jane, you are selfless by changing your name, but you don't have to. I should instead try to use the names you were given at birth." I'd expect the same. I'm not sure how I'd respond if someone said, "Wow, 'Richard' is too difficult. Can I just call you 'Sweaty Guy on Camera'? Or 'Loo'?"

THE WORD MIRROR

Want to get better at being selfless with your words? Record yourself. It will be painful at first. At CNN, we'd have a few coaches routinely come in to help us work through our storytelling skills. Each had a different curriculum and came from a different region of the country. On the face of it, getting a call to set up a coaching appointment simply meant the broadcast coach was in town and talent development wanted to see when you had time to meet. But to me, that call meant, *You need help.* I heard that message loud and clear in my first couple of coaching sessions, but I also found the sessions helpful. In fact, when I heard from colleagues that a coach was in town, I began to ask if they had extra openings. (I had this sweating problem, you see.)

One of the most helpful exercises we did was a tape review. "Bring two or three of your reports you like," the coach said—which meant, *You think that was good, hotshot? It wasn't.* When the coach and I listened to my tape, my crutch phrases really stood out. I referred more than I should have to my point of view rather than simply telling the story: "I saw"; "I spoke to"; "I went there." In reality, of course, it had taken a whole team to get the story. "We" would have been the far better choice in virtually all of those contexts. Dissecting everything I said on video wasn't my idea of a great time, but I was always glad I did it. It made me a better storyteller.

The experience of listening to recordings of what you say is like attending a Broadway play—you'll laugh and cry a lot. Mostly cry, actually. It's closer to *Les Misérables* than *Mamma Mia!* It will help you see how selfless the language choices you make are—or aren't.

Start by recording just your side of a phone call. For extra credit, consider going a step further, as my coaches would do, and transcribe your part of the conversation. If you prefer, you can use a transcription service such as Fiverr (fiverr.com) to do it for $20. Then stare at that transcript in amazement. What you say in black-and-white makes the words more real and bigger somehow. (Like looking at a pimple under UV light.) Now, count how many times you used the words "I," "me," and "myself." As the researchers did in the UCLA study, also count the "give" and "get" words to see how selfless your word choices are. Then listen to the recording once more, paying particular attention to the tone of the words. How did you say the "me" and the "get" words?

If you want to take it one step further, the next time you have a conversation with someone, try to *see* the words you are saying as you say them—as if they're typed on a screen in front of your eyeballs or in your head. This means you'll be listening to what you're saying as you're saying it. Talk more slowly to see if that helps. Seeing words makes us own our words and compels us to select them and then say them with our own unique intensity. This is another tactic that coaches counseled me to do when I'm on air. Communications advisers say we should pretend that everything we write or say on air would be printed in *USA Today*, reasoning that if the many people who read *USA Today* were to hear what we say, we'll be a bit more careful about our word choices.

. . . .

I remember the lessons I've learned from my coaches and mentors and try to apply them to the many words I write and say. But in some ways, I feel like it's still early on the word path. Especially when it comes to making better "enough about me" word choices. I started small—with my scripts at work, with people's names, with referring to myself in vulnerable ways, and with reading stuff that contains less meist language. In the end, I want people to take me at my selfless word.

Word Choices That Demonstrate Selflessness toward Others

Be specific when referring to race. For example, refer to "people of Vietnamese descent" rather than simply lumping everyone together as Asians. Say "Dominican" rather than Hispanic or Latino. At the same time, be specific only when necessary. Is ethnicity relevant to the story? Often it's not. For example, it's not necessary to say that a gunman is White or Black—unless you're asking the public to be on the lookout for someone who is at large and a physical description is needed.

Use "person-first" language. Person-first language puts a person before a diagnosis—for example, "people with disabilities" instead of "disabled people," or "a man who walks with crutches" instead of "a crippled man." Avoid referring to people as their diagnosis— "an epileptic," "a quadriplegic," "a Down's kid," "an autistic person," "the mentally ill"—and refer to them instead as "a person with" autism or epilepsy, and so forth. Doing so acknowledges that people with disabilities are more than their medical conditions.

Avoid emotionally loaded terms. For example, the phrase "confined to" a wheelchair can be the opposite of how a person feels. For a person who would otherwise have limited independent mobility, using a wheelchair may feel liberating (though "liberated" by a wheelchair is not a common expression). Similarly, exercise caution when using words such as *afflicted*, *stricken*, *restricted*, or *suffering* in connection with those who have a medical diagnosis. For example, if you are talking about someone with Alzheimer's disease, saying they were "diagnosed with Alzheimer's" is a better option than saying they are "afflicted with" or "suffering from Alzheimer's."

Focus on personal characteristics. You've probably heard those with disabilities described as "heroic" or "brave." However, those with disabilities may not want to be thought of as heroic or brave just for having a disability. Instead, they may prefer to be described for personal characteristics that are unique to them, just as we would describe anyone else.

Mention gender or sex only when relevant. Describe people by gender only when relevant. For example, it's appropriate to use "female police officer" when discussing gender in policing. Avoid phrases such as "you guys"—which I mistakenly use all the time and have to correct myself—unless everyone in the room is a man. Y'all (thanks to my Southern friends) works well as an alternative.

Avoid mentioning age first. This is another occasion when it's best to use people-first language. Refer to "people who are older" rather than "old people," "old men" or "old women," "the elderly," or "senior citizens."

Make frequent use of selfless words. Remember the study of virtue-related words—the one that revealed how selfless words are on the decline? Researchers found that words such as these convey selflessness:[12]

appreciation	fortitude	love
benevolence	generosity	modesty
charity	gentleness	perseverance
courage	gratitude	politeness
courtesy	helpfulness	sacrifice
diligence	hospitality	sincerity
faith	humbleness	thankfulness
faithfulness	humility	thoughtfulness
fidelity	kindness	

Chapter Fourteen

TEN STONES

L et's say we have to make a choice among three stocks, three flavors of buffalo wings (habanero, all the way), or three airlines. We've all been there—that fun debate among colleagues, friends, and family.

There are various ways to make choices, but what about the tried-and-true rock-paper-scissors approach? It's so popular it has multiple names—hick hack hock, ching chang chong (Chinese), and more. Or maybe we could take the approach of Gomer Pyle of the eponymous 1960s comedy series. When faced with a difficult choice, Gomer slapped his fingers—the same number of fingers as choices he had—on a table. The finger that hurt the most and longest was the choice. (Probably a sign of poor circulation, but I digress.)

Simply put, these imperfect decision-making games underscore how in many cases our choices do not require any attribution of value to each choice. Nor do they apply any specific rationale for one choice over another. It's a random chance, depending on how one's fingers form or ache after counting to three.

So here I am, along with the likes of Gomer Pyle and the inventors of rock paper scissors, ready to offer yet another fun decision tool: ten stones. Huh?

Using ten stones as an approach to decision making derives from managing "conjoint analyses" during my strategy-consulting days. It's a simplified extrapolation of how humans make decisions while using a whole host of factors. We just don't realize we're doing deep learning, quad-core chip stuff.

In market research, a conjoint analysis provides a better understanding of the value people give to their choices relative to each other. One of the longtime experts in the field, Sawtooth Software, describes conjoint analysis as a realistic questioning approach that "mimics the tradeoffs people make in the real world when making choices."[1]

In other words, if price is most important when choosing a car, when the price is higher, it's less preferable. But let's say I add in color as another variable; color may then be more important, but only up to a certain price point and within certain colors. If we add a third characteristic, like air-conditioning, where does that leave us? At some prices and with some colors, we may or may not care about having AC. A conjoint analysis can tell us which combinations of these three characteristics we prefer most. We don't have enough fingers to bang on the table to figure that out.

When it comes to selfless choices, we engage in the same debate. Do I donate ten dollars at the charity event to the blind auction, to the auctioneer, or just directly. You know the variables: Is it tax-deductible? Do I enjoy the auctioneer? Can I buy that sports jersey cheaper somewhere else? Sometimes I feel like I need to break out my computer to decide. The same can often be said with regard to volunteer decisions and encountering people who are homeless.

The "ten stones" method helps us make better, more efficient choices because it mimics a simplistic conjoint analysis. One more example. Let's say I'm looking for a new car and have three options, all of which cost the same amount.

- Choice A is a 2005 luxury car that has 120,000 miles.
- Choice B is a brand-new subcompact with no air-conditioning—bare bones.
- Choice C is my aunt's eight-year-old minivan.

Now let's give each choice a bucket. Using the "ten stones" method, I put more of my ten stones in the bucket for the car I like more. For example:

- choice A = 5 stones
- choice B = 3 stones
- choice C = 2 stones

Choice A it is. It's the bucket that got the most stones. It's not a ten-stone slam dunk, but it does show I value choice A the most—and by a good amount. Even when I translate the stones to simple math, choice A is the clear winner.

- I prefer choice A 66 percent more than choice B (5–3 = 2, 2 ÷ 3 = 66 percent).
- I prefer choice A 150 percent more than choice C (5–2 = 3, 3 ÷ 2 = 150 percent).

I know it's a crude conjoint analysis, but the number of stones does show I have a clear preference for the used luxury car with lots of miles. And if the luxury car is somehow sold before I get to the dealership, I can always go with the subcompact—the stones show I like it 50 percent more than my aunt's minivan after all (3–2 = 1; 1 ÷ 2 = 50 percent). She always ate foul-smelling durians while driving.

Forget the math for a second and focus on the simplicity of ten stones. I didn't have to answer several questions to determine which choice I valued most. Instead, I was able to intuitively assign relative value to each of my choices. Bottom line, buying a car is a complex process, but using the "ten stones" method helps simplify it and get to a clear decision.

Using the "ten stones" method removes the idea that a good choice needs to be a 10 (based on the 1 to 10 ranking construct) before going for it. And it suggests that a five-stone choice can actually be a more informed choice than a ten-stone choice in the sense that it takes the decision paralysis out of the all-or-nothing approach.

The "ten stones" method shows that choices don't have to be perfect, especially when all we have are imperfect choices. And this matters when it comes to selflessness. We don't have to attempt Mother Teresa, Nobel Prize–winning, mythological levels of selflessness. Given the choices in front of us, we can still decide on selfless stuff that's good and worthwhile.

PERFECTION PARALYSIS

Do you remember the Aesop's Fable story about a fox and a cat? The two animals discuss the tricks they use to escape bloodthirsty hounds. The fox boasts he has many ways to escape; the cat admits she has only one.

Then the hunters and hounds arrive. The fox can't decide which escape route is the best, and the hounds catch him while he's weighing his options. The cat scurries up a tree—her only option—and successfully escapes.

Turns out, human beings aren't all that different from the fox. We experience perfection paralysis daily when faced with decisions, both big and small.

Consider a decision as trivial as picking out a jam to buy at the grocery store. In an experiment, a Columbia University professor set up a jam-tasting booth that offered an assortment of two dozen different jams. Sixty percent of customers in the store stopped to sample the jams.

Every few hours, the professor and her research assistants pared down the selection to six different jams. Only 40 percent of customers stopped at the booth. But when it came to purchasing the jams, 30 percent of samplers bought from the pared-down offering, compared with only 3 percent of samplers who bought from the larger selection of jams.[2]

But jam is jam! All jams (except for traffic) are tasty, yet customers still got hung up on the perfect jam to put on their toast and ended up being unable to buy.

The same perfection paralysis happens in the more daunting choices in life. A study of young adults found that those who wanted the perfect career were more likely to experience career indecision. More than 31 percent of career indecision was explained by young adults' perfection paralysis.[3] Tell me about it. While perfectionism can sometimes lead to high performance, at other times it is "associated with a range of emotional difficulties, including anxiety and depression, eating disorders, fear of intimacy, and dysfunctional thinking," according to researchers.[4]

Whether we're making everyday decisions about jam or a career, we can suffer from decision paralysis. It's not a stretch then that our decisions about pursuing selflessness are vulnerable to the same malady—especially when looking for selfless people we believe are worthy of emulating.

Probably the most celebrated selfless person in the modern era was the small but mighty Mother "The Machine" Teresa. In 1950, Teresa founded the Missionaries of Charity, a Roman Catholic religious congregation whose members take vows of chastity, poverty, and obedience. They also vow to give "wholehearted and free service to the poorest of the poor."[5] In doing so, they provide homes for people dying of leprosy, HIV/AIDS, and tuberculosis, as well as running soup kitchens, mobile clinics, orphanages, and schools. Although some have criticized Teresa's use of funds and the quality of treatment provided, she will always be remembered for serving and living among the poorest of the poor. She fed, washed, and cared for the dying, respecting the dignity of every person.[6] She was awarded the Nobel Peace Prize and is one of only eight people in history to be given honorary citizenship by the United States.

Remembering such a giant of selflessness inspires me but also intimidates me at times. I have to remember that while she appeared to be perfect in so many ways, she was not perfect. In 1987, she was invited to speak at a conference on world hunger but stopped at the door of the building when she saw a hungry man lying by the door. Even though her coworker promised to take care of the man, Mother Teresa insisted on doing so herself, delaying her arrival to the conference by ninety minutes. So not a perfect decision maybe?

I have to stop to remind myself: she was an imperfect, super selfless person.

I'm a work in progress. Imperfect and wanting to find in myself just a piece of her selflessness.

THE BINARY WAY

Computer programmers use binary code to tell computers what to do. It's a two-symbol system that uses just ones and zeroes for virtually everything that happens in a computer. In any kind of binary system, there are only two options. Everything is either a yes or a no. A yin or a yang. A zig or a zag. That's a little polarizing for me. If selflessness is a binary condition and people like Desmond Tutu and Mother Teresa are ones, does that mean I'm a zero? And should I look at all of the choices in front of me that way?

When I've tried to choose between options based on which one is wholly good or bad, I'm like the fox in Aesop's Fable or the jam tasters—I freeze up and can't make a choice. Or I take the easy way out and just opt out of choosing at all. If the job opportunity isn't perfect, I don't consider it. If an acquaintance isn't perfect, they won't be invited into my friend circle. If the watermelons at the market don't have quite the right sound when I thump them with my knuckles, they're not getting into my cart. If I were to use a binary approach to make all of my decisions, I'd never have a job or friends. (Or, most tragic of all, have spit a watermelon seed—my greatest date trick.)

My binary view didn't stop at decisions. It was the way I saw people too. You were a one or a zero.

There I was—at Camp Koinonia in Santa Cruz for a church youth group retreat. It was my first time, and it was going to be a chance to meet others who were like me—ones in a sea of zeroes. I was an apostle, after all. I was converting people. I prayed morning, noon, and night. Despite this being the 1980s—the beginning of Jordache jeans, the Sir Jack's coats that only the cool kids wore, and the permed-hair hangover from the '70s—I was anti-materialistic. Day after day, I purposely wore the same hoodie and sweater my mom had knit for me. When my Sears jeans got holes in them, my mom just put patches on them. At one point, I even sewed two different pairs of pants together—black above the knee, blue below it. I was color-block before color-block was a thing. This was my pushback against materialism—a statement anyone could see a mile away.

At the retreat, I expected to see yet more sweatshirt-sporting, black/blue pants–wearing icons like myself. But I didn't. These people weren't ones; they appeared to be zeroes.

Cool haircuts, tanned, Quiksilver bikinis and boardshorts, hanging out by the pool, with Top 40 channels blaring on boom boxes. My fellow high schoolers at this church camp weren't what I thought folks who came to church camp should be. They were shysters, junior Judases in the making. They didn't fit my binary worldview.

That week felt like a rabbit hole of polemics and teenage existential crises. Each day got longer. The last day was the longest. It was midday, and my heart was beating too hard in my chest. I had a medical history of palpitations, and I was concerned. I was short of breath. The feeling of impending doom hit. This was it.

I called the staff, not knowing if they'd be able to help—after all, how many camp counselors moonlight as cardiologists? And as you may remember from your own summer camp days, the last thing a camp staffer wants to hear is, "Betty, it's urgent. One of the kids in tent 14 says he's having congestive heart failure with a potential myocardial infarction."

Minutes later, an ambulance arrived. The technicians plucked me out of my bunk and put me on the stretcher. They attached wires to my chest. I was breathless, still feeling like I was about to go home to see the Big Guy. They had to wheel the stretcher over a long gravel path from my cabin and through a gawking crowd of well-coiffed, California-groovy high schoolers. Even then, I was still mentally shaking my fist at them. *Look at what all you zeroes did to me! I'm fifteen, and I need a pacemaker.*

The ambulance door slammed shut, and I was on my way to the ER. What an exit! I couldn't have scripted it better.

It wasn't until recently, nearly thirty years later, that I realized what I experienced that day was a panic attack, not near-death by righteous indignation. I was driven to see things as either perfect or imperfect, good or bad, ones or zeroes. And when it came to religion, that rule applied in spades. So much so that I panicked when the people around me broke the binary mold. I haven't had one of these incidents since. (Though my broadcast job auditions are known to cause a bit of ischemia here and there.)

If I would have had a "ten stones" mindset back then, I could have characterized everyone more accurately—more realistically—as six or seven in the good bucket, and three or four in the bad. I wasn't supposed to judge other people, but I was, as I've already said, a big work in progress. I mean, give them a break. They were teens, and few things at that age are forever. But there I was, with the moral scales of justice hanging around my neck like a lucky charm. Many choices we face are a combination of both good and bad (like hot dogs, good taste, bad everything else, for example). But I couldn't see the mix. I was binary.

Having a "ten stones" mindset allows me to accept human beings for who they are—a complex mix of what is simplistically considered kind and inconsiderate, selfless and selfish. Using the "ten stones" method allows me to make decisions in an imperfect world. And to stay away from categorical judgments that would find few ones and leave many zeroes behind.

I had an opportunity to practice avoiding the binary when I began receiving invitations to speak. (As in, more than reciting the alphabet as a warm-up before a broadcast, and for more than six minutes—the normal extent of my stamina.) I was honored by the requests but worried I'd disappoint the inviters. I wasn't any smarter than I was before I was on TV. Remember, I was the guy who sewed two pairs of pants together, thinking it was the way to salvation. I also wrestled with whether or not, at the heart of it, these speaking opportunities were a chance to be selfish or selfless.

> **In the selfless category:** Bringing people together to accomplish a goal and discuss important topics is positive. And volunteerism is good.
>
> **In the selfish category:** It's good for my career. I enjoy standing up in front of groups of people and having my accomplishments recognized. It feels good when people ask to hear my stories and ideas.
>
> **Weighting:** six stones in the selfless bucket, four stones in the selfish bucket.

Even though it wasn't a "perfect ten" decision, the "ten stones" method propelled me into volunteering and community work as a broadcast journalist. It got me out of the high chair and into taking responsibility for the gifts and resources I had been given.

© Tak Toyoshima

UNDERSTANDING (RATHER THAN RATING) MY FATHER

Pastors are sometimes perceived as having holy halos—perfect in every way. Not my dad. He loved God, but he was imperfect. For us kids, living so many years at home gave us views under the brightest and most unflattering lights. I could tell my mom was sometimes frustrated that Dad wasn't as godly as she'd anticipated when she married him. That's human. When they met in the 1950s, he appeared to be the ideal Christian husband—a tall, handsome young man in seminary preparing to become a pastor. He was postcard-perfect. But for my mom, he ended up being less postcard and more cardboard—a little plain and not as colorful as she had imagined he would be.

Did my dad's occupation as a pastor make him a ten-stone, altruistic, godly man whose every word and deed was inspired by the Holy Spirit? No. Did he like to stand there and be important in front of the church? Yes. Did he want to be heard and respected? Yes, and yes. Did he respond with some anger when he was overlooked to be an elder? Of course. (Being an elder qualifies you for a discount at the movies.) And yet there was something inspiring about my dad's striving to live out his faith even in his imperfections. For much of his life, he was a six-stone man, but his six stones still made an impact. And seeing him that way allowed me to fully love and embrace him as my father and as a good person. But then his stone count changed.

When he was diagnosed with Alzheimer's disease, he began to take on a different tone. I noticed it when he said things like, "I'm sorry. I have Alzheimer's, and I forget." Most people with this disease don't admit they have it or don't remember they have it. But my dad was no longer afraid of vulnerability. He had lost much of his concern about commanding respect. Instead, he was concerned about authenticity and love.

My dad perfectly embodied the truth that transformation is a process, one in which we become progressively more like Christ. Like my dad, I'm not characterized by ten stones worth of trust, love, joy, and humility. It's an ongoing journey, not a destination. What matters is whether or not we're heading in the right direction.

Embracing the "ten stones" mindset allows me to understand and accept others in the full confidence that we are on the good side of the ledger, giving a net positive to the world. It's not a system for rating people in order to decide whether or not to spend time with them; it's a way of understanding the people I'm spending time with—my father included. We are moving forward together, even if it's only one stone at a time.

• • • • • • • • • •

One of the benefits of my job is being able to slip into the audience of *The Tonight Show Starring Jimmy Fallon* when friends and family are in town. It's always a good time, especially when cast member Seth Herzog does the audience warm-up before the show. He has a fun, P. T. Barnum approach to entertainment. He points out the applause signs, makes jokes, gets everyone laughing, and creates great energy in the audience.

I like Seth's approach, and I think there's a lesson in it for all of us who are trying to sort out what it means to be selfless. If we walk into a bookstore to try to find guidance about volunteering, we'll find shelves of books encouraging us to be "radical" and "sold out." These authors are trying to rev us up, sort of like Herzog. "Do more! Smile more! Serving others is awesome!" Sometimes that intensity is great; sometimes it isn't. If selflessness has to be either a one or a zero, people will never try. I think it's okay to have a balanced approach instead—a "ten stones" mindset. Using ten stones in decision making isn't a feel-good cover for doing things halfway; it simply acknowledges that I can do something, even if it's not perfect.

For you football fans, it's what the San Francisco 49ers refer to as a "West Coast offense"—using short, horizontal passing routes that enable a team to make punchy progress to the goal. The game is not all "Hail Mary" passes. A "ten stones" mindset is a way of making small choices more often. And therefore doing more . . . more often. Which means, in the end, gaining more toned selflessness muscles. Since we get to make a decision every fifteen minutes, that can be a whole lot of muscle.

I saw it happen recently with my oldest brother.

When we were kids, my dad went down to his study every morning to read and pray. If we had to knock on his door for lunch, he'd sometimes lay a verse on us he had just read. He was a human vending machine of Scripture. While his kids didn't have the same spiritual regimen (we were, marginally, four- to six-stone Christians for sure), each verse somehow moved the ball forward for my dad. He and Mom accepted the reality that their children were on a journey, and our parents were going to get onboard and help paddle the whole way.

A year ago, the wind caught the sails. My oldest brother shared a story on the family text thread about my dad. Dad had declined to the point where we could no longer care for him at home. Although we still spoke to him, he didn't seem to understand and rarely engaged with what we said. My brother had visited him at the care facility that day and made a surprising discovery. "I just read John 1 to Baba, and he tracked with me, looking at me midway through as I was reading," he texted. My brother, not known for reading anything out loud, had decided to read the gospel of John to my dad because he had named his son after the apostle in honor of my dad.

Ever since that day, it's become our tradition to read a Bible chapter to my dad when we visit. His faith is central to his life. These are words he has read over and over again throughout his life, and they are seared into his mind and heart. When Dad was still able to stand and sing, I marveled at how the disease had torn down walls of inhibition. How he was able to sing hymns in a way I had never seen him sing before, with hands and voice held high. Every time we read chapters of Scripture to him, it brings him back, keeps him closer to us, even if just for a verse.

I rarely give 150 percent, as my tennis coaches used to tell me to do, or get a 150 percent return on my investment—though sometimes I do. The other times, as it is with choosing jam, careers, and friends, approaching my choices with a commitment to pragmatic progress, not perfection, offers a healthy option. Reading John 1 to my father that day, my brother was able to do a little something. It wasn't a revival; it was a reading. Nothing of particularly great weight. But he did something, stone by stone.

Chapter Fifteen

ANATOMY OF
ACTION

Since the 1960s, San Francisco has had a well-earned reputation as the center of unprecedented sexual freedom. The "free love" and partying moved in in the 1970s and early 1980s. The time was ripe for a new, deadly virus silently spreading from person to person. It's hard to remember the fear and confusion that surrounded the onset of HIV, the human immunodeficiency virus, at that time. AIDS first made an appearance in 1981, but it didn't yet have a name. Doctors weren't sure how it was transmitted, speculating it could be passed through the air or a person's breath. People wondered if you could catch it through use of public toilets, water fountains, or swimming pools. Police officers refused to touch people who might have the disease.

In 1981, nine people in our city died of AIDS. By 1992, thirty people were dying every week. AIDS eventually killed more than twenty thousand San Franciscans, most of them gay men.

"Medically, this is a horror show," said David Denmark, a former nurse at San Francisco General Hospital, during the early days of the epidemic. When patients began pouring in, the hospital medical staff was initially reluctant. "We were afraid of them," he admitted. "Everybody was."[1] The medical staff wore suits that covered every part of their bodies—from the tops of their heads to the bottoms of their feet—since no one was sure how the disease spread. At some hospitals, patients were left in their own feces, since the auxiliary help was too fearful to go into their rooms to take care of them. In others, the cries of the sick and dying went unanswered.

At the time, AIDS was a death sentence. Upon diagnosis, patients were expected to live a few months or, if they were lucky, a few years before succumbing to a gruesome death. They had colds that never went away, rashes that never healed, weight that dropped and never came back. Many had been ostracized by their families and were dying utterly alone or surrounded by understandably fearful health care workers in hazmat suits.

In 1983, however, the medical staff at San Francisco General created a new ward called 5B, the first facility in the nation designed specifically to treat AIDS patients. The hospital put out a call for help, and all the nurses who worked in that ward did so voluntarily. They were given no assurances. Those with spouses were told to go home and talk to their loved ones before committing. They were warned they might contract the disease and die too.

"We were gay, we were straight, we were young, we were old," said nurse Alison Moed Paolercio, describing the coalition of caregivers who rallied to care for the dying. "And we were all kick-ass," said Cliff Morrison, a clinical nurse specialist. "Even the straight ones."[2]

The caregivers in 5B had a different perspective on caring for their dying patients. They knew they weren't there to restore the patients to health. Instead, they decided to love them well as they encountered death. Though nursing typically required a certain amount of professional distance, the 5B nurses broke with protocols. They held hands without gloves, rubbed patients' foreheads to give them comfort, and even crawled into bed to comfort the dying victims.

Hank Plante, a reporter with San Francisco's CBS affiliate KPIX, noticed other news stations that interviewed AIDS victims wouldn't even get close enough to pin a microphone on them.[3] As a member of the LGBTQ community, Plante knew many of the key players battling the disease. He filmed nurses holding hands with the patients, embracing them on camera as they attempted to destigmatize people with the disease. "Those nurses were subversive," he said.[4] Selflessness frequently is.

SHOWING UP

Not too long after the first generations of Irish who came to the United States during the nineteenth century landed on American soil, they were sworn in as soldiers and sent immediately to the front lines. Only they hadn't even been given citizenship. In spite of the intense discrimination these new immigrants felt, they served the country valiantly in the fight to end slavery. They joined the armed forces by the thousands, along with many other minority groups, including Native, Filipino, Chinese, and Pakistani Americans.

"This is my country as much as the man who is born on the soil. This being the case I have as much interest in the maintenance of the integrity of the nation as any other man," wrote one of these Irish American soldiers in a letter home to Ireland.[5] Their commanders had far less regard for their lives than for the lives of American-born troops. Fighting was a death sentence. The Catholic priests would give them their last rites before they headed to the front lines. The Fighting Irish gave all for their new country, one that hadn't yet even accepted them.

Colonel Jack Jacobs told me a similar story. He and I were collaborating on a report about Medal of Honor recipients, a large majority of whom are of Irish descent. Jacobs is one of the few living Medal of Honor recipients—there are just 103 as of this writing. He teaches at West Point, and he also teaches on our airwaves and in 30 Rock hallways. Standing five-foot-four-inches tall, his stature belies the magnitude of what he did during the Vietnam War.

When his company commander was injured on the front lines, Jacobs took charge to organize a retreat. During the melee, he was wounded by mortar fragments but still ran across open rice paddies to save fellow US soldiers—fourteen times. He couldn't see well because of bleeding from his head wounds, but he did well enough to avoid his own demise, even after encountering three enemy squads that tried to stop him. (He often reminds me that his sense of taste was affected. He says that's why he likes sweets—their flavor is stronger.)

When we were working on the Medal of Honor story, Colonel Jack always showed up an hour early to the studio. Always. Sometimes his segment would get pushed back or cut, but he always stayed until he was no longer needed. (And with a smile and a Tootsie Roll.) He wasn't just making an appearance or punching a clock. He showed up. And stayed late to help out, to teach us what only a decorated veteran could know. Just like he showed up fourteen times to save fourteen lives that day.

Showing up in person makes a difference. All of us know the value of having someone there for us. When we're feeling stressed, for example, we reach out to friends for support. Some friends make it a habit of sending quick texts to see if we're doing okay. Others show up in person. (The best ones bring Tootsie Rolls too.)

Interestingly, a team of Canadian researchers measured the difference between sending texts and showing up in person. A friend who showed their concern by coming in person was upward of 20 percent more effective at reducing stress than a friend who merely sent a supportive text message.[6] In a CBC interview, lead researcher Susan Holtzman said, "My suspicion is there's something really powerful about being with somebody, feeling or knowing you have that person's full attention, seeing a smiling face . . . and giving us support."[7]

Since the 1990s, business has been trying to put a figure on the value of showing up—specifically, the degree to which employee productivity rises or falls when employees work from home or in the office. The management of a Chinese travel agency with more than 16,000 employees tried something in 2010 that might shed some light. They did a nine-month study with a group of employees in which half of the group was assigned to work from home, and the other half to work from the office. When the participants reported back at the end of nine months, those who worked from home had added nearly a full day of productivity each week relative to the group working from the office. In addition, turnover in the home office workers group decreased 50 percent relative to the office workers.[8]

Even so, it wasn't good for all of the "work from home" group. Half of them actually wanted to return to normal office work, even though doing so required an eighty-minute round trip commute. They felt isolated and depressed. And there was concern about losing creativity (and those free office supplies to boot).[9]

Showing up has benefits.

· · · · · · · · · ·

When I got a job in Los Angeles in my twenties, my maternal grandmother let me move in with her. I didn't speak Cantonese, and she didn't speak English. Yet we were able to communicate pretty well. We pointed a great deal, nodded, and smiled. I didn't want to be a burden, so when I noticed she was carrying heavy bags of groceries home to cook for me, I decided to cook at least once a week to give her a break.

Since I had limited culinary skills at the time, I made boiled chicken. (It was as exciting a dish as it sounds.) "Do you like dark meat or white meat?" I asked her. Of course, she had no idea what that sentence meant, so I pointed. She pointed. We smiled. I figured out that she liked white meat, which was good since I liked the dark meat. Thighs, drumsticks, and backs all the way. Living with my grandmother for three months was such a great time in my life, as we developed a real relationship in spite of the language barrier—and some horrible cooking.

When she fell and broke her hip three years later, nothing was quite the same again. My family and I drove down from San Francisco to visit her. When I walked in the door, she didn't greet me or smile as she always had when I lived with her. There were no hugs with my little grandma. The strong head of that household I had come to know and love was gone. She could no longer carry heavy bags of groceries home. In fact, she couldn't walk at all. She could only sit there, uncharacteristically inert in her chair, her legs swelling with fluid like a slowly sinking ship. There wasn't much the family could do. Although she had once been the center of our interactions when we visited, we were left to speak among ourselves, pretending all was okay when it truly wasn't.

My sister said, "I wish I could speak Chinese to her." I knew what she meant. There really wasn't anything we could do to help, and it hurt.

"It's okay, Kristen," I said. "She knows we're here. I spent a whole summer sitting next to her. Sometimes we just stared at each other; other times we giggled. She knows we're here, and she knows we love her."

That was enough. To simply be there.

TASTE OF KINDNESS

Grandma died not too long after our visit. My mom told me then that Grandma didn't actually like white meat. She was a wing woman!

By eating the white meat, she was just doing what most grandparents do for their grandchildren, especially this freeloader who was trying to cook once a week. Each time, she just smiled, grabbed an overboiled chicken breast, took a bite, and nodded with fake enjoyment. This wasn't a language barrier; it was that selfless grandma gene kicking in. She would've eaten shoe leather rather than deprive her grandson of a juicy thigh.

Love and miss you, Grandma.

Making and sharing food with others may be the oldest act of selflessness. (Right up there with drawing a cave painting with animal fat for your best friend.) No matter where one stands when it comes to Christianity, Islam, Buddhism, and most other religions, food has been gathered and given since way back when. We're built to give food. It's a fundamental way we give and receive love. When we linger over food with family and friends, we enhance our relationships with every single helping.

At my parents' house in San Francisco, there's a painting of a dinner party. It's a reproduction of da Vinci's *Last Supper*—history's most famous meal. You can't miss it when you walk in. It hangs over the couch I sleep on whenever I go home to help take care of my mom and dad. And every time I wake up, it's an opportunity to enjoy brunch with Jesus.

I've spent some time examining the details. The salt spilled by Judas on the table. The small sack he clutches that contains his reward for betraying Jesus to the authorities. The knife in the apostle Peter's hand, which he'll use later to defend Jesus during his arrest. With each detail, Leonardo (not the one of Ninja Turtle fame) offers insight into the biblical scene. What about that delicious food sitting there on the table? The Last Supper was a Passover meal. In biblical times, lamb was on the menu. A plate of fish to the left. Pieces of fruit. Plenty of bread and wine. To the right, a plate of grilled eel topped with orange slices. (Wait a second! Leonardo made a glaring error—eels aren't kosher! Jesus and his disciples would never have eaten that entrée.)

Glancing at the painting one night, I thought there had to be a reason Leonardo included so many details that related to the food. My father told us about Jesus' last meal many times. Jesus knew one of his apostles would betray him. Yet even during his final meal, he still fed others. World-famous Savior, underrated host.

The thing is, food often epitomizes acts of kindness. Meals are deliberate ways to love others as we spend hours, sometimes days, preparing.

GREETINGS ARE GIVING

For various reasons, it sometimes feels like an awkward dance when someone I know approaches me. What if the other person reaches out to shake hands? The Centers for Disease Control and Prevention has said, "Hands off!" That's because a "glad hand" greeting transfers ten times more bacteria than a fist bump, and about twice as much as a high five.[10] So what was left if I couldn't shake hands? I couldn't just ignore folks. I had to greet them somehow. I decided to do some research to find out how people in other parts of the world acknowledge friends and new acquaintances.[11]

People in Zimbabwe greet each other by clapping once, and then the other person responds by clapping twice. In northern Mozambique, people clap three times before they verbally greet one another. I could get used to applause with every greeting.

Okay, here's one that would drive all elementary school teachers crazy. Since the ninth century, people in Tibet have been sticking out their tongues at each other in greeting. This is because an unpopular king who was known for having a black tongue had died. People began sticking out their tongue to prove they weren't the king, or his reincarnation. Though sticking out one's tongue in the West is a sign of disrespect (unless you're sixteen and like Skittles or are an Instagram influencer), it has been a sign of respect in Tibet for centuries.

In Vietnam, holding two fingers in a V-shape is a pun-oriented way to say hi. That's because the number two is pronounced "hai," which sounds like the way English speakers say "hi." Or simply nod your head (and wave when you leave). Nodding and waving happens in many places. In fact, 60 percent of participants in a 2014 study were made comfortable by a robot solely on the motions it made to wave to and greet them.[12] (Maybe that's why we're giving them so many of our jobs.)

In the Philippines, people greet their elders by bowing and pressing their foreheads against their knuckles. In Liberia, the young drop to a knee to demonstrate honor to people older than they are. And though each country has its own variation, people in Nepal, Cambodia, India, Laos, Thailand, and Japan all bow to each other.

· · · · · · · · · ·

Before COVID-19, my dad and I weren't able to greet each other by exchanging conversation. Though I talked to him the entire time I was in his room, the greeting that really seemed to matter was touch.

I would put my hand on his head in the same way I had seen him do when he placed water on children's foreheads during baptism. It seemed to comfort him. He closed his eyes once my palm touched his forehead. Baba had wanted to baptize me when I was a baby, but my mother objected. She wanted her children to make that decision on their own, to find our own way.

I wasn't able to even be in the same room with Dad during the pandemic, so I stood outside the window of his room in the garden of his care facility. I waved at him. I smiled.

I never did get baptized, and now it's too late for my father to do it. But I can imagine what it might have been like. The glint in his eyes, the earnest expression of love and hope. As I stood outside on the other side of the glass, feeling in many ways my need for my father, Baba's eyes locked with mine—like an invisible hand reaching out to me. I didn't move. He didn't move. The edges of his mouth formed an impish smile. He was trying to smile back through his disease's confines.

We were separated by glass—just two feet away from each other. I stood there motionless for thirty minutes, trying to see beyond the disease and the years and all that was lost, and we connected in that moment so sacred and human.

Selflessness can be so physical. The way we look at and embrace each other. Our arms and legs, even if we're not touching, can show that it's not about us. It's intuitive to those who are affected by our movements or who are watching our movements. In the subway, at the supermarket, in the streets, we can watch the ways people actively express the anatomy of selflessness, manifesting their view on thinking outside themselves. It will make you smile.

Chapter Sixteen

STORIES THAT STICK

According to Dr. Paul J. Zak, founding director for the Center for Neuroeconomic Studies, oxytocin is "produced when we are trusted or shown a kindness."[1] Oxytocin is the chemical behind empathy, and repeated studies have found that higher levels of oxytocin mean more empathy.

The interesting thing is, when we do these acts of kindness, we get hooked. A natural high occurs. Our brain triggers the release of even more oxytocin, which drives our EQ (emotional intelligence). It's the stuff that is released when we hug or cuddle, or when we form emotional or social connections. The strength of the bond between mother and child, for example, is connected to oxytocin levels in mothers during the first trimester of pregnancy. Mothers with higher levels are more likely to sing to, bathe, or protectively monitor their children.[2] In a way, the best mothers are also the biggest users of oxytocin.

Though I'm not planning on becoming a mother anytime soon, I'll settle for becoming an oxytocin junkie. It turns out we can boost our oxytocin levels by inhaling an oxytocin spray. Apparently this is how scientists typically study the effects of oxytocin in humans. These nasal sprays are widely available, so I bought a tiny bottle of the spray—$35 online. A small price to pay for science-backed selflessness. Still, dear reader, please don't try this at home. I checked with a medical professional on the side effects and moved forward.

Ten minutes before I used the spray, I took some surveys measuring my emotional and mental state. I responded to questions about how secure, calm, amicable, or attentive I was feeling—from low to high.

And with the squeeze of the trigger and a small spritz into my right nostril, my personal test of oxytocin began. I waited for a little bit. I was wondering if I'd start feeling like I could fly or want to crochet at high speeds. Or start peeling sacks of potatoes with one hand. I may have mixed up this drug's effects with another one. I did have the kind of feeling you get after you let out a nice big sigh. With all these fascinating thoughts passing through my mind, ten minutes passed. I then took the same surveys as before, trying to be as honest and spontaneous with my responses as possible.

This clearly was not a serious scientific endeavor (I'm not expecting my Nobel Prize for science soon), but I was still curious whether the spray would lead to any measurable changes in how I felt. Well, it did.

Comparing my responses before and after the oxytocin, it seemed that I was feeling calmer, happier, and more secure after inhaling this bond-building hormone. What's more, I observed a huge effect on the measure of how amicable (versus antagonistic) I was feeling. There was a 36.6 percent jump in my post-oxytocin levels of amicability. It's not that I had started out hating everybody. But while my pre-oxytocin score was slightly above the midpoint of the scale, after the inhalation I was at a solid 91 percent. (I was Mr. Friendly. Like an unmeltable Olaf.)

Clearly, oxytocin had something to do with empathy. But just how strong is that association? A study of fifty-five adult Jewish Israelis revealed that after inhaling oxytocin, the Israelis' empathy for the suffering of Arabs increased to similar levels as their feelings toward the suffering of other Jews or Europeans.[3]

Dr. Paul Zak and his team wanted to go one step further and find out whether storytelling could activate this powerful hormone. They did blood draws before and after showing participants a film and discovered that the amount of oxytocin released by the brain directly predicted how much participants were willing to take action to help others in situations similar to those they had observed in the film.[4]

Additionally, the University of Toronto's Keith Oatley found that engaging with stories in novels improves empathy and theory of mind.

"When we read about other people, we can imagine ourselves into their position and we can imagine what it's like being that person," Oatley said. "That enables us to better understand people, better cooperate with them."[5]

There is powerful brain chemistry behind why good stories with selfless themes pay off. And it's because of one of today's most popular hormones—oxytocin. (Eat your heart out, adrenocorticotropic hormone.) Indeed, if my personal oxytocin trial is any (unscientific) indication of what happens when we empathize, as researchers Paul Zak and Keith Oatley discovered, the power of story to create empathy and selfless understanding seems legit. It's a good place to start in our exploration of stories that stick.

· · · · · · · · · ·

One of the jobs of a journalist is to report on stories that fly under the radar but that need to be heard. Most stories are assigned to a correspondent by a producer, based on the events of the day. A typical day starts with an editorial meeting in which each journalist pitches stories to the team. Ultimately, it's the executive producer and other higher-ups who make the final decisions about which stories to pursue. Roughly 5 to 10 percent of the stories seen on air are what we call enterprise stories, the ones that don't necessarily fit "news of the day."

When I began to pitch enterprise stories on Asian Americans more frequently, one of them had to do with a group of illegal immigrants known as "paper sons." These were Chinese people who illegally immigrated to the United States, using fraudulent documentation to claim they were sons or daughters of Chinese Americans who had US citizenship.

In 2007 while working at CNN, I reported on the history of the paper sons.[6] My crew and I flew to San Francisco and took a ferry to Angel Island. Angel Island was to Asian immigrants crossing the Pacific what Ellis Island was to European immigrants crossing the Atlantic. From the ferry, we climbed more than a hundred wooden steps and then walked a mile along a curvy, uphill road. Below us to our left, we saw the blue water of the Bay, sailboats bobbing in the distance.

Finally we saw a small sign on the ground: Angel Island Immigration Station. Beside it was a rebuilt foundation of where the main administration building once stood. There I interviewed a man named David Leong, a paper son when he arrived at Angel Island by ship in 1940 as an eight-year-old after a nearly three-week journey. While sailing to America, he memorized a detailed cheat sheet that outlined who his fake parents and siblings were and who lived on certain blocks of his purported family village in China.

He remembered the barracks. "I heard that people committed suicide in the bathrooms because they couldn't get off the island. At night, I wouldn't go to the bathroom at all."

The barracks, which had fallen into dangerous disrepair, were undergoing remodeling. From the outside, we filmed the fumigation drapery that covered the dilapidated walls. On the inside I later saw poems the detainees had chiseled there, their weeping evident in their words. Some weren't sure why they were detained; others were angry; and still others wanted to take their own lives. These seventy-year-old poems revealed melancholy retrospectives of life in China, punctuated by simple hopes of freedom.

Next we visited Erika Gee, a woman who learned as a high school student that her grandparents had come to the United States illegally. We stood in San Francisco's Chinatown, where many first-generation Chinese Americans hung out, practiced tai chi, smoked, and played intense games of thirteen-card poker. (Not all at the same time, though it would be an incredible act on *America's Got Talent*.)

"Are you glad your grandfather committed the crime?" I asked Erika.

"In some ways, no, because it was a crime," she said. "But I'm fortunate he did, and I have a tremendous amount of respect for the risks he took in order to come to the United States and to provide a better opportunity for his family."

"What do you think about modern-day immigrants who are illegally trying to do what your grandfather did a century ago?"

"I don't know," she grinned uncomfortably. "I don't feel comfortable saying it's okay for people to come in."

"It's perplexing for you, isn't it?" I asked. She nodded yes.

The stories of David and Erika echo those of an estimated one in three Chinese Americans who are descendants of the paper son system—which makes it a story applicable to one million Americans.

The story resonated. CNN International picked it up for broadcasting globally. It was also one of the stories that the Angel Island Immigration Station Foundation posted on its site—for more than a decade now. Hopefully the brains watching the six-minute report were spitting out oxytocin so they could remember and share the context of the importance of immigration, legal and illegal, to the country.

STORYTELLING PRACTICES

"I'm a storyteller." That's something many people say. In fact, it's probably right up there with "I'm an influencer," or "My brand is . . ." But just because we claim to be storytellers doesn't mean we are.

We've all been cornered by that "I'm a storyteller" guy (let's call him Uncle Ramble) who relays seven loosely tied anecdotes with no ending. And yet we all have the potential to tell life-changing stories. We just have to work on them, build them, edit them, and tell them. Good stories don't come easy. Ask any editor.

Stories are a fundamental aspect of what it means to be human. People have handed down stories to the next generation from the beginning. It's how we pass on our values. It's how we pass on our traditions. (And most importantly, it's how we scare the spit out of kids while toasting marshmallows around a campfire.)

Telling a story is different from building a story. *Telling* is saying, publishing, delivering the story—which essentially means you're past "building" something and are ready to push it out. *Building* means making the parts and then piecing together the parts of a story.

Reporters build and tell their stories. Then they get feedback from readers or viewers in the form of ratings, social media comments (some angry), and letters to the editor (sometimes even angrier). This feedback helps them build better stories over time.

To do better also can mean how well we're able to gather the essence of the profile and not of ourselves. The journalist's DNA is to exclude themselves from the story altogether, to be the ether in the room. If the story is about Denver and you lived there for five years, it's not relevant to the story. It's about the story, never about the journalist. In a way, it's part of journalism's selfless tradition.

To that end, here are a few tips on how to build stories, many of which the amazing coaches at NBC News (that's you—M. L. Flynn, Martin Fletcher, Ed Deitch) have passed down through the years:

- *Why you?* Why are you the right person to build and tell the story? There's enough unoriginal content. Tell the story only you can tell.
- *Write down your story.* Writing down a story makes it more real. Like building that storage shed, it's much easier to talk about it than to build it. But once you do, how you talk about it is much more informative.
- *Practice telling your story out loud.* Saying it out loud makes it more real. Plus, you'll know what it sounds like to friends you've cornered at a dinner party.
- *Throw out your sacred cows.* Sacred cows are those two or three parts of the story you're convinced are sacred and can't be deleted. The problem is, they sometimes get in the way, and few story items are indispensable.
- *Know your audience.* What matters to them? What do they like to do? How do they live? Tailor your story to their needs and interests.
- *Show, don't tell.* Telling says, "He was angry." Showing says, "He clenched his fists and screamed." Few enjoy being told new ideas; more often we like to be shown them.
- *Lead with your best pictures.* Visually or in words, start with your best stuff.
- *See Say; Say See.* Say what you are seeing. And see what you are saying. Say "the barn was on fire." See a picture of a barn on fire. And vice versa. Words must match pictures.
- *Use muscular verbs.* Yes, I know—again with the muscles. Muscular verbs are specific, and they typically convey images and actions. For example, instead of, "The child sat on the stool," you can say, "The child plopped on the stool." *Plopped* conveys something more specific than *sat*.
- *Use shorter sentences.* Not dumber sentences, just not long sentences. It's the way humans talk. (Unless you are Uncle Ramble.)
- *Follow the porpoise.* Just as a porpoise leaps and dives above and below the water, a good story moves back and forth between the

big picture and the details, the surface and the deep. Keep moving, and don't stay low or high too long.

- *Express facts and statistics simply and strategically.* Statistics and facts don't make a story; emotions do. Fifty percent of people agree. (I made that up.)
- *Use quotes that express passion and emotion.* Don't pull quotes that only major in statistics and facts. Use short quotes that give context and convey the human experience in the story.
- *KISS: Keep It Simple, Stupid.* Can you say what you mean in ten rather than fifteen points? (Apparently, some of us need work in this area.)

If you can master these skills, you'll have every right to make the claim, "I'm a storyteller." It's an approach that may cause people to drop a little oxytocin and as a result find empathy and a story that sticks.

One more thought. If your stories have the power to inspire audiences to be selfless, what kind of effect do you think they could have on you? Without getting into more science, one clear benefit is that when we tell a story that highlights others rather than ourselves, we give our selflessness muscles a workout. Marvel Comic's Stan Lee by these standards is "The Rock" of storytellers. His stories only got told better and better.

Lee was all in on inspiring selfless values in his craft. Going as far back as the 1960s, readers would find Marvel creator Stan Lee's cartoon likeness on the pages of the comics. The artist drew himself in for fun, but it later became something much more meaningful. Beginning in the early 2000s, when Hollywood popped out a Marvel film just about every summer (making *Iron Man* more popular, finally!), Lee made cameos in almost every Marvel film. He appeared as an old geezer running a hot dog stand (*X-Men*), a man at the fair (*Spider-Man*), a man reading a newspaper at a crossing (*Daredevil*), and a security guard (*Hulk*). And in the great 2008 *Iron Man* film, when Lee gets out of a limo, Iron Man mistakes him for Hugh Hefner. By the time of Lee's death in 2018 at the age of ninety-five, he had amassed more than a thousand cameos.

Lee wanted to build, tell, and share these heroes' journeys as his comic book creations put themselves in danger to help and save the world. Against all odds. These great stories were built at a cost of $2 million per minute of screen time. (Better and better ain't cheap. And if you think that's a waste of money, go to the "federal budget" section at Congress. gov.) Good stories take an investment—sometimes in money and most often in time and energy. Stan Lee was involved in this craft for the better part of a century.

This kind of investment pays off. Researcher Paul Zak found that if a story captivates, the audience is "likely to continue mimicking the feelings and behaviors of those characters."[7] It's why as you leave the theater after watching *Iron Man*, you suddenly have the desire to become a billionaire playboy superhero trying to save the galaxy with repulsor blasts from your hands. In Zak's words, great stories "affect behavior after the story has ended: we have put ourselves into the narrative."[8]

Zak's research was funded in part by the US Department of Defense's secretive research agency, DARPA (Defense Advanced Research Projects Agency). Why would DARPA, an agency best known for funding research of stealth aircraft or military robots, be interested in storytelling? "Governments often use stories to present information, so understanding how we comprehend them is important," explained Georgia Institute of Technology psychology professor Eric Schumacher to the *Washington Post*.[9]

How can we use the power of (DARPA and Stan Lee) stories to highlight otherishness? Instead of posting the latte pic, a political rant, or your fat Christmas hen baby, post a story. Ideally, it could be about selflessness. Did you observe a person at a grocery store who was helping someone out? Do you have a family member in the military? Did you make a decision that hurt you financially but benefited others? Did you witness a random act of kindness? It's worth telling the story—even if it's as seemingly insignificant as a stranger on a train giving up their seat to someone else. Such everyday stories of selflessness are little jolts of inspiration that jump-start the soul.

Social media is an easy and accessible way to share stories of selflessness with the larger world. Your main audience is the people who love you. (Unless you're in politics.) Even if you don't want to put such stories on Facebook or Twitter, start making it a habit to tell stories at dinner with your family or over coffee with friends. You may be surprised how your stories of selflessness resonate with your loved ones.

Philosopher James K. A. Smith wrote, "Shaping of our character is, to a great extent, the effect of stories that have captivated us, that have sunk into our bones—stories that 'picture' what we think life is about, what constitutes the 'good life.' We live *into* the stories we've absorbed; we become characters in the drama that has captivated us."[10] Or, more succinctly, he wrote, "When our imagination is hooked, *we're* hooked."[11]

Telling stories of bravery inspires bravery in the hearts of the listeners. Telling stories of honesty creates listeners who want to be truthful. What are the stories that hook you? What are the stories you want to live into and be shaped by? Go find them and share. I'd love to read your stories of selflessness in the comments section below. (Oh, whoops! I forgot I wasn't on social media.)

OWNING OUR OWN STICKY STORY

Much of my life, I've been crafting one story. It's the story of someone in my family who was unsure of himself, took a risk, and made the best of difficult conditions. I tell this story because there was a time when I used to make fun of him, and I didn't even realize I was doing it.

I've already mentioned how I became an ugly American as a teenager. I made fun of the new Asian immigrants who came to my middle and high school. They ate funny foods, smelled different, dressed like FOBs—people "fresh off the boat," a prejudiced, derogatory term. *I wasn't like them*, I thought. I wanted to be viewed as an American. I was born here, and I needed to make sure my friends knew that. Instead of carrying around my birth certificate, I joined with the chorus of others who were mocking the immigrants. Only later did I begin to realize that I was also indirectly making fun of my grandfather. He, like these immigrants, came to the United States with little treasure and a lot of risk.

There's no excuse for the way I acted back in the day, but I wish I had known more of my grandfather's story. Cognitive psychologists have determined that hearing and reading other people's stories increase our ability to imagine what it's like to be someone other than ourselves. Deprived of my grandfather's true story, which is also my story, I wasn't able to tap into the empathy that may have saved me from becoming the ugly American.

Here is the story that helped me embrace and understand who my grandfather was—a man who was in some ways selfish but in other ways selfless in that he ultimately made it possible for me to be born an American.

. . . .

My parents named their first child Mark, and the next one Robert. By the time I arrived, I was two weeks past my due date and weighed in at a hefty nine pounds, eleven ounces. I was fatter than a Christmas hen— the unit of measure back then. The wide-eyed doctor said to my father, "Mr. Lui, you have a sumo wrestler! He's a big one." (Yes, I'm Chinese, and sumo is a sport from Japan—only thirty seconds old, and already I'm dealing with this stuff.)

"What's his name?" the doctor asked.

My father shrugged his shoulders. He was just glad he could give away those now clammy-handed cigars he had been holding for fourteen days in the third-floor waiting room of the baby ward. For three days after I was born, he and my mother couldn't decide on a name. As I lay in my plastic box next to other babies in plastic boxes behind the glass window, my name card remained blank. Finally, on my fourth day there, my parents decided on Richard Lui. My identity was settled.

Or so it seemed. I learned my true identity later when I was eight. But I was also too young to know what true identity meant.

I never knew my grandfather on my dad's side. He died at the age of fifty-three from lung cancer. But I did know my grandmother. A broad woman, she was six feet tall. You've heard the comparisons to linebackers? That was Grandma. Having birthed thirteen children of her own, she must have been downright fatigued by the time I met her. It initially scared me that she didn't smile much, didn't speak English, and kept her house dark—three traits that come in handy on Halloween. Over time, as I spent more time cooking with her, I saw her smiling and laughing. By the time she died, I knew she was a kindhearted woman.

I was amazed to see the hodgepodge of Chinese grieving rituals mixed with American ones. As a grieving family, we weren't supposed to shower for a certain amount of time, and we weren't supposed to wear red, yellow, or brown. In the United States, appropriate grieving attire has historically been black. As a Christian family, we participated in some rituals but not others.

Weeks after the burial, as is traditional, we returned to my grandmother's grave. We brought our grandmother's and grandfather's favorite foods. (Asian folks are the only ones I know who have cemetery picnics.) Chicken. Noodles. Vegetables. Whisky. Cigarettes. We set it all on the grave for thirty minutes for the enjoyment and in the honor of the deceased. Then we ate it. Finally, we burned paper money for them to spend in the afterlife. Twice a year, it was like we were in an Asian hip-hop video.

My grandmother was laid to rest next to my grandfather. When the tombstone was installed, we returned. When I first approached the plots to inspect the new stone, I made an unwelcome discovery. The tombstone had an error—and it was etched in the granite. Instead of Lui, the last name was Wong.

"They made a mistake on our name!" my siblings and I exclaimed. (I know we're cheap, but did we have to get a refurbished model for this tombstone?) My father went over to speak with his eight sisters and three brothers in a sideline huddle. He came back expressionless. "It's not a mistake."

My dad's parents were not who we thought they were. Me neither. At the age of eight, I learned I was not Richard Lui. (After all the name drama when I was born.) My real name was Richard Wong!

I had the Wong name.

My grandparents had participated in an immigration hoax to get into the United States and had gotten away with it. They were illegal immigrants. I am the grandson of illegal immigrants. (I'm a hit at cocktail parties when I bring this up.) My grandparents committed a crime. They were scared about being discovered and kept it secret until their deaths—even from their own children. Only the oldest of the thirteen knew the truth and connected the dots for my dad.

The first dot was laid back in the late 1800s, when thousands of Chinese immigrants lived in America, building railroads and working in mines under conditions now considered to be indentured servitude. They were made to live outside of the city limits in Chinese areas—out of sight and out of mind. As jobs began to be abandoned by previous immigrant groups such as the Irish, the Chinese took them on. Laundry was a good example. Then as the economy weakened, people saw how they had filled the laundry market gap and began to worry that Chinese workers would "take" yet more jobs. Plus, they didn't look like everyone else, often spoke a different language, and ate smelly food. They became targets of racism and violence, even lynchings. California passed a pole law, so if you used a pole to move two baskets of laundry down the street over your shoulder, you had to pay a fine. (Guess who used poles in their laundry businesses.)

California Senator John Miller described the Chinese as a "degraded and inferior race" when he introduced the Chinese Exclusion Act of 1882.[12] The act stated that Chinese laborers endangered "the good order of certain localities" and prohibited them from entering our country.[13] It was the only law in our nation's history to ban a single country's citizens and, in effect, a single ethnicity from immigrating to America.

Then in 1906, an earthquake with an estimated force of 7.9 on the Richter Scale rocked San Francisco, causing major damage and fires. City Hall, with almost all of Chinatown's public records, went up in flames. Sensing an opportunity to secure themselves in a nation brimming with anti-Chinese sentiment, many Chinese immigrants claimed they were born in San Francisco and therefore had birthright citizenship. The government had no records to determine whether or not they were lying.

Reluctantly, the government gave them the stamp of approval. Practically every Chinese American went down to City Hall and claimed they had six, seven, or even eight children "on paper" back in China. Since they now had birthright citizenship, they were allowed to bring those children over to the United States legally. However, for their claims to be true, every Chinese woman in California prior to 1906 would have had to have birthed six hundred sons.[14] (My grandma was clearly a slacker, coming up 587 kids short.)

One of these claimants, a Mr. Lui, told government officials he had children in China. Using a middleman, he sold the immigration slots for his fictitious children to people in China for today's equivalent of about $1,800 each.[15] My grandfather, Wong Lee, bought one of Mr. Lui's seven slots, becoming a "paper son" to this complete stranger.

On the treacherous journey across the Pacific Ocean, my grandfather was given little books and maps with detailed information about his "paper parents." From those, he memorized key details about his "paper family"—details that included geography of the village he supposedly came from, the layout and look of his fictitious family home, and his other pretend brothers and sisters. He was instructed to throw these training booklets and maps overboard when he reached the Golden Gate. His voyage, like that of so many others, ended at Angel Island. I stood on the grounds of the same immigration station when I did my story on paper sons and daughters for CNN nearly a century later.

If the officials reached a conclusion that the immigrants were frauds, they put them back on a boat to China. My grandpa passed the interrogation and was permitted to enter as a United States citizen. It must have been frightening to know he was committing a criminal act before even taking a single step on American soil.

My grandfather first worked at a restaurant and then became a barber in a one-chair shop in Ross Alley, now the oldest and most famous alley in San Francisco's Chinatown. In the 1960s, it became home to the Golden Gate Fortune Cookie Factory, where tourists still flock to watch women hunched over the machines, folding the quickly cooling batter and tucking a little paper fortune inside before it hardens. The printing shop for the fortunes is next door. My grandfather's nondescript barber shop is still there, now run by different people, tucked behind a red door under a red awning in a building painted green like a dragon.

My grandparents always feared their children would be sent back because of their deception. They promised each other they would take their illegal immigration secret to their grave—and they did. The first time their actual names were revealed was on their tombstone. In a way, it was their coming-out party.

As did so many others, Grandpa came to the United States thinking, *I don't want my grandchildren to be like me, a poor Chinese farmer.* Thank you, Grandpa, for risking it all. Your dream came true. I am a national news anchor, not a poor Chinese farmer.

Thank you.

• • • • • • • • • •

It took me thirty years to fully decipher that story. Every five or ten years, I'd ask a question that would bring me to a new chapter about where I came from. After I pieced a large part of the story together when I was in my late thirties, I think I found a good part of myself. Maybe better to say, I accepted a good part of myself. An interesting thing I'm learning today is that well-thought-out stories help us understand people who are significantly unlike us, but they can also help us understand *ourselves*. For me, that moment of understanding and accepting my "illegal immigration" past meant I understood what was happening in the millions of other communities working through it.

"Honey, you have to read this...they like chewing slippers too."

© Tak Toyoshima

If a little extra oxytocin can drop for those who hear sticky stories so that they embrace others, the same can be said of those who are telling sticky stories.

Section Five

GREEN PATCHES

Chapter Seventeen

GRATITUDE

B rian was too shy to give me his number," Rocio said with a smirk. "He gave his phone number to his friend to give me after he walked out. But his friend decided to give it to me while he was still there." Brian, with a six-foot height befitting his Marine Corps roots, blushed as he looked at his wife.

Sitting side by side in front of the camera, the Alvarados looked like they had come straight out of the interview scenes in *When Harry Met Sally*. "He was going to get deployed. So we interacted by emails, letters, and phone calls. That was basically our courtship."

Now in their early forties, the Alvarados routinely get attention in public. They pinch each other's cheeks and cabooses, but that's not why they get people pointing. It's Brian, who has an incurable disease that has stolen half his weight. Brian gets the "ugly stares," as Rocio calls them. Brian is one of an estimated tens of thousands of men and women from the armed forces believed to be suffering from diseases after working in burn pits. Burn pits were used to incinerate everything from plastics to chemicals and human waste—all without wearing protective equipment or masks. Today Brian battles throat cancer. The disease has stripped him of his voice. He communicates with what sounds like grunts, understood only by Rocio and their preteen daughter, Rhianna. He breathes through a tracheal tube and eats through a feeding tube.[1]

I asked them how they managed to find the silver lining. "For us, it is more being home together and just thanking God for giving us another year with him being here," Rocio said humbly. She was thankful for the time she has with him to raise their daughter together.

Displays of gratitude are actually fairly common today. The hashtag #Blessed fills social media timelines, "offering cover to revel in schadenfreude: I'm grateful for *my* safe home, *my* great family, *my* good job, as opposed to some other sucker's terrible life," as the *Atlantic*'s Sonya Huber puts it.[2] When sincere, gratitude has been associated with benefits ranging from "fewer aches and pains to improved sleep to better cardiovascular health."[3] But here's a twist. Instead of asking "What have I been blessed with?" consider, "What would life be like without the blessings I have?"

Psychologists call this "mental subtraction." By considering how different our lives would be without something or someone, we learn more about why we appreciate those things and people so much. Addition by subtraction. (It's enough to make an arithmetic student's head explode.) One study asked participants to consider what life would be like if a positive event, such as meeting a romantic partner, had never happened. The participants reported elevated feelings of gratitude. Some were "surprised by how unlikely that meeting actually was," and how "lucky [they] were that it happened as it did."[4]

At the end of my interview with the Alvarados, I asked Rocio to consider the same mental subtraction question: "What would life be like without Brian?"

She answered hesitantly. "I haven't really . . . don't want to think about it, basically." Rocio didn't need to imagine it. Her husband's disease could take him at any time, and she had done the mental subtraction math in her mind over and over. But each day they had together was enough.

A SELFLESS COUSIN

When I was but a young, self-proclaimed missionary attending church, my mother would play the piano and we'd sing the hymn "Count Your Blessings," which encouraged us to name our blessings "one by one" to "see what God hath done." The hymn writer knew it wasn't ideal to acknowledge your blessings in bulk. (After all, this is church, not Costco.) The hymn points to an important truth: gratitude is essential for a happy and healthful life.

Gratitude, the first cousin of selflessness, simply means being thankful. When you feel it, you're buoyed by what others have done for you or given to you. Gratitude stands on the shoulders of selflessness, since you can't be grateful if you believe people owe you something. Gratitude requires the death of entitlement, which is then replaced by the awe of generosity. We recognize the beauty of what we have instead of being jealous of what others have. In her novel *Gilead*, author Marilynne Robinson put it this way: "I don't know exactly what covetise is, but in my experience it is not so much desiring someone else's virtue or happiness as rejecting it, taking offense at the beauty of it."[5]

Gratitude is not just a Christian notion. "Gratitude is a highly prized human disposition in Jewish, Christian, Muslim, Buddhist, and Hindu thought . . . Indeed, the consensus among the world's religious and ethical writers is that people are morally obligated to feel and express gratitude in response to received benefits," wrote psychologists Robert Emmons and Michael McCullough.[6]

The researchers found that the "Count Your Blessings" hymn was right. They discovered that cultivating gratitude in college students helped boost optimism and exercise levels and made the students feel better about their lives. Since gratitude is also associated with positive relationships with others, its practice is a win-win—for the individual and the community.

Another happiness researcher, Barbara Fredrickson, agrees: "When you express your gratitude in words or actions, you not only boost your own positivity but [other people's] as well. And in the process you reinforce their kindness and strengthen your bond to each other."[7] It stands to reason that when expressing gratitude to a romantic partner, it enhances this special bond too. Writ large, gratitude helps strengthen community bonds. It is Fixodent for the community. When we see others more positively and charitably than before, interdependence and cooperation with others grow.[8] Call it the gratitude-selflessness two-way street.

LITTLE THINGS

Thank you, blue chair. You held me up for more than a year. I spilled chili on you. Even a Diet Coke here and there. You kept working. I will find a good home for you.

Thank you, chili. You were delicious. Sorry I spilled you on my blue chair.

Goodbye, bicycle. You took me to many places across Manhattan. You brought home groceries. You stopped quickly to keep me from getting hit by Manhattan taxis. Thank you, brown bike. I will find you a good new home.

I started the Marie Kondo process of living simply by letting go of things in my small apartment. I watched her streaming series as the organizing guru came into people's homes to help organize their lives. She knelt on the ground and bowed to different corners of the home to thank them for keeping its inhabitants safe. At first, it's a little strange to watch the petite consultant talk to inanimate objects as if they're old friends about to embark on a cross-country move. (Then again, I'm known to speak—while locked in a room for hours—to cameras and lights, with no one else around. Who's the crazy one?)

Gratitude today is a multimillion-dollar industry, ranging from Marie's KonMari website to the dozens of gratitude-logging apps available for download on the App Store.

I decided to try out one of these gratitude apps. I'm now in my third week. It's simple. I write down five things or people I'm grateful for. I do it while I'm waiting for a taxi or in the bathroom or during credits to the eightieth streaming series I've watched in the last several months. Each day's session takes about two minutes. It doesn't take long to think of people and things I'm grateful for. Here are some things I wrote down over the last three weeks:

1. I'm grateful for my brother Rob for giving all of his energy selflessly to care for my parents.
2. I'm grateful for health so I can get up every day and try to make things better for people.
3. I'm grateful for clean water.
4. I'm grateful for Mom, whose kindness and faith inspire me.

I noticed I tended to list people as opposed to things some days, and vice versa other days. Clean water was definitely on the list the day I changed my water filter cartridge. A week in, I wanted to do more to put my gratitude into action. I began to be more deliberate about saying thank you to coworkers. I planned to get a gift for Elaine, who has been a custodian at 30 Rock for thirty-plus years and who just this year decided to retire. She stopped me in the halls as she was emptying a garbage can to say with a smile, "Goodbye." So far so good with this app.

The Wharton School found that employees whose supervisors expressed gratitude for their hard work were 50 percent more productive.[9] And there are school lesson plans for gratitude journals available from the George Lucas Educational Foundation.[10]

Practicing gratitude is not some New Age hokum. In the times of Julius Caesar, statesman and philosopher Cicero wrote, "This one virtue [gratitude] is not only the greatest, but is also the parent of all the other virtues."[11] Consider the mental subtraction tool here to understand what Cicero meant by that. What would virtues be without gratitude? Could we have loyalty without gratitude for the people to whom we are loyal? Compassion without appreciation of those who care for us?

My dad stopped talking about a year ago. We weren't sure if he was still in there. On my visits, I wore a name tag to remind him, "I'm Richard, your son." As my brother had done, I read his favorite Bible passages, hoping to bring him back from the blank stares with something he loved and knew well. I knew he was watching and listening. But I wanted more confirmation he was there, that he was still okay. On one of my visits to the care facility, I read a passage from 2 Corinthians, speaking through a little battery-powered amplifier so he could hear.

"Dad, if you can hear me, *blink*." His eyes closed slowly and stayed shut for two seconds, then opened as he looked at me.

"Dad, if you can hear me, blink again." I took out my phone to record it. He looked at me and did it again with another long, deliberate blink. I shared the video with the family.

He's still fighting. There's still life in him. And I'm grateful for that hope.

GRATITUDE VISITS

On my next visit to the nursing home, I came armed with my usual kit: name tag, shaver, amplifier. But with a new addition. A letter. I wanted to express in writing why I was grateful for everything Dad has done. Teaching me to defend myself when I was a kid. Showing me how to shave. And most recently, showing me how to care for others. This prolonged illness is not what any of us would have chosen, but Dad is still teaching me. He is teaching me the unexpected power of selflessness.

Researchers suggest taking time every six months to do a "gratitude visit." The steps are simple:

- Write your letter: "Dear _____."
- Describe why you are grateful—specificity and details are key.
- Be heartfelt and go for depth.
- Get personal.
- Try mental subtraction—what would life be like without them?
- Plan your visit. Let the recipient know you have a surprise.
- Read the letter out loud when you meet.[12]

One study on young adults found that even for those who were normally unhappy, a gratitude visit significantly raised their spirits for up to two months.[13] It's easy to see why these visits have shown such promising results. When we show gratitude, we're giving thanks for someone else and the way they have cared for us. "The letter affirms positive things in your life and reminds you how others have cared for you—life seems less bleak and lonely if someone has taken such a supportive interest in us," write researchers at UC Berkeley.[14]

So I unfolded the sheet of paper I had spent fifty years living and six years writing in my mind. A celebration of what he had given me but had only recognized now.

Dear Dad . . .

Chapter Eighteen

PASSING IT ON

When I was a kid, we would on occasion hop in the car and head to my maternal grandparents' house in Los Angeles. When we arrived at their little house, my grandfather would lift his wrinkled finger and point to a picture he had hung over the fireplace mantel back in 1943. It was a California Shipbuilding Corporation print that showcased a Liberty ship. These fairly inexpensive cargo ships delivered much-needed supplies to Allied troops in the Pacific and Atlantic during World War II.

"Look," he'd say, pointing to the cargo ship, though it had been decades since he had forged the metal. "I built that." My grandfather made guns for those Liberty ships. Each of the ships had one main deck gun, which was at the tip of the bow. In the 1940s, his Los Angeles shipyard hosted a special family day so workers' families could see the work they were doing to support the war effort.

"See this metal?" my grandpa had said to his children as he knocked on a large, round sheet, causing the eyes of his eight-year-old daughter Rose to widen. "I bolt it, weld it, and make it into a gun to put on the ship. This is its only line of defense in the open ocean."

Though my grandfather had been born in China, he passed on his patriotic pride for his new country to his children. Four of his sons enlisted in the Army and Navy, and he placed their enlistment photos proudly on the mantel—each of the sons sharply dressed in their uniforms. Those old black-and-white military photos of my uncles were a little dusty but still proudly displayed. Two of my dad's brothers served in the military too.

While her brothers were off in the service, Rose, my mother, took care of the home. As the youngest daughter, she cooked all of the family meals as soon as she was able to reach the stove. She put in twelve hours a day at their corner store and—somehow—still attended school. (I'm still petitioning Marvel to feature her as their next superhero.) Only at midnight, when her other daily tasks were done, did she finally have the chance to study.

When that hardworking young girl was ten, she also attended church, even though none of her siblings did. Once, in an "only in America" kind of moment, a teenage Shirley Temple came and sang in the choir with her, an unforgettable moment. But the most life-changing church moment happened later at Chinese First Presbyterian in Los Angeles. It was where she met a young man named Stephen.

Stephen was attending Fuller Theological Seminary, and became a Reverend during a time when there were few faces like his in seminary. My mom, a young choir singer, must have looked at my father and thought he was a catch. A tall, young Reverend who was Chinese American? Not a common character in 1958 America. They married soon after in a ceremony with all of the American traditions—white dress, big cake, everything—but with Chinese flair.

Immediately, they encountered financial hardship. The demand for youth ministers was practically nonexistent. Even when my dad finally did get a job, his salary was so low that the newlyweds lived with my grandparents until I was born eight years later.

My siblings and I had a happy childhood. Even though Dad's church salary wasn't much, Mom set aside her career as a schoolteacher to stay home and care for us kids. Among other things, she taught us how to bake. My brothers were allergic to milk and butter, so prepackaged grocery store treats were out of the question. We learned to bake cookies and make apple pie from scratch, perfecting the flaky crust with ingredients that were safe for my brothers. My dad's parents may have come over from China in the elaborate "paper sons" immigration scheme I mentioned earlier, but we were as American as the apple pie we made weekly.

My mother, a Southern California girl, loved diner food, though she would occasionally make something unexpected like ratatouille. I think my dad wished she would make more traditional Chinese food, such as tomato beef chow mein.

"Why am I cooking every night?" she asked my dad. Even when she resumed teaching, she was still cooking for everyone. That's how Fridays became my dad's designated dinner night. At first, he attempted to make fairly simple meals—Lawry's chicken wings and spaghetti with bottled sauce. But even those dishes were a stretch for him. Eventually, he gave up and bought pizza. (Laziness: 1; Chinese Traditions: 0. Fridays got way better.)

Mom was musically gifted, picking up a new instrument every five to ten years—piano, jazz guitar, acoustic guitar, violin. She drew the line at tuba. She also played the piano for church services, even though the choir, as I would kiddingly say to her, was one only God could love. We kids could barely restrain ourselves as the off-key notes wafted through the church to our back row—the audio version of expired mayo. Sometimes Mom would catch my eye, but I knew I wouldn't get in trouble for cutting up. She had perfect pitch and could detect the flat notes better than anyone. Yet she faithfully played or sang every Sunday morning.

After dinner, Mom left the plates on the table and pans on the stove. With her work for the day done, she went to the front room and sat down at her upright piano. She'd run her hands over the worn wooden keys and play hymns. "Rosey is tickling those ivories," my brother and I would say.

"O Lord my God," she sang, "when I in awesome wonder consider all the works thy hands have made." While these after-dinner songs wafted through the house, I cleaned the kitchen. Dad helped me clear the plates. Most of the time, I didn't feel full, so if there were remnants left on anyone's plate, they usually ended up in my mouth rather than in the garbage. As we cleaned up, Dad and I chatted about big things and little things. I'm not sure I ever stopped to fully absorb those ordinary moments. I probably never paused to listen to my mom's hymns, nor really appreciated what it felt like to be in a conversation with Dad. I was just a kid—worried more about licking the plates clean and the Russians attacking us than spending much time in reflection. Real kid stuff.

I appreciate those ordinary times now though.

My parents made very little money, but they loved us—imperfectly, yet consistently. They sent me to summer camp whenever we could afford it. Affording it required my dad to sell 150 cans of toffee peanuts to other social workers. "My son wants to go to summer camp, and he's selling these amazing peanuts to make his way there." I heard him say that for weeks, all so he and my mom could afford to send me to camp. Camp set me more or less on a good path. (Okay, okay, one of those year's camps was the site of that infamous panic attack, yes. But it wasn't bad enough to keep me away—and it was good enough for me to go the toffee peanut route of entrepreneurial fundraising.)

One year at camp, my friend and I started a daily newspaper. (Secretly, of course, because that's more exciting.) Everybody wants to be the editor of an underground press. We worked into the dark of night, kept our sources close, and didn't reveal our daily schedule in order to make our early-morning clandestine printing deadlines. (I may be overplaying it a bit here, but hey, we were high schoolers and had a love for Christian folkloric drama with the best of them.) Admittedly, our "paper" was an 8-1/2 x 14 piece of notebook paper with a hand-drawn masthead. We were teens at a church camp. And a bit crazy. At 6:00 a.m., after being awake all night, we'd head to the copy shop and rush back. (Yes, this was before you could buy printers for less than the price of a dinner at Waffle House.) Then we'd fold them and stick them under the doors of the cabins and watch as people woke up and began wondering who on earth was behind such a literary masterpiece.

The *Daily Bugle* was full of humor and jokes, because if church camp isn't funny, nothing is. This is when I first marveled at the power of the written word, as poorly written as our words were, replete with bad grammar and cheesy puns. Though I do remember many nights when we would laugh for hours. My parents laughed at us and knew it was good, clean fun. They'd save money to send me to this camp each summer.

This annual experience helped me grow in my passions. I discovered my passion for politics when the controversial Proposition 13 was passed in California. I didn't know whether I was left or right, but I did know that Prop 13 meant less money for my teacher-mom, which meant less money for me. I expressed my strong opposition on bus rides to school to my friends. I dreamed of one day writing about policy and foreign affairs for prestigious publications. Clearly I was trying to upgrade from the *Daily Bugle*.

The principal allowed me to graduate—thanks to my parents' interference—but I didn't go to college after high school. One of my first jobs after graduation happened when I was seventeen years old.

And that first job was also the result of my parents' love and their relationships with others in the community. "Uncle Alan" Wong asked me to work for his campaign for the board of City College of San Francisco. Though we weren't related, he treated me like we were. He and my parents had gone to church together since they were teens themselves. I jumped at the chance, eager to learn about the inner workings of politics. My interest in the subject grew, along with my understanding of what it takes to be a real-life politician.

Two years later, I was as surprised as anyone when he asked me to be his official campaign manager. He had already won in two previous elections, and he thought I was ready to handle the pressures and strategy of mounting a third campaign. Though I knew it was a big job for someone my age, I loved having a bigger title and more responsibility. And so after just a little deliberation, I stepped up to the plate.

Uncle Alan overestimated me. The victory slipped out of our hands on Election Day, and I was devastated. It's one thing to lose a campaign; it's another to lose one for a dear family friend who had taken a chance on me.

When I think of Uncle Alan's mentorship, I realize the world could accuse him of giving me responsibility when he shouldn't have. He lost the election under my "leadership." Even so, I can't help but believe I'm where I am now because he took a chance on me. Knowing how much he valued investing in others, his mentorship could be considered successful. In a way, he truly did triumph many decades later through teaching me such crucial lessons.

My meandering, eclectic path went from being an unsuccessful campaign manager to a fired Mrs. Fields manager. After four years—at age twenty-two, the age at which many students graduate from college—I realized I couldn't work in cookies forever. Like the cookies themselves, this job was going to get stale eventually.

I decided I wanted to go to college. But I hadn't taken the SAT. Plus, with my dismal high school grades, no university would take me. City College of San Francisco, at dollars a credit, did.

At CCSF, I rediscovered education. Because I was a shy kid in high school, I took a speech class taught by a professor named Ethel Beal, hoping it would jolt me out of my shyness. I was so into the class that I did my homework—which was to practice speaking. I practiced in the parking lot, orating my heart out to parked cars. It was the only "A" I got in my first semester. In the end, not only did I win several speech awards for CCSF, but I also went on to find myself in a career in public speaking in front of a camera and lights and with lots of makeup.

Another professor, Mimi Riordan, inspired me to stretch my abilities and enjoy English, and she encouraged me to read national papers such as the *Washington Post* and the *Wall Street Journal.* I took three inspirational English classes from her. She grabbed my mind and shook it. "You now have the responsibility to learn on your own," she told me. "I'm teaching you how to do it."

After two years, I completed an associate's degree in 1990.

When I finally graduated from college, my parents (in many ways, my *long-suffering* parents) sat in the stands beaming at me. They didn't even act embarrassed when I did a cartwheel across the stage. (Those were the days. Now I cramp up just bending over to tie my shoelaces.)

Eventually, I got my BA from the University of California, Berkeley and then earned an MBA from the University of Michigan Ross School of Business. Several years later, after I had become a journalist, I got an award in San Francisco for community volunteerism.

By this time, "Uncle Alan" had become a wheelchair user because of a late-night fall that left him only able to move his head. It took a lot of planning to get to the venue for the award ceremony in his mechanical wheelchair, but he was there. Though he couldn't really move anything except his head and his lips, he gave the introductory speech for my award. Somehow he was smiling at me and telling me that the election loss we had experienced twenty-five years earlier was all part of a plan.

While writing this book, I got a text informing me of Uncle Alan's passing. It brought back many fond memories of him mentoring me. I was blessed by the people who surrounded me, the people who invested in my life and helped build my character, the people who saw past what looked like failure and taught me how to fulfill my destiny.

Destiny is a funny thing. It is a quiet friend most of the time. But then it winks at you.

October 2020 it did it again. In a twist of roles, I was now the presenter of an award from the same organization (Asian, Inc.) that gave me the award that Uncle Alan presented to me. Except this time I'd be presenting to Uncle Alan posthumously. I was floored by the symbolism.

So I started my research for my remarks. Along the way, I discovered an old website for Alan Wong's campaign for college board. Only it wasn't old; it was new.

In the same year my uncle Alan Wong left us, a new, fresh-faced Alan Wong was running for the same elected seat! Not spelled Allen Wong. Not spelled Allan Wang. But the very same spelling—ALAN WONG!

Uncle Alan was winking at me.

Destiny was winking at me.

God was winking at me.

Pass it on, Richard.

When I think of my parents, I imagine them as the support crew on the side of the marathon course, throwing me bottles of water and power bars as I negotiated some tough hills and valleys. And yes, they're Asian! Did they not get the Asian parenting manual? You know, rule number one: scowl and scream when the grade point average is below 4.9. (Asian parents think it goes that high.) Rule number two: if he doesn't go to class, make him stare at the wall for eight hours while balancing a plate on his head.

Instead, they let me fail, and learn.

One of the fondest childhood memories I have is of my father reading *The Story of Babar* to me. Babar was the kind, talking French elephant king in a three-piece suit with a crown and pants. There was something comforting about my father's proximity, his cadence as he read.

Years later, when Dad got sick, I'd sit next to him on the couch. Instead of him reading to me, teaching me the alphabet, I helped him read and do a third-grade-level crossword puzzle on an iPad. It was one of the last normal activities we were able to do, and he laughed and smiled. I knew it would be one of the last of a lifetime of side by sides.

Dad was always proud that I had ended up becoming a journalist on television—that Asian American man with his broadcast. Especially considering the fact his parents had come here illegally in such a dramatic way. And considering my own youthful struggles.

© Tak Toyoshima

A few months ago, I was taking a bus from New York to the nation's capital. As the city came into view, I realized I had come a long way from the days when I went to bed with my stomach not quite full. Now I was carrying forward the precious package my parents had given to me—to remember to be selfless. And in a way, I was fulfilling even my grandparents' selfless yearnings for a better life for their children. The seat next to me was empty. But it wasn't. They were with me. Holding me. I felt it.

I felt the warmth of all the people who had poured love into me over the years.

In a way, I am a paper son too.

I wake up some days and realize that I am not who I thought I was.

Reflecting at the halfway point, I now know the second half will also be built on the shoulders of those who are selfless.

ACKNOWLEDGMENTS

I want to thank my parents and siblings. For being good people. For dividing and tackling the tasks of caregiving—doctor appointments, test results, medicines, activities, visitors, and more. I'm honored to be fighting the good fight with you. I also want to thank our extended family of close to two hundred people who have always made us laugh and learn and appreciate working as a team.

I'd like to thank the entire team at HarperCollins Zondervan, especially Carolyn McCready, who understood this book in its soul and provided wonderful edits to make it the best it could be. She always exuded a can-do attitude and practical approach; it was an honor to work with such an experienced practitioner. Thank you to Paul Fisher, Webb Younce, Dirk Buursma, Trinity McFadden, Andrea Kelly, Alyssa Karhan, and all the others at Zondervan who have given so much of themselves to get this done. And to Robin Barnett and Shannon Stowe for your commitment to getting the good word out.

Thank you to the UTA team—Brandi Bowles and Pilar Queen—for your vision for this book. I would never have been able to accomplish this without your expertise and guidance. Much gratitude to Rick Ramage for being a friend and listening and rooting while keeping me honest in the whims of my life and career. You are the best in the business.

Thank you to my 30 Rock, NBC News, MSNBC, and Comcast NBCUniversal family: ML Flynn, for teaching me how to consider journalistic writing as poetry and for blowing open my mind over the power of words; Martin Fletcher, for being there to guide me when I first joined; Elena Nachmanoff and Jessica Kurdali, for finding me, bringing me in, and making sure I succeeded to the best of my ability; Yvette Miley, for always believing in me, reminding me that as a journalist I could do almost anything, and supporting my caregiving for my father and my career development simultaneously; and to Cesar Conde, for his encouragement and his groundbreaking thinking and work, for being a great barometer for us in the news industry.

To all of those close to me who had to listen to me talk about the book endlessly—Ly, Mic, Jeanette, Kevin, Laura, and others who heard me tell these stories. Again. And again. And again. This includes the gajillionaires—Bob, Chad, Jen, Venkat—who suggested I shouldn't become a journalist but who stuck with me when I did it anyway; they have helped me through this first book. To my Ross Business School family—so many of you to thank. And to anyone who has gone to the University of Michigan, ever—thank you.

To Mike Breslin for giving me my first job out of college, for letting me implement a Kanban scheduling system, and for taking me to a shooting range for the first time. To the kind employers after that, thank you, Mercer Strategy, Oliver Wyman, Citibank, Singapore Technologies / Green Dot, and CNN Worldwide. To my film family at Prisca Productions and *Sky Blossom*—thank you for inspiring me to make movies, to commit to the time to get it right.

Thank you to the community organizations that brought me in to volunteer and that pushed me to think big—Plan International USA (Judithe Registre, Meg Cangany, Robin Costello, Because I Am a Girl campaign), Alzheimer's Association (Kate Meyer, Jen Wirth, Ashley Bryan), AARP (Daphne Kwok, Ron Mori, Bob Stephen), Wallace H. Coulter Foundation (Sue Van, Susie Van, Dennis Van), Asian American Journalists Association, the United Nations and UN Women, and the Elizabeth Dole Foundation (Senator Elizabeth Dole, Steve Schwab, Hidden Heroes campaign). And to Emil Lin, who for more than a decade has encouraged me to give back to hundreds of organizations and gatherings.

Thank you to Lorraine Nam for the cover and interior art that help shape the book's dynamic visual identity. Thanks to Wendi Gu, who connected us. The combination of Lorraine and Curt Diepenhorst made the book's cover look beautiful. Also to Kait Lamphere for designing the interior to make it inviting and comfortable, Paul Cheung and Io Kurihara for creating the informative graphics that grace these pages, and Tak Toyoshima for your creativity and humor in the cartoons. Working through the creative process with you all was great fun.

Thank you to Dhaya Lakshminarayanan and Matt Koff for helping shape this book's humor, and for all the laughing out loud we did along the way. I met this duo through Ronny Chieng, who gives so much not only in making our lives more jocular but also heartier. Thank you to Analicia Sotelo, Josè Olivarez, and Eloisa Amezcua, who helped bring poetic grace and the idea of alternate stanzas to the book. To my DDB buddies David George and T Vasabhuti for your guidance through word and visual design on this project and so many other projects.

Thank you to Pelin Kesebir, researcher at the University of Wisconsin, for being a stalwart partner in undertaking our original research for this book, as well as for making sure the data and research we quoted served our goal of achieving a greater understanding of selflessness.

Thank you to Alex Lo for taking on the role of assistant researcher, yeoman drafter, and all-around book utility player at any moment's notice, as well as for the big and small ideas offered along the way to get this book to market and beyond.

And last but certainly not the least, to my indefatigable collaborator, Nancy French. You have been a trusted sounding board for all my ideas, a more than enthusiastic participant in my harebrained plans. And most importantly, you've been the best inspiration and encouragement one could ever hope for. Your humble and humorous advice during our trips around the country and our writing process are the bedrock of why this book made it this far. You are the best book sherpa in publishing. I'm so grateful to have learned from the best.

Finally to all the journalists—those who give their all for free speech and facts—even as we mourn the more than sixty journalists who are killed each year, we carry forward your passion for selfless truth.

Appendix One

OAR PLAYBOOKS

This section gives a glimpse into various playbooks you may have picked up from *Enough About Me*. Think of these as little mind cards to carry with you, bite-sized plans to help you move forward. And while you're at it, try putting together some of your own. Like the oar we put in the water with our boatmates, synchronized for forward movement, use **O** for objective, **A** for action, and **R** for result. I would love to hear about the OARs you put in the water. Send your stories to OAR@richardlui.com. I'm looking forward to learning from them.

PLAYBOOK 1: RELATIONSHIPS

Three Lunches	*Gratitude Journaling*
Objective: To make connections with people who are different from you.	*Objective:* To count and appreciate your blessings.
Action: Make a list of three people you'd never imagine hanging out with. Invite them to lunch.	*Action:* Once a week, write a list of at least three things you're grateful for.
Result: You will have potential new friends! And a greater ease around those who are different from you that is the result of the reduction or elimination of the stress hormone cortisol.	*Result:* You will have a more optimistic outlook, an increased appreciation for the people in your life, and fewer doctor visits.

(cont.)

Local Five	No-Go Zones
Objective: To find a place to start doing some things differently, because it can seem daunting to try to decide.	*Objective:* When some places, groups, and people are considered off-limits, try to learn what is really "no go."
Action: Select the closest five people (typically from your inner circle—family and close friends).	*Action:* Spend an afternoon in the no-go zones in your life and community.
Result: You will achieve a higher return on investment, because the "local five" are high-touch, high-frequency, intimate relationships.	*Result:* You will tangibly see what you have in common with people in the no-go zones . . . and how what you don't share is *not* "no go," just different.
"Too Selfless" Test	*Gratitude Visit*
Objective: Understand why you can't say no to requests even when you are physically and mentally exhausted.	*Objective:* To understand who you are most grateful for and why.
Action: Take the "Are You Too Selfless?" test (pp. 73–74).	*Action:* Every six months, write a letter of gratitude to someone. Get personal, use details, and read it in person. Consider what life would be like without them.
Result: Afterward, reflect on a possible realignment of self-care expectations so you can develop healthier habits and relationships.	*Result:* Your happiness will be significantly increased for up to six months.

PLAYBOOK 2: DAY-TO-DAY

Four Choices	Five Ds
Objective: Decide where to start making more selfless decisions.	*Objective:* To act appropriately when you see an extremely selfish incident.
Action: We make four choices every hour. Consider each choice as an opportunity to decide, based not only on "I" but also on others.	*Action:* Start with *direct* intervention; *distract* by engaging with the targeted person; *delegate* by turning to third-party help; *delay*; then *document* with your phone.
Result: You will begin to see selflessness as single, small wins. This bite-sized approach makes it easier to achieve a more selfless lifestyle.	*Result:* You will be prepared to engage in safer, right-sized conflict resolution.

Muscle Memory	*Ten Stones*
Objective: To tone your selflessness muscles by little, repetitive actions.	*Objective:* To avoid decision-making paralysis when the options aren't perfect.
Action: Look for the selfless things that are accessible. Do "small" selfless things like choosing to take the stairs if there isn't enough space for everyone on the elevator.	*Action:* You have ten stones, as well as buckets representing the three choices; place stones in buckets based on preference.
Result: You will build stronger selfless muscles that prepare you to do bigger, sometimes even heroic selfless acts.	*Result:* The bucket with the most stones leads you to a decision and simulates scientific conjoint analysis. You may become up to ten times more effective in your decision making.
Touch	*Showing Up*
Objective: To make family and friends feel appreciated.	*Objective:* To help you decide whether or not to attend a function or event.
Action: Use human touch that respects personal space (e.g., a longer hug, a pat on the back, a two-handed handshake, a side hug, a touch on the back of elbow in a friendly manner).	*Action:* Go! A text to check in is a backup option, but show support. Above all, do not ghost.
Result: As the "empathy hormone" oxytocin is released, you and others are opened up to show vulnerability, and your relationships are strengthened.	*Result:* By showing up, you are reducing stress in a person in need 20 percent more than a text.

PLAYBOOK 3: LANGUAGE

Greetings	*Telling Stories*
Objective: To say hello in ways other than shaking hands.	*Objective:* To make a point, express a position, or further an argument.
Action: Smile, clap three times (Mozambique), stick your tongue out (Tibet), say namaste (India/Nepal), bow (Asia), wave.	*Action:* Select a story containing a selfless, empathetic element; if possible, use a video or short film.
Result: One study shows that 60 percent felt more comfortable with these greetings. Another shows that these greetings trigger the brain's "pleasure center." A third shows that others instinctively/reflexively return the greeting.	*Result:* Stories that release the "empathy hormone" oxytocin spur people to action, making it likelier they will help.

(cont.)

The Selfie	*"I"*
Objective: To use body language selflessly.	*Objective:* To make a point, express a position, or further an argument without using personal anecdotes.
Action: Record audio and video of your communication with others (only with approval); review home videos of your communication (this is based on best practices of CNN coaches) and evaluate.	*Action:* Avoid "I believe," "I think," and other "I"-focused sentence structures. Use fact-based assertions: "Study A or expert B found that . . ."
Result: This review will reveal what you thought was the way you communicate versus the way you actually communicate.	*Result:* People who use "I" less are more emotionally stable. People- and subject-first language reduces defensiveness.
Names	*Dreaming on Paper*
Objective: To connect with new colleagues, acquaintances, and friends who have difficult-to-pronounce names.	*Objective:* To plan ahead for selflessness.
Action: Ask how to pronounce their names. Try to pronounce along with them as they help you. Use their given names, not a lazy adaptation of their challenging name (e.g., say Zhengyu, not "Z").	*Action:* Create a "career log." Write down three dream jobs, along with steps to reach them in two years. Add position/salary/firm details, and be sure to note target steps that overlap. Include selflessness goals. Revisit this annually.
Result: Using given names shows vulnerability, effort, respect, and a high level of caring for the other person.	*Result:* You will become more likely to speak with stakeholders. Your language and knowledge will be memorialized, and your selflessness objectives will be thought out and documented.

ALTERNATE
STANZAS

I originally wanted these poems to be in the body of the book. But I came to realize they fit better in a reflective section. These creative pieces help us discuss *Enough About Me* in a more unconventional way during gatherings or as we walk along the way. My collaborators on these poems were gracious and embraced why "we" is usually better than "me."

PLANTS
José Olivarez and Richard Lui
(from section titled "Watering Three Plants" in chapter 6)

we live on the clock,
shuffling between dreams and bills.
rent taps on our shoulders,

so do our unfinished screenplays.
the price of bread memorized like songs
stuck on repeat as we enter the office.

we are midnight marauders
indulging passions
only the moon watches.

if life is a garden,
this is for those of us afraid
of plants that might never pay.

it's the green patches,
though we eat fruits of one
others give flowers.

we live fearful of bill collectors,
fearful of dying like we live:
working to live off the clock.

it's the flowers of others
growing not one or two
watering three.

we will go soon,
do not delay
living.

A STONE

José Olivarez and Richard Lui
(from chapter 14 titled "Ten Stones")

how many times did i start
to add birds to words
to subtle the metaphor
to laugh track lines
to sparkle rhymes
to glitter the sun
to spice the stew
to slam the drums
to fertilize the soil
to backspace delete quit altogether.

an ironic friend
wanting the mountain
but cannot summit
still climbs
reaches
builds.

so this
of a mountain
of a hill.
a stone
for the world we want

NAMES
Analicia Sotelo and Richard Lui
(from chapter 3 titled "Behind the Camera")

We don't need
to be seen. We need

to go. We need to do something
with our names. *Peter. Anita.*
Amir. Tiffany. Stephen.

Across the country, we wave
like flags even after
the smoke rises.

Across the room, we rise
and walk toward our children.

This is the last time
we will lose ourselves
to find that the roads have become maps;

to find the maps are simply
this room again, where the books
are filled with water, and the ocean

is here, too, bringing
the waves in. Bringing in
Peter. Anita. Amir. Tiffany. Stephen.

READING BY THE WINDOW
Analicia Sotelo and Richard Lui
(from chapter 1 titled "Halftime")

I read him the news.
I couldn't tell which year it was

we felt the worst, or the most,

or both. Nor could Dad remember
which year was the year

I decided on Bolognese
and turnip soup for dinner.

We're all a little mixed-up.

At the table,
our opinions dance

at the sight of blooms—
with no way of knowing

if these are our new
centerpieces and if so, how we

made them happen. Did we do it
together, through sheer

concentration, like a window
left open to the air

and the elements and whatever else
might happen today,

which could be tomorrow,
or even yesterday?

NOTES

Chapter 1: Halftime

1. Acts 20:35.
2. Cited in Sheena Iyengar, "How to Make Choosing Easier," TEDSalon NY2011, November 2011, www.ted.com/talks/sheena_iyengar _how_to_make_choosing_easier.

Chapter 2: Is Selflessness Possible?

1. Quoted in Johnny Diaz, "Peter Wang, Florida School Shooting Victim: Brave Teen Seen Holding Door Open for Others During Shooting," *South Florida Sun Sentinel*, February 15, 2018, www.sun-sentinel.com /local/broward/parkland/florida-school-shooting/fl-florida-school -shooting-peter-wang-obit-20180215-story.html.
2. See Sammy Mack, "Peter Wang, Who Died Protecting Other Children, Given Military Honors," WUSF Public Media, February 20, 2018, wusfnews.wusf.usf.edu/2018-02-20/peter-wang-who-died-protecting -other-children-given-military-honors.
3. "Peacock Surprise: What Females Like in a Male," National Geographic Society Newsroom, July 30, 2013, https://blog.nationalgeographic.org /2013/07/30/peacock-surprise-what-females-like-in-a-male.
4. Richard Dawkins, *The Selfish Gene* (Oxford: Oxford University Press, 1976), ix.
5. Richard Dawkins, *The God Delusion* (New York: Houghton Mifflin, 2006), 252.
6. Dawkins, *Selfish Gene*, 2.
7. See Peter Turchin, "Selfish Genes Made Me Do It! (Part 1)," Evolution Institute, December 4, 2013, https://evolution-institute.org/blog/selfish -genes-made-me-do-it-part-i.

8. See Dan Falk, "The Complicated Legacy of Herbert Spencer, the Man Who Coined 'Survival of the Fittest,'" Smithsonian, April 29, 2020, www.smithsonianmag.com/science-nature/herbert-spencer-survival-of -the-fittest-180974756.

9. The phrase "Nature red in tooth and claw" comes from Alfred, Lord Tennyson, "In Memoriam A. H. H.," Canto LVI; see Lilian Nattel, "Darwin and Poetry," https://liliannattel.wordpress.com/tag/nature-red -in-tooth-and-claw.

10. Russell Moore, "God Doesn't Want Us to Sacrifice the Old," *New York Times*, March 26, 2020, www.nytimes.com/2020/03/26/opinion /coronavirus-elderly-vulnerable-religion.html.

11. Cited in Jonah Lehrer, "Kin and Kind: A Fight about the Genetics of Altruism," *New Yorker*, February 27, 2012, www.newyorker.com /magazine/2012/03/05/kin-kind.

12. See John Annese and Leonard Greene, "FDNY Legend Jimmy Boyle, Two-Time Head of NYC Firefighter Union Who Lost Bravest Son on 9/11, Dead at 80," *New York Daily News*, October 28, 2019, www .nydailynews.com/new-york/ny-retired-firefighter-jimmy-boyle-dead -20191028-6ehbigljjvebfckhmywzvj26v4-story.html.

13. See Michael B. Sauter and Charles Stockdale, "The Most Dangerous Jobs in the US Include Electricians, Firefighters and Police Officers," *USA Today*, January 8, 2019, www.usatoday.com/story/money/2019/01/08/most -dangerous-jobs-us-where-fatal-injuries-happen-most-often/38832907.

14. Michael T. Ghiselin, *The Economy of Nature and the Evolution of Sex* (Berkeley: University of California Press, 1974), 247.

15. Charles Darwin, *The Descent of Man*, vol. 1 (New York: Appleton, 1871), 157.

16. Matthew 20:26; 20:16.

17. "SPLC on Campus: A Guide to Bystander Intervention: The Five Ds of Bystander Intervention," Southern Poverty Law Center, October 5, 2017, www.splcenter.org/20171005/splc-campus-guide-bystander-intervention #bystander.

18. Stefan Klein, *Survival of the Nicest: How Altruism Made Us Human and Why It Pays to Get Along* (New York: The Experiment, 2014), xiv.

Chapter 3: Behind the Camera

1. James W. H. Sonne and Don M. Gash, "Psychopathy to Altruism: Neurobiology of the Selfish-Selfless Spectrum," *Frontiers in Psychology* 9, no. 575 (April 19, 2018), www.frontiersin.org/articles/10.3389/fpsyg.2018 .00575/full.

Chapter 4: Goodness Meets Gorgeous

1. See Kevin M. Kniffin and David Sloan Wilson, "The Effect of Nonphysical Traits on the Perception of Physical Attractiveness: Three Naturalistic Studies," *Evolution and Human Behavior* 25, no. 2 (March 2004): 88–101, www.sciencedirect.com/science/article/abs/pii/S10905 13804000066.
2. Kniffin and Wilson, "Effect of Nonphysical Traits."
3. Kniffin and Wilson, "Effect of Nonphysical Traits."
4. Cited in David Moore et al., "Selflessness Is Sexy: Reported Helping Behaviour Increases Desirability of Men and Women as Long-Term Sexual Partners," *BMC Evolutionary Biology* 13, no. 182 (2013), https://bmcevolbiol.biomedcentral.com/track/pdf/10.1186/1471-2148-13-182.
5. Matthew 7:12.
6. 1 Peter 3:3–4.

Chapter 5: Longevity and Youth

1. Cited in Stephen Post and Jill Neimark, *Why Good Things Happen to Good People: The Exciting New Research That Proves the Link between Doing Good and Living a Longer, Healthier, Happier Life* (New York: Broadway, 2007), 48.
2. Doug Oman, Carl E. Thoresen, and Kay McMahon, "Volunteerism and Mortality among the Community-Dwelling Elderly," *Journal of Health Psychology* 4, no. 3 (July 1999): 301–16, https://journals.sagepub.com/doi/pdf/10.1177/135910539900400301.
3. Cited in Sara Konrath et al., "Motives for Volunteering Are Associated with Mortality Risk in Older Adults," *Health Psychology* 31, no. 1 (January 2012): 87–96, https://pdfs.semanticscholar.org/bfa6/f50d859 60b7b7622b4b8dc902ed56542bada.pdf.
4. See B. Grace Bullock, "Loving-Kindness Meditation May Protect Your Genes and Slow Aging," *Mindful*, September 12, 2019, www.mindful.org/loving-kindness-meditation-may-protect-your-genes-and-slow-aging.
5. See Khoa D. Le Nguyen et al., "Loving-Kindness Meditation Slows Biological Aging in Novices: Evidence from a 12-Week Randomized Controlled Trial," *Psychoneuroendocrinology* 108 (October 2019): 20–27, www.sciencedirect.com/science/article/abs/pii/S0306453019300010?via %3Dihub.
6. See Elizabeth B. Raposa, Holly B. Laws, and Emily B. Ansell, "Prosocial Behavior Mitigates the Negative Effects of Stress in Everyday Life," *Clinical Psychological Science* 4, no. 4 (July 2016): 691–98, http://ebraposa

.blogs.wm.edu/files/2016/03/Clinical-Psychological-Science-2015
-Raposa-2167702615611073.pdf.

7. See Rachel L. Piferi and Kathleen A. Lawler, "Social Support and
Ambulatory Blood Pressure: An Examination of Both Receiving and
Giving," *International Journal of Psychophysiology* 62, no. 2 (November
2006): 328–36, https://pubmed.ncbi.nlm.nih.gov/16905215.

8. Quoted in Vicki Contie, "Brain Imaging Reveals Joys of Giving," June 22,
2007, www.nih.gov/news-events/nih-research-matters/brain-imaging
-reveals-joys-giving.

9. "Why Giving Is Good for Your Health: Studies Show How Giving Affects
Your Body," Cleveland Clinic: Health Essentials, October 28, 2020,
https://health.clevelandclinic.org/why-giving-is-good-for-your-health.

10. See Justin Kruger, "Helper's High: Why Doing Good Makes Us Feel Good,"
Project Helping, August 9, 2017, https://projecthelping.org/helpers-high.

11. See David R. Topor, "If You Are Happy and You Know It . . . You May Live
Longer," Harvard Health Blog, October 16, 2019, www.health.harvard.edu
/blog/if-you-are-happy-and-you-know-it-you-may-live-longer-2019101618020.

12. Cited in Amy Patterson Neubert, "Money Only Buys Happiness for a
Certain Amount," Purdue University News, February 13, 2018, www
.purdue.edu/newsroom/releases/2018/Q1/money-only-buys-happiness
-for-a-certain-amount.html.

13. Cited in Sarah Jane Gilbert, "Spending on Happiness," Harvard Business
School, June 2, 2008, https://hbswk.hbs.edu/item/spending-on-happiness;
see Elizabeth W. Dunn, Lara B. Aknin, and Michael I. Norton,
"Prosocial Spending and Happiness: Using Money to Benefit Others Pays
Off," *Current Directions in Psychological Science* 23, no. 1 (2014), www.hbs
.edu/faculty/Publication%20Files/Dunn%20Aknin%20%20Norton%20
-2014%20CD_bfccfc43-4139-476a-904b-ebcf855ab7c3.pdf.

Chapter 6: Career Payoff

1. See "Estimated Average Annual Salary of Teachers in Public Elementary
and Secondary Schools: Selected years, 1959–60 through 2008–09,"
National Center for Education Statistics: Digest of Education Statistics,
https://nces.ed.gov/programs/digest/d09/tables/dt09_078.asp; see also Ed
Hurley, "Teacher Pay 1940–2000: Losing Ground, Losing Status," National
Educational Association, http://ftp.arizonaea.org/home/14052.htm.

2. Del Jones, "CEOs Say How You Treat a Waiter Can Predict a Lot about
Character," *USA Today*, April 17, 2006, https://usatoday30.usatoday.com
/money/companies/management/2006-04-14-ceos-waiter-rule_x.htm.

3. See Kimmo Eriksson et al., "Generosity Pays: Selfish People Have Fewer Children and Earn Less Money," *Journal of Personality and Social Psychology* 118, no. 3 (March 2020): 532–44, http://www.diva-portal.org /smash/get/diva2:1253120/FULLTEXT01.pdf.

4. See Joseph B. Fuller and Manjari Raman, "The Caring Company: How Employers Can Help Employees Manage Their Caregiving Responsibilities—While Reducing Costs and Increasing Productivity," Harvard Business School, January 16, 2019, www.hbs.edu/managing-the -future-of-work/Documents/The_Caring_Company.pdf.

5. Fuller and Raman, "Caring Company," 4.

6. Cited in Chenlu Gao, Nikita Y. Chapagain, and Michael K. Scullin, "Sleep Duration and Sleep Quality in Caregivers of Patients with Dementia: A Systematic Review and Meta-Analysis," JAMA Network, August 23, 2019, https://jamanetwork.com/journals/jamanetworkopen /fullarticle/2748661.

7. Cited in Alyssa Rapp, "Be One, Get One: The Importance of Mentorship," *Forbes*, October 2, 2018, www.forbes.com/sites/yec/2018 /10/02/be-one-get-one-the-importance-of-mentorship.

8. *Monty Python and the Holy Grail*, directed by Terry Gilliam and Terry Jones (1975).

9. Kabir Sehgal, "Why You Should Have (at Least) Two Careers," *Harvard Business Review*, April 25, 2017, https://hbr.org/2017/04/why-you-should -have-at-least-two-careers.

10. George Beahm, ed., *I, Steve: Steve Jobs in His Own Words* (Chicago: Agate, 2011), 73.

Chapter 7: Personal Relationships

1. See Heidi L. Fritz and Vicki S. Helgeson, "Distinctions of Unmitigated Communion from Communion: Self-Neglect and Overinvolvement with Others," *Journal of Personality and Social Psychology* 75, no. 1 (July 1998): 121–40, https://psycnet.apa.org/record/1998-04530-009.

2. See Justin Newsome, "Gender Stereotypes and Relationship Equity and Satisfaction," Dominican University of California (2019), https:// scholar.dominican.edu/cgi/viewcontent.cgi?article=1099&context=ug -student-posters.

3. See Ari Berkowitz, "Over 100 Years of Searching Hasn't Found Key Differences between Male and Female Brains," *Science Alert*, August 9, 2020, www.sciencealert.com/a-century-of-studies-on-male-and-female -brains-has-turned-up-no-major-intrinsic-difference.

4. Cited in "Caregiving in the U.S.: 2020 Report," AARP, May 2020, 10, www.aarp.org/content/dam/aarp/ppi/2020/05/full-report-caregiving-in -the-united-states.doi.10.26419-2Fppi.00103.001.pdf.

5. Cited in "Caregiving in the U.S.: 2020 Report," AARP, May 2020, 4.

6. Judson Mills et al., "Measurement of Communal Strength," *Personal Relationships* 11 (2004): 213–30, https://clarkrelationshiplab.yale.edu /sites/default/files/files/Measurement%20in%20communal%20strength .pdf.

7. See "What Is Bronfenbrenner's Ecological Systems Theory?" Psychology Notes HQ, May 21, 2020, www.psychologynoteshq.com/bronfenbrenner -ecological-theory.

8. Deuteronomy 15:11.

9. Émile Durkheim, *The Elementary Forms of the Religious Life* (1915; repr., Mineola, NY: Dover, 2008), 214–39.

10. Durkheim, *Elementary Forms of the Religious Life*, 10.

11. See Andrew G. Thomas et al., "Mate Preference Priorities in the East and West: A Cross-Cultural Test of the Mate Preference Priority Model," *Journal of Personality* 88, no. 3 (June 2020): 606–20, www.comparative cognition.com/Thomas%20et%20al%202019.pdf.

12. Cited in Allison Linn, "Why Married People Tend to Be Wealthier: It's Complicated," *TODAY*, February 13, 2013, www.today.com/money /why-married-people-tend-be-wealthier-its-complicated-1C8364877.

13. See Pádraig MacCarron, Kimmo Kaski, and Robin Dunbar, "Calling Dunbar's Numbers," *Social Networks* 47 (October 2016): 151–55, www .sciencedirect.com/science/article/pii/S0378873316301095.

Chapter 8: A Meism Era

1. James 1:17.

2. Bodhidharma, *The Zen Teaching of Bodhidharma* (New York: North Point, 1987), 49.

3. Sukhmandir Khalsa, "Seva in Sikhism," Learn Religions: Sikhism, February 12, 2019, www.learnreligions.com/seva-selfless-service-2993078.

4. "Jessie's Girl," lyrics by Rick Springfield (1981).

5. Quoted in "Now, the California Task Force to Promote Self-Esteem," *New York Times*, October 11, 1986, www.nytimes.com/1986/10/11/us /now-the-california-task-force-to-promote-self-esteem.html.

6. Cited in Steve Chawkins, "John Vasconcellos Dies at 82; Father of California Self-Esteem Panel," *Los Angeles Times*, May 25, 2014, www.la times.com/local/obituaries/la-me-john-vasconcellos-20140526-story.html.

7. Jesse Singal, "How the Self-Esteem Craze Took Over America and Why the Hype Was Irresistible," *The CUT*, May 2017, www.thecut .com/2017/05/self-esteem-grit-do-they-really-help.html.

8. Quoted in Singal, "How the Self-Esteem Craze Took Over America."

9. Quoted in Singal, "How the Self-Esteem Craze Took Over America."

10. Cited in "Now, the California Task Force to Promote Self-Esteem."

11. Quoted in Singal, "How the Self-Esteem Craze Took Over America."

12. Quoted in "'Starving for Affection' of *Terrace House*," April 7, 2020, www .sandyrie.com/notes/starving-for-affection-of-terrace-house.

13. The study was led by Ernst Fehr at the University of Zurich and based on research done with 229 Swiss children. See Ernst Fehr and Bettina Rockenbach, "Egalitarianism in Young Children," *Nature* 454, no. 7208 (September 2008): 1079–83, www.researchgate.net/publication/23222622 _Egalitarianism_in_Young_Children.

14. "Children's Sense of Fairness Makes Them Egalitarian but Not Generous," *Nature*, August 27, 2008, www.nature.com/articles/7208viiia.

15. See Kelly Wallace, "What Your Baby Knows Might Freak You Out," CNN, February 14, 2014, www.cnn.com/2014/02/13/living/what-babies -know-anderson-cooper-parents/index.html.

16. Cited in Paul Bloom, "The Moral Life of Babies," *New York Times Magazine*, May 5, 2010, www.nytimes.com/2010/05/09/magazine/09babies-t.html.

17. Bloom, "Moral Life of Babies."

18. See Lin Edwards, "Psychologists Say Babies Know Right from Wrong Even at Six Months," *Medical Xpress*, May 10, 2010, https://medicalxpress .com/news/2010-05-psychologists-babies-wrong-months.html.

19. Rick Warren, *The Purpose Driven Life: What on Earth Am I Here For?* (Grand Rapids: Zondervan, 2002), 148.

20. Cited in Sam Thomas Davies, "To Solve Problems, Look in the Mirror," June 24, 2020, www.samuelthomasdavies.com/elevator-waiting-times.

21. See Alex Stone, "Why Waiting Is Torture," *New York Times*, August 18, 2012, www.nytimes.com/2012/08/19/opinion/sunday/why-waiting-in -line-is-torture.html.

22. "You're So Vain," lyrics by Carly Simon (1971).

Chapter 9: Communities of Others

1. Robert D. Putnam, *Bowling Alone: The Collapse and Revival of American Community* (New York: Simon & Schuster, 2000), 24, 27.

2. Cited in Jacinta Francis et al., "Creating Sense of Community: The Role of Public Space," *Journal of Environmental Psychology* 32, no. 4 (December

2012): 401–9, www.researchgate.net/publication/266620692_Creating
_Sense_of_Community_The_role_of_public_space.

3. Cited in Julianne Holt-Lunstad and Timothy B. Smith, "Loneliness and
Social Isolation as Risk Factors for Mortality: A Meta-Analytic Review,"
BYU ScholarsArchive (March 23, 2015), 14, https://scholarsarchive.byu
.edu/cgi/viewcontent.cgi?article=3024&context=facpub.

4. See Jonathan Glancey, "Is This the Perfect City?" BBC, December 11,
2015, www.bbc.com/culture/article/20151211-is-this the perfect city.

5. "Free Speech Monument: Berkeley, California," Atlas Obscura, www
.atlasobscura.com/places/free-speech-monument.

6. See Kashmira Gander, "How Architecture Uses Space, Light, and Material
to Affect Your Mood," *Independent*, May 16, 2016, www.independent.co
.uk/life-style/design/how-architecture-uses-space-light-and-material-to
-affect-your-mood-american-institute-architects-a6985986.html.

7. See "Place of Birth for the Foreign-Born Population in the United States,"
US Census Bureau, https://data.census.gov/cedsci/table?q=United%20
States&t=Place%20of%20Birth&g=0100000US&tid=ACSDT1Y2018
.B05006.

8. Cited in Jemima Kelly, "France Elects Record Number of Women to
Parliament," Reuters, June 18, 2017, www.reuters.com/article/us-france
-election-women/france-elects-record-number-of-women-to-parliament
-idUSKBN19911E.

9. See Robert P. Spunt, Meghan L. Meyer, and Matthew D. Lieberman,
"The Default Mode of Human Brain Function Primes the Intentional
Stance," *Journal of Cognitive Neuroscience* 26, no. 6 (June 2015): 1116–24,
www.mitpressjournals.org/doi/full/10.1162/jocn_a_00785.

10. See Stuart Wolpert, "Even When We're Resting, Our Brains Are
Preparing Us to Be Social," UCLA Newsroom, May 15, 2015, https://
newsroom.ucla.edu/releases/even-when-were-resting-our-brains-are
-preparing-us-to-be-social-ucla-psychologists-report.

11. Quoted in Emily Esfahani Smith, "Social Connection Makes a Better
Brain," *Atlantic*, October 29, 2013, www.theatlantic.com/health/archive
/2013/10/social-connection-makes-a-better-brain/280934.

12. Cited in Michael Harré, "Social Network Size Linked to Brain Size,"
Scientific American, August 7, 2012, www.scientificamerican.com/article
/social-network-size-linked-brain-size.

13. See Jenny Gross, "Colorado Paramedic Who Came to Help New York
Dies from Covid-19," *New York Times*, May 2, 2020, www.nytimes.com
/2020/05/02/nyregion/paramedic-paul-cary-coronavirus-nyc.html.

14. See Lucy Harley-McKeown and Melissa Korn, "Medical Students in Europe and U.S. Graduate Early to Join Coronavirus Front-Lines," *Wall Street Journal*, April 18, 2020, www.wsj.com/articles/medical-students -in-europe-and-u-s-graduate-early-to-join-coronavirus-front-lines -11587233541.
15. "Physician Oaths: A Modern Hippocratic Oath by Dr. Louis Lasagna," Association of American Physicians and Surgeons, https://www.aaps online.org/ethics/oaths.htm.

Chapter 10: Republicans and Democrats

1. See Richard Lei, "The Commander in Briefs," *Washington Post*, April 20, 1994, www.washingtonpost.com/archive/lifestyle/1994/04/20/the -commander-in-briefs/04219ef3-aa61-4f28-8869-6217476c1b47.
2. Cited in "How the Clintons Cheated on Their 'Used Underwear' Tax Return," Americans for Tax Reform, October 27, 2016, www.atr.org /ClintonsUnderwear?amp.
3. Cited in "Cost of Living 1986," The People History, www.thepeople history.com/1986.html.
4. "Address of Senator Nixon to the American People: The 'Checkers Speech,'" American Presidency Project, September 23, 1952, www .presidency.ucsb.edu/documents/address-senator-nixon-the-american -people-the-checkers-speech.
5. Quoted in Andrew Glass, "Nixon Says He's 'Not a Crook,' Nov. 17, 1973," *Politico*, November 16, 2016, www.politico.com/story/2016/11 /nixon-says-hes-not-a-crook-nov-17-1973-231309.
6. Cited in Mark Murray, "Flashback: Richard Nixon Released Tax Returns While under Audit," NBC News, May 12, 2016, www.nbcnews.com /politics/2016-election/flashback-richard-nixon-released-tax-returns -while-under-audit-n573036.
7. See Antonia Noori Farzan, "Trump, the First President in a Century with No Dog, Explains Why: 'I Don't Have Any Time,'" *Washington Post*, February 12, 2019, www.washingtonpost.com/nation/2019/02/12 /trump-first-president-century-with-no-dog-explains-why-i-dont-have -any-time.
8. Cited in Sarah Pruitt, "6 Surprising Facts Found in Presidential Tax Returns through History," History Channel, September 29, 2020, www .history.com/news/presidential-tax-returns-facts.
9. Cited in David Cay Johnston, "The 2000 Campaign: The Financial Situation; Bush Campaign Makes Public Candidate's 1999 Tax Return,"

October 21, 2000, www.nytimes.com/2000/10/21/us/2000-campaign
-financial-situation-bush-campaign-makes-public-candidate-s-1999.html.

10. See "How Much Is Given? By Whom? For What?" Charity Choices,
www.charitychoices.com/page/how-much-given-whom-what.

11. Cited in Josh Gerstein, "Romney Gives More to Charity Than Obama,
Biden," *Politico*, September 21, 2012, www.politico.com/story/2012/09
/romney-gives-more-to-charity-than-obama-biden-081529.

12. Cited in Grant Williams, "Barack and Michelle Obama Donated
$240,000 to Charity Last Year," *Chronicle of Philanthropy*, March 25,
2008, www.philanthropy.com/article/BarackMichelle-Obama/163177.

13. Cited in Lisa Chui, "Obamas Donated 14 Percent of Their Income
to Charity in 2010," *Chronicle of Philanthropy*, April 18, 2011, www
.philanthropy.com/article/Obamas-Donated-14-of-Their/195393.

14. Cited in Gerstein, "Romney Gives More to Charity Than Obama, Biden."

15. Michael LaBossiere, "Democrats & Republicans: The Philosophy of the
State," A Philosopher's Blog, November 1, 2012, https://aphilosopher
.wordpress.com/2012/11/01/democrats-republicans-the-philosophy-of
-the-state/.

16. James H. Fowler, "Altruism and Turnout," *Journal of Politics* 68, no. 3
(August 2006): 674–83, http://fowler.ucsd.edu/altruism_and_turnout.pdf.

17. Meri T. Long, "Who's More Compassionate, Republicans or
Democrats?" The Conversation, January 10, 2019, https://theconversation
.com/whos-more-compassionate-republicans-or-democrats-99730; see
Meridith Taylor Long, "Compassion in Red and Blue: The Politics of
Who Cares about Whom" (PhD diss. Vanderbilt University, August
2016), https://ir.vanderbilt.edu/bitstream/handle/1803/12979/Long.pdf.

18. Long, "Compassion in Red and Blue."

19. Cited in Danny Hayes, "Candidate Qualities through a Partisan Lens:
A Theory of Trait Ownership," *American Journal of Political Science* 49,
no. 4 (October 2005): 908–23, www.jstor.org/stable/3647705.

20. Larrie D. Ferreiro, "The Radical Theory of Evolution That Explains
Democrats and Republicans," *Atlantic*, June 11, 2012, www.theatlantic
.com/politics/archive/2012/06/the-radical-theory-of-evolution-that
-explains-democrats-and-republicans/258307.

21. See Laurie E. Paarlberg et al., "The Politics of Donations: Are Red
Counties More Donative Than Blue Counties?" *Nonprofit and Voluntary
Sector Quarterly* 48 (April 2019), https://journals.sagepub.com/doi/abs
/10.1177/0899764018804088.

22. Quoted in Paul Sullivan, "How Political Ideology Influences Charitable

Giving," *New York Times*, November 3, 2018, www.nytimes.com/2018 /11/03/your-money/republicans-democrats-charity-philanthropy.html.

23. See Leslie Albrecht, "The U.S. Is the No. 1 Most Generous Country in the World for the Last Decade," MarketWatch, December 7, 2019, www.market watch.com/story/the-us-is-the-most-generous-country-but-americans-say -debt-is-keeping-them-from-giving-more-to-charity-2019-10-18.

24. Cited in Marianne Hayes, "Lending Tree Says, 'American Generosity Is Unprecedented,'" Inside Charity, September 8, 2020, https://inside charity.org/2019/10/26/lending-tree.

25. Gautam Nair, "Most Americans Vastly Underestimate How Rich They Are Compared with the Rest of the World. Does It Matter?" *Washington Post*, August 23, 2018, www.washingtonpost.com/news/monkey-cage /wp/2018/08/23/most-americans-vastly-underestimate-how-rich-they -are-compared-with-the-rest-of-the-world-does-it-matter.

26. "We Are the Lucky Ones," Canadian Red Cross, www.redcross.ca /crc/documents/What-We-Do/Emergencies-and-Disasters-WRLD /education-resources/lucky_ones_povdisease.pdf.

27. Luke 12:48.

Chapter 11: Three Lunches

1. Cited in John Whitesides, "From Disputes to a Breakup: Wounds Still Raw after U.S. Election," Reuters, February 7, 2017, www.reuters.com /article/us-usa-trump-relationships-insight/from-disputes-to-a-breakup -wounds-still-raw-after-u-s-election-idUSKBN15M13L.

2. Cited in "Partisanship and Political Animosity in 2016," Pew Research Center, June 22, 2016, www.pewresearch.org/politics/wp-content/uploads /sites/4/2016/06/06-22-16-Partisanship-and-animosity-release.pdf.

3. "Partisanship and Political Animosity in 2016."

4. James Mattis, "The Enemy Within: Our Grasp on What It Takes to Sustain a Democracy Is Slipping," *Atlantic*, December 2019, www .theatlantic.com/magazine/archive/2019/12/james-mattis-the-enemy -within/600781/.

5. Cited in Branka Vuleta, "How Much Data Is Created Every Day? [27 Powerful Stats]," SeedScientific, January 30, 2020, https://seed scientific.com/how-much-data-is-created-every-day.

6. Cited in David Reinsel, John Gantz, and John Rydning, "The Digitization of the World: From Edge to Core," Seagate (November 2018), 3, www.seagate.com/files/www-content/our-story/trends/files/idc -seagate-dataage-whitepaper.pdf.

7. See Rohin Dhar, "The Science of Headline Writing: Does A/B
Testing Headlines Work?" *Priceonomics*, September 27, 2016, https://
priceonomics.com/the-science-of-headline-writing-does-ab-testing.
8. Martin Bashir, "Lui: Why Jeremy Lin Transcends Sport," February 20,
2012, www.msnbc.com/martin-bashir/watch/lui-why-jeremy-lin
-transcends-sport-43878979719.
9. Rodney E. Hood, "How Financial Institutions Can Help America Heal,"
Wall Street Journal, June 4, 2020, www.wsj.com/articles/how-banks-can
-help-america-heal-11591311103.
10. Arthur Brooks, *Love Your Enemies: How Decent People Can Save America
from the Culture of Contempt* (New York: HarperCollins, 2019), 205.
11. See Elizabeth Page-Gould, Rodolfo Mendoza-Denton, and Linda R.
Tropp, "With a Little Help from My Cross-Group Friend: Reducing
Anxiety in Intergroup Contexts through Cross-Group Friendship," *Journal
of Personality and Social Psychology* 95, no. 5 (November 2008): 1080–94,
https://stanford.app.box.com/s/1iupcxgs89yf74fc3nmugoxup6wm19aa.
12. See Richard T. LaPiere, "Attitudes vs. Actions," *Social Forces* 13, no. 2
(December 1934): 230–37, www.jstor.org/stable/2570339?seq=1.
13. See Peter T. Coleman, *The Five Percent: Finding Solutions to Seemingly
Impossible Conflicts* (New York: Public Affairs, 2011), 2.
14. Quoted in Amanda Ripley, "Complicating the Narratives," Solutions
Journalism, January 11, 2019, https://thewholestory.solutionsjournalism
.org/complicating-the-narratives-b91ea06ddf63.
15. Francesca Gino, "The Business Case for Curiosity," *Harvard Business
Review* (September–October 2018), https://hbr.org/2018/09/curiosity.
16. Ripley, "Complicating the Narratives."
17. Greg Miller and Souad Mekhennet, "One Woman Helped the Mastermind
of the Paris Attacks. The Other Turned Him In," *Washington Post*, April
10, 2016, www.washingtonpost.com/world/national-security/one-woman
-helped-the-mastermind-of-the-paris-attacks-the-other-turned-him
-in/2016/04/10/66bce472-fc47-11e5-9140-e61d062438bb_story.html.

Chapter 12: Muscle Memory

1. David Bayles and Ted Orland, *Art and Fear: Observations on the Perils (and
Rewards) of Artmaking* (Santa Cruz, CA: Image Continuum, 1993), 29.
2. Ainslie Johnstone, "The Amazing Phenomenon of Muscle Memory,"
Oxford University, December 14, 2017, https://medium.com/oxford
-university/the-amazing-phenomenon-of-muscle-memory-fb1cc4c4726.
3. See Sara Chodosh, "Muscle Memory Is Real, but It's Probably Not

What You Think," *Popular Science*, January 25, 2019, www.popsci.com
/what-is-muscle-memory.

4. Aristotle, *Nicomachean Ethics*, book II, http://classics.mit.edu/Aristotle
/nicomachaen.2.ii.html.

5. Benjamin Franklin, *Wit and Wisdom from Poor Richard's Almanack*
(Mineola, NY: Dover, 1999), 42.

6. See NCCS Team, "The Nonprofit Sector in Brief," National Center
for Charitable Statistics, June 18, 2020, https://nccs.urban.org/project
/nonprofit-sector-brief.

7. Aristotle, *Nicomachean Ethics*, book IX, http://classics.mit.edu/Aristotle
/nicomachaen.9.ix.html.

8. See my article, "Richard Lui: King's Dream Shared by Many," *USA
Today*, August 22, 2013, www.usatoday.com/story/news/nation/2013/08
/22/march-on-washington-richard-lui/2690219.

9. Chinua Achebe, *Things Fall Apart* (1958; repr., London: Penguin, 2001).

10. Quoted in Douglas Brinkley, "Selma's Historic Bridge Deserves a Better
Name," CNN Opinion, March 6, 2015, www.cnn.com/2015/03/05
/opinions/brinkley-selma-bridge-john-lewis/index.html.

11. Sharon Pian Chan, "The Yellowface of 'The Mikado' in Your Face,"
Seattle Times Opinion, July 13, 2014, www.seattletimes.com/opinion
/the-yellowface-of-ldquothe-mikadordquo-in-your-face.

Chapter 13: One Word at a Time

1. I learned this from M. L. Flynn, the longtime award-winning producer
at NBC News, who taught correspondent classes, which I was fortunate
enough to be in. It changed my journalism life forever.

2. See Patricia M. Greenfield, "The Changing Psychology of Culture
from 1800 through 2000," *Psychological Science* 24 (August 7, 2013):
1722–31, https://greenfieldlab.psych.ucla.edu/wp-content/uploads/sites
/168/2019/01/54-Greenfield-The-changing-psychology-of-culture-from
-1800-through-2000-1....pdf.

3. Pelin Kesebir and Selin Kesebir, "The Cultural Salience of Moral
Character and Virtue Declined in Twentieth-Century America," *Journal
of Positive Psychology* 7, no. 6 (November 2012): 471–80, www.dropbox
.com/s/osmzym686mss78o/The%20Cultural%20Salience%20of%20
Moral%20Character.pdf.

4. See Katherine Loughead, "State Individual Income Tax Rates and
Brackets for 2020," February 4, 2020, https://taxfoundation.org/state
-individual-income-tax-rates-and-brackets-for-2020.

5. James W. Pennebaker, "Your Use of Pronouns Reveals Your Personality," *Harvard Business Review*, December 2011, https://hbr.org/2011/12/your -use-of-pronouns-reveals-your-personality.

6. See Gabriel Cortes, "How Many Times Do Presidents Say 'I' in Their State of the Union Speeches?" APM Research Lab, February 5, 2020, www.apmresearchlab.org/state-of-the-union.

7. See Anna Bruk, Sabine G. Scholl, and Herbert Bless, "Beautiful Mess Effect: Self-Other Differences in Evaluation of Showing Vulnerability," *Journal of Personality and Social Psychology* 115, no. 2 (2018): 192–205, https://psycnet.apa.org/record/2018-34832-002.

8. Brené Brown, *Daring Greatly: How the Courage to Be Vulnerable Transforms the Way We Live, Love, Parent, and Lead* (New York: Avery, 2012), 113.

9. Quoted in Kimmy Yam, "Americanizing Asians: The Mental Toll of Being Asked to Change Your Name," NBC News, June 26, 2020, www .nbcnews.com/news/asian-america/americanizing-asians-mental-toll -being-asked-change-your-name-n1232116.

10. Rita Kohli and Daniel G. Solórzano, "Teachers, Please Learn Our Names! Racial Microaggressions and the K-12 Classroom," *Race, Ethnicity, and Education* 15, no. 4 (2012), www.tandfonline.com/doi/abs /10.1080/13613324.2012.674026.

11. Quoted in Yam, "Americanizing Asians."

12. See Kesebir and Kesebir, "Cultural Salience of Moral Character and Virtue," 4.

Chapter 14: Ten Stones

1. "What Is Conjoint Analysis?" Sawtooth Software, https://sawtoothsoft ware.com/conjoint-analysis.

2. Cited in Alina Tugend, "Too Many Choices: A Problem That Can Paralyze," *New York Times*, February 6, 2010, www.nytimes.com/2010/02 /27/your-money/27shortcuts.html.

3. Cited in Ilana Lehmann and Varda Konstam, "Growing Up Perfect: Perfectionism, Problematic Internet Use, and Career Indecision in Emerging Adults," *Journal of Counseling and Development* 89, no. 2 (April 2011): 155–62, www.researchgate.net/publication/215722798.

4. Lehmann and Konstam, "Growing Up Perfect."

5. "The Spiritual Family Founded by Mother Teresa: Missionaries of Charity Sisters," www.motherteresa.org/active-sisters.html.

6. See Christine Galeone, "Seven Insights from Mother Teresa on Being Merciful," Beliefnet, www.beliefnet.com/faiths/catholic/7-insights-from -mother-teresa-on-being-merciful.aspx.

Chapter 15: Anatomy of Action

1. See "Cannes 2019: '5B,' a Monument to the Early Heroes of the AIDS Crisis," *Encore!* France24 English, YouTube video, May 17, 2019, www.youtube.com/watch?v=DWBE3tylww0.
2. "Cannes 2019: '5B,' a Monument."
3. "Cannes 2019: '5B,' a Monument."
4. Quoted in Pat Padua, "In 1983, a Hospital Opened the First Ward Exclusively for AIDS Patients. This Documentary Tells That Moving Story," *Washington Post*, June 10, 2019, www.washingtonpost.com/going outguide/movies/in-1983-a-hospital-opened-the-first-ward-exclusively-for-aids-patients-this-documentary-tells-that-moving-story/2019/06/10/5bdfa882-8a06-11e9-a491-25df61c78dc4_story.html.
5. Quoted in James M. McPherson, "Citizen Soldiers of the Civil War: Why They Fought," National Park Service, www.nps.gov/parkhistory/online_books/rthg/chap4.htm.
6. Cited in Susan Holtzman et al., "Emotional Support during Times of Stress: Can Text Messaging Compete with In-Person Interactions?" *Computers in Human Behavior* 71 (June 2017): 130–39, www.sciencedirect.com/science/article/pii/S0747563217300559.
7. Quoted in "In-Person Support Better Than Texting for People under Stress, Study Finds," CBC News, May 15, 2017, www.cbc.ca/news/canada/british-columbia/stress-study-texting-1.4116807.
8. See Nicholas Bloom et al., "Does Working from Home Work? Evidence from a Chinese Experiment," *Quarterly Journal of Economics* 130, no. 1 (March 2013), https://nbloom.people.stanford.edu/sites/g/files/sbiybj4746/f/wfh.pdf.
9. See Adam Gorlick, "The Productivity Pitfalls of Working from Home in the Age of COVID-19," Stanford News, March 30, 2020, https://news.stanford.edu/2020/03/30/productivity-pitfalls-working-home-age-covid-19.
10. Cited in Sara Mela and David E. Whitworth, "The Fist Bump: A More Hygienic Alternative to the Handshake," *American Journal of Infection Control* 42 (2014): 916–17, www.apic.org/Resource_/TinyMceFileManager/Fist_bump_article_AJIC_August_2014.pdf.
11. See Jason Woods, "How to Greet People Around the World," Heifer International, *World Ark*, July 14, 2017, www.heifer.org/blog/greetings-around-the-world.html.
12. Cited in Ritta Baddoura and Gentiane Venture, "Human Motion Characteristics in Relation to Feeling Familiar or Frightened during an Announced

Short Interaction with a Proactive Humanoid," *Frontiers in Neurorobotics* 8 (March 2014), www.ncbi.nlm.nih.gov/pmc/articles/PMC3960492.

Chapter 16: Stories That Stick

1. Paul J. Zak, "Why Your Brain Loves Good Storytelling," *Harvard Business Review*, October 28, 2014, https://hbr.org/2014/10/why-your -brain-loves-good-storytelling.
2. See Catherine West, "Level of Oxytocin in Pregnant Women Predicts Mother-Child Bond," *Observer*, Association for Psychological Science, November 1, 2007, www.psychologicalscience.org/observer /level-of-oxytocin-in-pregnant-women-predicts-mother-child-bond-2.
3. Cited in University of Haifa, "Oxytocin Increases Empathy, Researchers Find," San Diego Jewish World, February 13, 2014, www.sdjewishworld .com/2014/02/13/oxytocin-increases-empathy-researchers-find.
4. See Zak, "Why Your Brain Loves Good Storytelling."
5. Quoted in "World Kindness Day," Words Alive! November 13, 2017, www.wordsalive.org/blog/tag/World+Kindness+Day.
6. "'Paper Sons': Chinese American Illegal Immigrants," YouTube, November 14, 2009, www.youtube.com/watch?v=Hhc-om3SXKw.
7. Zak, "Why Your Brain Loves Good Storytelling."
8. Paul J. Zak, "Why Inspiring Stories Make Us React: The Neuroscience of Narrative," *Cerebrum* (Jan.–Feb. 2015), www.ncbi.nlm.nih.gov/pmc /articles/PMC4445577.
9. Quoted in Ariana Eunjung Cha, "Why DARPA Is Paying People to Watch Alfred Hitchcock Cliffhangers," *Washington Post*, July 28, 2015, www.washingtonpost.com/news/to-your-health/wp/2015/07/28/why -darpa-is-paying-people-to-watch-alfred-hitchcock-cliffhangers.
10. James K. A. Smith, *Imagining the Kingdom: How Worship Works* (Grand Rapids: Baker Academic, 2013), 32.
11. James K. A. Smith, *Desiring the Kingdom: Worship, Worldview, and Cultural Formation* (Grand Rapids: Baker Academic, 2009), 54.
12. See Erika Lee, "The Chinese Must Go!" *Reason*, March 2016, https:// reason.com/2016/02/17/the-chinese-must-go.
13. "Transcript of Chinese Exclusion Act (1882)," OurDocuments.gov, www .ourdocuments.gov/doc.php?flash=false&doc=47&page=transcript.
14. See Lisa See, "'Paper Sons,' Hidden Pasts," *Los Angeles Times*, August 2, 2009, www.latimes.com/archives/la-xpm-2009-aug-02-oe-see2-story.html.
15. For a similar tale, see "Fat Family: Early History," Sacramento State Library, https://library.csus.edu/fatfamily/history.html.

Chapter 17: Gratitude

1. See David Whiting, "Burn Pits Are the New 'Agent Orange' for Cancer-Stricken Veterans, Marine from Long Beach Says," *Orange County Register*, July 21, 2017, www.ocregister.com/2017/07/21/burn-pits-are-the -new-agent-orange-for-cancer-stricken-veterans.

2. Sonya Huber, "Does 'Counting Your Blessings' Work?" *Atlantic*, January 4, 2018, www.theatlantic.com/technology/archive/2018/01/does -counting-your-blessings-work/549638.

3. Summer Allen, "Is Gratitude Good for Your Health?" *Greater Good Magazine*, March 5, 2018, https://greatergood.berkeley.edu/article/item /is_gratitude_good_for_your_health.

4. "Mental Subtraction of Relationships: Why It Works," Greater Good in Action, https://ggia.berkeley.edu/practice/mental_subtraction _relationships.

5. Marilynne Robinson, *Gilead: A Novel* (New York: Picador, 2004), 223.

6. Robert A. Emmons and Michael E. McCullough, "Counting Blessings Versus Burdens: An Experimental Investigation of Gratitude and Subjective Well-Being in Daily Life," *Journal of Personality and Social Psychology* 84, no. 2 (2003): 377–89, https://whish.stanford.edu/wp -content/uploads/2018/11/GratitudeArticle.pdf.

7. Barbara L. Fredrickson, *Positivity: Top-Notch Research Reveals the 3-to-1 Ratio That Will Change Your Life* (New York: Three Rivers, 2009), 186–87.

8. See Sonja Lyubomirsky, *The How of Happiness: A Scientific Approach to Getting the Life You Want* (New York: Penguin, 2007), 129.

9. Cited in Harvard Health Publishing, "In Praise of Gratitude," Harvard Mental Health Letter, November 2011, www.health.harvard.edu/mind -and-mood/in-praise-of-gratitude.

10. See Owen M. Griffith, "Gratitude: A Powerful Tool for Your Classroom," Edutopia: George Lucas Educational Foundation, November 17, 2014, www.edutopia.org/blog/gratitude-powerful-tool-for-classroom -owen-griffith.

11. Cicero, *The Orations of Marcus Tullius Cicero*, trans. C. D. Yonge (London: Bell, 1981), 80–81.

12. Adapted from "Gratitude Letter: How to Do It," Greater Good in Action, https://ggia.berkeley.edu/practice/gratitude_letter.

13. Cited in Jeffrey J. Froh et al., "Who Benefits the Most from a Gratitude Intervention in Children and Adolescents? Examining Positive Affect as a Moderator," *Journal of Positive Psychology* 4, no. 5 (October 2009):

408–22, www.researchgate.net/publication/228345154_Who_benefits_
the_most_from_a_gratitude_intervention_in_children_and_adolescents
_Examining_positive_affect_as_a_moderator.

14. "Gratitude Letter: Why to Try It: Why It Works," https://ggia.berkeley
.edu/practice/gratitude_letter.